Swipe This!

The Guide to Great
Touchscreen Game Design

Swipe This! The Guide to Great Touchscreen Game Design

This edition first published 2012

© 2012 John Wiley and Sons, Ltd.

Registered office

John Wiley & Sons Ltd, The Atrium, Southern Gate, Chichester, West Sussex, PO19 8SQ, United Kingdom

For details of our global editorial offices, for customer services and for information about how to apply for permission to reuse the copyright material in this book please see our website at www.wiley.com.

A catalogue record for this book is available from the British Library.

ISBN 978-1-119-96696-8 (paperback); ISBN 978-1-119-94054-8 (ebook); 978-1-119-94052-4 (ebook); 978-1-119-94053-1 (ebook)

Set in 10 pt. Chaparral Pro by Indianapolis Composition Services

Printed in the United States by Bind-Rite

Swipe This!

The Guide to Great Touchscreen Game Design

Scott Rogers

WILEY

A John Wiley and Sons, Ltd, Publication

Game Copyrights

Angry Birds (Rovio Entertainment, 2009)

ARDefender (int13, 2011)

Barry Steakfries, Jetpack Joyride, Fruit Ninja (Halfbrick, 2012)

Beat Sneak Bandit (simogo, 2012)

Bejeweled (Pop Cap Games, 2001)

Bumpy Road (simogo, 2011)

Canabalt (Semi Secret Software, 2009)

Columns (SEGA, 1990)

Crash Bandicoot (Sony Computer Entertainment, 1996)

Crush the Castle (Armor games, 2009)

Cut the Rope, Om-Nom (Chillingo, 2012)

Dance Pad (EA, 2012)

Die Zombie Die (Andy Reeves, 2011)

Doodle Jump (Lima Sky, 2009)

Draw Something (OMGPOP, 2012)

Dude with Sword, Bedbug, Grave Robber, Steampunch, Farm Wars (Scott Rogers, 2012)

Enviro-Bear 2010 (Blinkbat Games, 2011)

EPOCH. (Uppercut Games Pty Ltd, 2012)

Family Guy (20th Centruy Television, 1999)

Flight Control, Flight Control Rocket, Real Racing 2 (Firemint, 2012)

Formula Nova (Gil Beyruth, 2012)

Fruit Ninja (Halfbrick, 2010)

G.I. Joe and all related characters (Hasbro, 2012)

Game Dev Story (Kairosoft Co. Ltd, 2011)

God Finger (ngmoco, 2010)

Helsing's Fire (Click Gamer, 2011)

Henry Hatsworth in the Puzzling Adventure (EA games, 2009)

Homerun Battle 2 (Com2uS, 2012)

Indiana Jones Adventure: Temple of the Forbidden Eye (Disney/Lucasfilm, 1995)

Jason Call (Gameloft, 2010)

Keyboard Cat (Brad O'Farrell, 2007)

Killer Moth, Batman (DC Comics, 2012)

Knight's Rush (Chillingo, 2011)

Link (Nintendo, 1986)

Mickey Mouse, Where's My Water?, Swampy, Cars 2 AppMATEs (Disney, 2011)

MiniGore (Chillingo, 2009)

Nathan Drake (Sony Computer Entertainment, 2007)

NeverMIND (Erin Reynolds, 2012)

No, Human (vol-2, 2011)

Puzzle Juice (Colaboratory, 2012)

Rolando (ngmoco, 2008)

Scribblenauts (WB Games, 2009)

Sonic & SEGA All-Stars Racing (SEGA, 2011)

SpellCraft School of Magic (Appy Entertainment, 2011)

Spider: The Secret of Bryce Manor (Tiger Style, 2009)

SpongeBob Squarepants, Patrick Star, Squidward Tentacles (MTV Networks International, 1999)

SPYMouse (EA 2012)

Star Wars Arcade Falcon Gunner (THQ, 2011)

Star Wars, Darth Vader, Obi-Wan Kenobi and related characters and vehicles (Lucasfilm Ltd., 2012)

Super KO Boxing 2 (Glu Games Inc., 2012)

Super Monkey Ball (SEGA, 2001)

They Live (Universal, 1988)

Triple Town (Spryfox, 2012)

WarioWare: Touched! (Nintendo, 2004)

Wizard of Oz (MGM, 1939)

Publisher's Acknowledgements

Some of the people who helped bring this book to market include the following:

Editorial and Production

VP Consumer and Technology Publishing Director: Michelle Leete

Associate Director–Book Content Management: Martin Tribe

Associate Publisher: Chris Webb

Assistant Editor: Ellie Scott

Development Editor: Gareth Haman

Copy Editor: Debbye Butler

Technical Editors: Graham Jans, Paul O'Connor, Noah Stein

Editorial Manager: Jodi Jensen

Senior Project Editor: Sara Shlaer

Editorial Assistant: Leslie Saxman

Marketing

Associate Marketing Director: Louise Breinholt

Senior Marketing Executive: Kate Parrett

Composition Services

Compositor: Erin Zeltner

Proofreaders: Jessica Kramer, Tricia Liebig

Indexer: Potomac Indexing, LLC

About the Author

Once upon a time, **Scott Rogers** played video games, Dungeons and Dragons and drew comic books without realizing he could do these things for a living. After being "discovered" in a coffee shop and realizing game designers have more fun, Scott helped design video games including Pac-Man World, the Maximo series, God of War, Darksiders and the Drawn To Life series. A lecture about his two favorite things – level design and Disneyland – led to writing "Level Up! The Guide to Great Video Game Design," lecturing at the prestigious Interactive Media Division at the USC School of Cinematic Arts and employment with the Walt Disney Imagineering R&D team. Scott is currently living happily ever after in Thousand Oaks, CA with his family, action figure collection and an iPad full of games.

Evelyn and Jack – Thank you for being so patient while Dad worked on this book. I love you both. Now let's play!!

Contents

Swipe This Book!

Well, don't literally *swipe* this book.

Swipe This! The Guide to Great Touchscreen Game Design is all about making touchscreen games, like the kind you play on tablets such as your iPad, on smartphones such as your iPhone, and on handheld gaming systems like the Nintendo DS or Sony PS Vita. You'll learn how to design gameplay that's as simple as moving your finger (or stylus)—or *swiping* it—across a screen. It's a *pun*. Ugh. Now I've just explained the title of the book to you: that's as bad as explaining the punch line of a joke.

Look, would it help if I told you that it took a long time to write this book? I (and my publisher) would prefer that you buy *Swipe This!* rather than actually swiping it . . . or pirating it electronically, or memorizing it in the bookstore, or borrowing it from a friend and never giving it back. What can I do to convince you to not swipe *Swipe This!*?

I know! In a previous video game design book I wrote,[1] I explained that every good book has to start off with an excerpt so gripping, so exciting, so thrilling that the reader has to keep reading it to its conclusion. An excerpt that has zombies in it! Preferably something like this:

> *Jack leapt aboard the helicopter as two dozen zombies reached out, entangling the struts. "There's too much weight!" yelled Evelyn from the cockpit. "We'll never be able to take off!" Jack hew at the clawing creatures and yelled back, "Working on it!" He wasn't sure whether zombies could feel pain, but they sure couldn't hold onto the helicopter strut without hands. As the zombies dropped off one by one, Jack waved them goodbye, calling out: "Good-bye! Toodle-loo! See you later!" Splat. Splat. Splat. The 'copter rose into the sky and Jack collapsed to the floor. "I must be losing it," he muttered. "Face it, Jackie boy. The zombie apocalypse isn't as much fun as you thought it would be." That's when the skeletal dragon swooped in front of the 'copter, spreading its enormous bat wings with a sound not unlike knuckles cracking. Jack thought "Nuts. I shouldn't have opened that book."*

Okay, so maybe you didn't pick up *Swipe This!* to read about zombies, dragons, or helicopters,[2] but the good news is there *are* zombies, dragons, and helicopters in this book—just not right this second.

What I am sure of is that you picked up this book (or are previewing the first few pages on your e-browser) for one of the following reasons:

---

[1] *Level Up! The Guide to Great Video Game Design* (John Wiley & Sons, Inc., 2010) available everywhere books are sold! <End advertising mode>

[2] Though I don't blame you if you did, because they are awesome!

Some Possible Reasons You Picked Up Swipe This!

1. You don't know anything about tablet games but want to learn all about them.

2. You've played tablet games and want to make one of your own, but don't know where to start.

3. You already create tablet games and want to make your games even better.

4. *Swipe This!* has an awesome cover.

5. *Swipe This!* has zombies, dragons, and helicopters in it.

6. _____.[3]

If you have picked up this book for any of these reasons, then we're off to a great start. *Swipe This!* is definitely the book for *you*.

Who Is This Book For?

You![4]

And since there are four types of people who enjoy reading books about video games, you are probably one of the following: **nerd**, **geek**, **otaku,** or **fanboy**. I'm kidding! What I meant to say is that you are probably a **gamer**.

---

[3]Please write in your own reason here. I can't think of everything.

[4]Didn't I just say that?

What (or who) is a gamer? According to that source of all knowledge, Wikipedia,[5] the term gamer is "commonly used to identify those who spend much of their leisure time playing or learning about games." That said, you don't have to be a gamer to read *Swipe This!* You just need to fit into one of my four easy-to-stereotype classifications:

Working Video Game Professionals

These hard-working men and women can be found fighting the good fight in development studios around the world. As experienced game creators, you'd think they would already know everything there is to learn from a book such as this. But, as I've learned over the years, no one can know *everything*. And even if they think they do, no one can *remember* everything. The human brain is a very slippery thing[6]—which is why books exist in the first place!

Books (like this one) can be very helpful because game creators often develop what I call **designer blinders**. Designer blinders happen when a game developer becomes so engrossed in his work that he overlooks important details. For example, developers spend so much time playing their games that they end up tolerating their sloppy controls. Sometimes they don't realize their controls could be better. Other times they're just satisfied that the darn things are working at all. They might neglect ways to improve their gameplay because they are so focused on getting features into a game under a tight deadline. They're like Luke Skywalker flying down the trench of the Death Star, so hyper-focused on shooting that photon torpedo into the exhaust port[7] that they fail to notice Darth Vader and his wingmen have just flown into the trench behind them and have them in their sights! But never fear! *Swipe This!* is your Han Solo, flying in for the assist, knocking Vader and his wingmen out of your way so you can make the shot, blow up the Death Star, and be the hero!

[5]Before you judge me for using Wikipedia as a source, I'll have you know that I first referenced a copy of *Webster's New Universal Unabridged Dictionary* that weighs 5 lbs. and can kill a man if you drop it on his head. The definition for gamer wasn't even listed in there.

[6]Have you ever tried to hold one?

[7]Right below the main port.

Despite my blatant pandering-to-nerds analogy, I hope that *Swipe This!* will help inspire an idea, a gameplay feature, or merely provide some reassurance to the working professionals that they are on the right track and that the exhaust port is still in their sights.

Future Video Game Designers

The future of tablet games is wide open, and in this group are those brave pioneers who are ready to take flight! These pioneers come from all walks of life. Maybe they're game developers who have decided to "take a break" from the grind of producing "triple A" games and strike out on their own. Perhaps they are programmers, artists, or designers who feel their creative ideas and self-expression are being crushed under their day jobs and they want to create something of their own. Maybe they're wannabe game developers who just need a push in the right direction.

When I started out in games (the ancient 16-bit days), it wasn't easy to learn how to make games. It was black magic, a secret art practiced by programmers and the Japanese. Heck, I didn't even realize video games were a career path until I was actually working in the industry! There sure as heck weren't places like game schools or products like DVDs on how to design games, and only a precious few magazines and books.[8]

But I was lucky enough to have a mentor—someone who had a few successful games under their belt, enough experience to know what worked and what didn't, and (thankfully) didn't have a huge ego to be offended when a very eager (and slightly frustrated) video game artist walked into their office and told them he wanted to be a game designer. Since then, I've been inspired by my mentor and learned that it's important to pass knowledge on and help those who ask for help. The information in this book is based on many years of experience making games on touchscreen devices. With each game, I made mistakes, learned something new, discarded what didn't work, and applied what did. And that's what you'll find in this book. Everything I've learned. So, let me be your mentor. All you need to do is follow my advice, work hard, and take advantage of opportunities when they eventually arrive.

---

[8]Most of them were about chess or how to get a high score in *Donkey Kong*.

Students of Game Design

Are you a student going to one of the many universities and trade schools that offer a program in video game design? LUCKY!! Man, I wish they had that when I was a student! Go to school to make video games? That is so freakin' cool! Jealous! Ahem. But I digress. As a video games student, you are going to dive deep into the study of all aspects of video game development. You'll sit through courses on the history of gaming; critically discuss why a game was a successful or failure; take labs to learn coding or character animation; get into adult beverage-fuelled debates with your dorm mates why *Angry Birds* was a lucky fluke or the most calculated game design ever created. And while you will be learning, learning takes time. You know what accelerates learning? Books.

Now there are lots of textbooks on video game design. Some pretty good books filled with academic theory on why games are fun. You should read those books[9]. But first, you should read *Swipe This!* The information, tips, and tricks you will find in these pages will enhance all of those classes, labs, and discussions. I think you'll find *Swipe This!*'s practical approach to game design to be the antidote to that heavy diet of theory your teachers are going to be feeding you. Theory is great for the classroom, but the reality is, what matters most in the trenches of the video game industry is practical advice. *Swipe This!* brings you that advice from some of the industry's best and brightest. This is why *Swipe This!* will be indispensable over the course of your academic career.

Besides, I've read those dry game design textbooks, and I can guarantee you that none of them contains a picture as awesome as this:

People Who Love Video Games

Just because you aren't a working professional, student, or future game developer, that doesn't mean you can't love video games, much less not read a book about them. As with movies and art, the more I learn about how something is made, the more I appreciate it. The saying goes "Knowing is half the battle."[10]

Besides, what's not to love about video games? The best games make your wishes come true. They make you feel smart, strong, rich, and athletic. They'll take you to places you've never been, and will allow you to experience lives you'll never have in the real world. This is why video games are the most popular form of entertainment in the world[11]: They make you awesome.

I hear some of you more skeptical readers thinking[12] "I need more proof!" And while I'm generally not a statistics person, try these on for size:

○ Goldman Sachs's research indicates that 79.2 million touchscreen devices will be sold in 2012.[13]

○ A Google survey reports that 84% of touchscreen owners use their devices primarily for gaming.[14]

○ Nintendo reports that 144 million DSs (including DSi, DS Lite, and DSi XL) have sold worldwide as of early 2011.[15]

---

[10]The other half of the battle is shooting lots of red and blue lasers.

[11]http://www.telegraph.co.uk/technology/video-games/8421458/Video-games-sell-more-than-DVDs-and-albums.html

[12]I know it's unnerving, me reading your mind, but get used to it.

[13]http://www.intomobile.com/2010/12/14/goldman-sachs-tablets/

[14]http://www.guardian.co.uk/technology/appsblog/2011/apr/08/tablets-mainly-for-games-survey

[15]http://www.vg247.com/2011/01/27/nintendo-lifetime-ds-sales-hit-144-million-wii-almost-85-million/

That's a lot of people who love tablet games! And they aren't alone. I've said it before, and I'll say it again: I love video games too! I love to play them and I love to make them. I love to read about making them. Wouldn't you rather read a book written by someone who loves video games than one that wasn't?

So would I.

Why Another Book on Game Design?

No one has written a book quite like *Swipe This!* before: a book **specifically** about the design of tablet and handheld games.

Over the years, I have learned that designing games for touchscreens and handheld gaming systems is very different than designing the types of games played on consoles and computers. Everything from the genres of games people like to play, to the do's and don'ts of designing gameplay for handheld devices, to thinking about how the player interacts with the controls is different.

As more and more game developers embrace tablet gaming, they will need to know how to make great games for these devices. *Swipe This!* is the place to learn it. I've been creating games for a very long time, so let me be your guide into the brave new frontier!

What You Won't Find in This Book

Books can be many things. Paper weights, door jams, anti-squid projectiles. But did you know the insides of a book are often useful too? You will find lots of useful information on how to design tablet games in *Swipe This!* On the flip side, here are five things you *won't* find:

1. Very deep theory.

2. The complete history of video games.

3. How to program tablet games.

4. How to create art for tablet games.

5. Lameness.

Very Deep Theory

To quote cultural theorist Johan Huizinga from his seminal *Homo Ludens*: "Poiesis, in fact, is a play-function. It proceeds within the playground of the mind, in a world of its own which the mind creates for it. There, things have a different physiognomy . . . zzzzzzzz." I'm sorry. I must have dozed off. I'm sure ludic theory has its place . . . in academia or during dinner conversation with the royals,[16] but when it's time to roll up your sleeves, and get to work, theory can stay home and clean the house. Lord knows it needs it.

This isn't to say that this book doesn't have *some* theory in it. I've been known to come up with a theory or two of my own: *The Theory of Unfun. The Triangle of Weirdness. The Rule of Three*. You can find all these (and probably more than I care to admit) in my previous video game design book.[17] But the point of this book is not to overwhelm you with theories. It's to overwhelm you with helpful, practical, factual designing goodness that will help make designing a tablet game a breeze.

The Complete History of Video Games

There are already dozens of books on this subject, and at least three of them are good.[18] Besides, you can find a truncated history of arcade and console games in *Level Up!* If you are looking for another invocation of the holy quartet of video gaming[19], you can look elsewhere. However, since *Swipe This!* is a book about touchscreen gaming, I *will* be covering the origins and evolution of touchscreen games. As philosopher and *Bejeweled*-enthusiast George Santayana once said "Those who cannot remember the past are condemned to replay it." Or something like that.

---

[16]http://www.guardian.co.uk/uk/2011/jul/10/william-kate-stars-los-angeles

[17]See footnote #1.

[18]*Replay* by Tristan Donovan (Yellow Ant, 2010), *The Ultimate History of Video Games: From Pong to Pokémon* by Steven Kent (Three Rivers Press, 2001), and *All Our Bases Belong To Us* by Harold Goldberg (Three Rivers Press, 2011).

[19]Chant along with me: Higinbotham, Russell, Bushnell, Baer. Higinbotham, Russell, Bushnell, Baer.

How to Program Video Games

By trade, I am a game designer, not a programmer. I don't know how to code games, so I'm not going to pretend to include "how to program a game" in this book. I wouldn't want to steer you in the wrong direction. But as a functioning member of a creative team, you still need to know what a programmer is talking about. You should know the difference between iOS (Apple's mobile operating system) and an SDK (Software Development Kit). You should know that games can be programmed in Cocoa, Open GL ES 2.0, and Objective-C. The more you can understand *programmer-ese,* the easier it will be to communicate your design needs to a programmer. If you want to learn more or go deeper, many good books on the topic[20] will help you gain some working knowledge. Feel free to learn a programming tool to really learn how things work, or to program the game yourself.

How to Create Video Game Art

Like I said, I'm a game designer, and although I used to create game art for a living (waaaay back in the 16-bit days), this book does not get into the technical aspects of creating art for your tablet game: topics like "How to create 3D models," "How to texture and shade objects and environments," or "How to draw bitmaps or create alpha layers." But that doesn't mean I am not going to discuss game art. I talk about choosing an artistic style for your game, deciding what kind of art works best on those little tiny mobile touchscreens, applying lighting tricks, and understanding color theory, UI design . . . all types of artsy topics. Once again, there's nothing stopping you from learning about this yourself and, just like with programming, the more you know, the easier it is to communicate your ideas.

Lameness

I'm hoping this one is self-explanatory.

What You Will Find in This Book

1. Practical information (check out the following section)

2. Tips and tricks

3. Interviews

4. Analysis

---

[20]Like *iPhone & iPad Game Development For Dummies* by Goldstein, Manning & Buttfield-Addison (John Wiley & Sons, Inc., 2011).

5. Helpful documentation

6. Lots and lots of drawings

7. Lists[21]

Practical Information

Swipe This! will guide you through the entire process of designing a tablet and touchscreen game, from coming up with your initial (dare I say brilliant?) idea to learning strategies on how to best release your game into a fiercely competitive market. And how are we going to do this? By using the following three methods:

1. *Designing games.* First and foremost, *Swipe This!* will teach you how to create a design *exclusively* for a tablet and touchscreen video game. Unlike console and PC games, tablet and touchscreen games have very different design requirements and their players have very different needs. We will take these exceptions into consideration; this, in turn, will help make your game much more successful. I have created documentation to give you a headstart on creating your game designs. We're gonna design some games! Exciting, right?

2. *Talking to people who design games.* You may not know many game developers in real life, but I do. I have interviewed many of the game industry's top and up-and-coming tablet game developers about their games to learn what worked and what didn't, where they draw their inspiration from, and what they would do differently now that they know better. And they've got a lot of good stuff to share. It's like having a Game Developers Conference in a book!

3. *Playing and evaluating games.* I always say, "You can learn a lot from playing a game, even a bad one." I've played a lot of tablet games—both good and bad. We'll look at many of these games, and I will provide in-depth analysis to figure out why they work, why they don't, what could have been done better, and what was done right. And, for absolutely free, I'll give you the analytical tools, documentation, and some creative exercises to learn from other games in order to make yours the best it can possibly be.

As you read *Swipe This!*, you will find many examples where I write "When I designed so-and-so . . . ." Please be aware that this is an oversimplification. Video games are created by many, many, many talented people, and to give the impression that I did all the work myself is not only incorrect, but it's also egotistical. Although there are tablet games made by a single creator, that was not the case on the titles I was involved with. Whew. I'm glad I got that off my chest!

---

[21]Like this one.

Something else you might have noticed already about *Swipe This!* is that there are lots of drawings. Look! There goes one of them now!

Over the years working as a video game designer, I've learned that the best way to get people to read something like a ***game design document***[22] or a book on video game design is to draw cartoons and diagrams of VERY IMPORTANT game play concepts. This is why you will find lots and lots of drawings in this book, so you will continue reading and understand the ideas I present. When you understand, then you can apply them when making your own game designs and become a great tablet game designer! Oh, I almost forgot. There's one other thing in this book that you won't find in most other video game design books:

Good News!

Here's the good news. Thinking about designing tablet game video games brings the following quote to mind:

> *There has never been a better time for someone to design, develop, and publish a video game in the history of the medium.*
>
> —*Me (I just said it right now)*

I have been preaching this wisdom to countless students, professionals, and wannabe video game developers since 2008. And I wouldn't tell it to them (or you) if I didn't believe it.

When I first started working in video games, it used to be near impossible to make one without money, a team, experience, equipment, a developer's license, a publisher, more money, a team, and another team.

---

[22]And what, pray tell, is a ***game design document***? Hold your horses, cowboy. We'll get to that!

Many of my peers used to yearn for the "good old days" when a couple of friends could sit in a garage, armed with some computers and the passion to make something fun for all to enjoy. I'm happy to say that things have come full circle. Teams as small as one person are creating tablet games these days. There's room for everyone in the video game industry, provided you . . .

1. Have the passion to create something great.

2. Love video games.

3. Are not an idiot[23].

Now that we've gotten that out of the way, are you ready to start learning how to design some tablet video games?

Let's go!

---

[23]You've already proven to me that you aren't an idiot, because you're reading this book.

chapter 1

Hardware Wars

Sigh.

I hate to do this to you because you seem like such a nice person, but every book has to start with the writer assuming that the reader knows *little or nothing* about the topic the book is about. My fondest wish is that you already know enough about tablet gaming that I can dive right into professional-grade tips and techniques delivered in the most obscure jargon and arcane argot.

Alas, I cannot. While I am sure that your head isn't completely devoid of even the most basic of knowledge . . . what a handheld device is, what a video game is, what a touchscreen tablet is, and so forth, this is where I write the literary equivalent of talking . . . very . . . slowly . . . and for that, I deeply apologize.

Okay, future game design genius, let's start with some basic definitions:

Video game: A game people play on a video screen.

Touchscreen: An electronic visual display that can detect the user's touch.

Tablet: A light, thin portable computer consisting mostly of just a touchscreen. Also known as a tablet computer.

Smartphone: A phone that (often) features a large touchscreen interface, possesses a fast processor, and provides additional features such as apps, access to the internet, and video playback. Of course, this book only applies to designing for smartphones with touchscreens.

Handheld gaming system: A dedicated video game playing device that users hold in their hands.

Sorry about that, but it had to be done. I believe that if you want to learn *how* to design a game for one of these gaming devices, you first need to know a little about the hardware and where it came from.[1] So let's pack some snacks and turn the dial on the way-back time machine to that brisk day in the fall of 1888 when not-so-young inventor Elias Gray burst into the Oval Office with a startling proclamation:

---

[1] "The electronics store" is not an acceptable answer.

At least that's the way I heard it.

The **_telautograph_** was a pretty awesome invention for the 1800s. A machine that could write . . . with a pen. Okay, maybe it wasn't as cool as a giant mechanical steam-powered spider, but the telautograph enabled users to transmit a drawing electronically. Documents could be signed over long distances, essentially making it the first fax machine. This is why we fought the robot civil war, to prevent machines from having better penmanship than us! Over the years, the technology stemming from Gray's invention split into two directions—handwriting recognition technology and image reproduction. The copyright for telautograph was eventually bought by a brash start-up called Xerox. I wonder how they did?

Flash forward to the 1950s: the atomic age, the era of three-piece suits and three-martini lunches. It is against this backdrop that a member of the think-tank known as the RAND Corporation barged into the Oval Office with another astounding announcement:

Next dateline: 1962. The Lincoln computer lab of the Massachusetts Institute of Technology (MIT) saw the birth of two significant technological advances that would eventually converge almost 25 years later. *Spacewar!*, one of the earliest video games, was created on the lab's DEC PDP-1 computer by three students: Steve "Slug" Russell, Martin "Shag" Graetz, and Wayne Witaenem. Meanwhile, Ivan Sutherland[2] presented his Ph.D. doctorate thesis, "Sketchpad: A Man-Machine Graphical Communication System," which allowed the user to input simple lines and curves by drawing directly onto a CRT screen with a light pen. Although originally two dimensional, Sketchpad was upgraded to display all three dimensions. Sutherland's invention created the field of ***computer-aided design*** (or *CAD*). Since a single graphical display CRT monitor cost $40,000, not including the computer you needed to run the software, CAD was not widely available except by computer scientists at universities and the military. Eventually, CAD found its way into commercial industries—automotives, aerospace, engineering, architecture, and film special effects.[3] These last two industries would later have a great influence on video game creators.

---

[2]Not only did Sutherland invent computer graphics, but he was the father of virtual reality, designing and building a VR headset in the late 1960s. This invention gave video games yet another gift: the concept of the word ***HUD*** *(heads-up display).*

[3]The democratization of 3D modeling and animation tools is one of the great success stories of the personal computer and an important moment in video game development. When I was a young university student in the 1980s, my art and design instructors foretold that the future was creating objects in 3D. However, finding a computer on which I could learn the available software proved to be extremely difficult. Many of the early 3D artists and architects guarded their systems as fiercely as Templar Knights protecting the Holy Grail. Fortunately, more affordable 3D modeling and animation tools like Alias and 3D Studio Max came along, pushing these Knights aside and allowing everyone a seat at the 3D party.

Next stop, Stardate: 1966. A time when *Star Trek* first aired on television and science fiction nerds were just climbing out of the primordial ooze. Even to these prehistoric Trekkies, tablet computers seemed like science fiction, like the tricorder used by the crew of the Enterprise. However, computer scientist Alan Kay must have visited the City on the Edge of Forever when he designed the ***Dynabook*** in 1968. The design for this early tablet laptop was way ahead of its time and provided inspiration and the technological foundation for today's e-readers and tablet computers.[4]

Sadly, the Dynabook never made it past the concept phase, but many of its ideas paved the way for the first Apple handheld device in 1993—the Apple Newton. This handheld PDA (personal digital assistant) was an electronic notepad, allowing its owner to use a pen to write notes, create spreadsheets, and keep an events calendar. Flinging angry birds was still many years off, however. Despite this significant omission, the success of the Newton gave Apple the confidence to give tablet technology a second try in the 2000s; this time, the company had phenomenal success with the creation of the iPod touch, iPhone, and iPad tablet.

---

[4]http://www.tomshardware.com/news/alan-kay-steve-jobs-ipad-iphone,10209.html

Hooray! We've returned back from the past and we didn't even have to watch our parents make out at the Enchantment-Under-The-Sea ball! Since one out of 43 U.S. presidents agree that touchscreen gaming is pretty keen, let's examine this amazing technology further.

Touch and Go!

The great thing about technology is there are different ways to achieve the same results. Want to get airborne? An airplane, helicopter, balloon, and catapult all do the trick![5] The same is true with touchscreens. While they all look the same on the outside, there is a difference depending on what's going on beneath those cold, shiny exteriors. Each technology has its own advantages and restrictions that are important for designers to be aware of. There are five types of tablets: capacitive, resistive, passive, electromagnetic, and inductive.

A *capacitive tablet* detects the electrostatic signal generated by porous materials such as conductive foam or . . . ick . . . human skin. Most modern tablet PCs use capacitive signals to detect user input, eliminating the need for a stylus; a human finger works just as well! Capacitive tablets can support multi-touch capability; the current iPad can detect up to 11 touch points! Disadvantages include having to frequently clean your tablet's screen due to the user's Cheetos-stained fingers.

iPhone touch screen

---

[5]Though your landing experience may be radically different in each case.

Resistive tablets are touchscreens that require physical pressure to operate and are found in devices like the Nintendo DS, low-end tablet PCs, and those pads at the supermarket that you have to sign if you use a credit card to buy your groceries.

Resistive touchscreens are created by layering two screens that activate when the top layer is forced into contact with the bottom layer. Styli are often used to increase precision on the screen although they don't need them to operate. They just help increase the accuracy as it's easier to be precise with the tip of a pen than it is with a big ol' sausage finger. Resistive screens are very cheap to produce, but they generally don't handle multitouch functionality and lack durability. Even worse, you can lose those styli under your couch.

Resistive screen tablet

Passive tablets are most commonly found in drawing tablets that use a stylus or "light pen." The battery-powered stylus generates a **resonant circuit** or **LC circuit** that reacts with criss-crossed wires inside the tablet. The wires act as receiving coils for the LC circuit and cause electromagnetic induction. In other words, the tablet becomes an electromagnetic tuning fork. A passive tablet is so sensitive the user doesn't even have to touch the surface of the tablet to draw. By changing pressure on the stylus nib or pressing a switch on the stylus, the signal generated by the pen changes, allowing for different line effects such as line weight, which simulates adding or removing pressure. It's much like drawing with a pencil (except you never have to sharpen your pencil!).

Wacom tablet

Passive tablets like those made by Wacom and THQ's UDraw are not tablet computers, but rather peripherals that require additional software or a gaming console to operate. These devices are included in *Swipe This!* because (a) they are touchscreen gaming systems and (b) you design games for them as you would any other touchscreen device.

Electromagnetic tablets are cousins to passive tablets, but the tablet detects the pen rather than vice-versa with the passive tablet. In other words, the EM tablet is "smart" and its pen is "dumb."

An ***inductive touchscreen tablet*** differs from the passive tablet in that their "smart pen" stylus houses electronics that transmit an electromagnetic signal to the tablet to determine the user's position.[6] It constantly watches every move you make![7] The pen transmits information about pressure, button presses, and the user's movements to the tablet. These active tablets allow users to draw smoother lines and their screens have the highest precision, but they are very expensive. This is why professional artists use them. These artists do not have time for video games. They're too busy mak-

Active tablet

ing them, which is also why you don't see too many games designed specifically for these devices. Sure, there are a few games you can play on an active tablet: browser games like *Line Rider* (Boštjan Čadež, 2006) and *Scribble* (Nitrome, 2006). Any game that can be played on a computer monitor can be played on an active tablet because it is an accessory, not a PC. A bummer about active tablets is that if you lose or break an active tablet stylus, it can be expensive to replace. You don't want to risk that happening, so maybe you're better off not playing games on an inductive touchscreen.

More Things to Be Touchy About

There are a few other input systems that live with (or at least in the same neighborhood) as the ones listed above: ***optical*** and ***acoustic*** systems.

An ***optical tablet*** uses a small camera in the stylus to match an image being drawn on the tablet. The camera tracks the motions and marks created by the user and then translates them to data that is reproduced on-screen. While optical tablets are the great-great-grandchild of the telautograph, the technology is still in use today. For example, the Nintendo Wii uses similar technology[8] to track the movement of the Wii Remote for drawing games such as *Drawn to Life: The Next Chapter* (THQ, 2008) and *Okami* (Capcom, 2008). However, precision drawing is not always possible with an optical control system. I talk about techniques and tricks to overcome this challenge in Chapter 3.

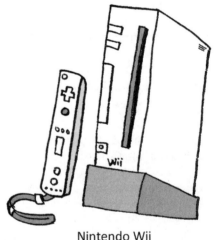

Nintendo Wii

---

[6]This might be the most scientific sentence I write in this book.

[7]It might be time to start up the robot civil wars again.

[8]Keep in mind that I'm not calling the Wii Remote a tablet, I'm just illustrating that it uses the motion camera system. Geez, you're so literal!

An **acoustic tablet** uses microphones to determine the placement of the stylus, allowing for greater fidelity in determining the stylus's position in 3D space. Acoustic transducers can be used to register distinctive finger taps and scrapes to control functions formerly done with traditional buttons or other control mechanisms.[9] Currently, no existing game systems use this technology, but some recent tablet PC patents indicate that they might be in the near future. Start growing those fingernails and get prepared now!

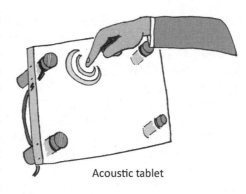

Acoustic tablet

And this is just the beginning! Touchscreen technology will evolve even further as the tablet-arms race ramps up. How many touchpoints will future touchscreens be able to support? Just how many digits will it take to satisfy touchscreen users? Twelve? Thirteen? Toes? Now that we've examined the types of touchscreens available, just what can we play on them?

Game On!

Why, games of course! A common misconception is confusing a game with an app. "What about apps? Where do they fall into all of this?" I hear you cry. To learn the difference, here are some more of those ever-useful definitions:

Mobile optimized: A website or web application specifically designed and developed for the dimensions, interactions, and performance of a web browser on an Apple iPod touch, iPhone, or iPad. By creating content for use on multiple platforms, development costs are reduced and money and content can be regularly updated via the website rather than the user. Less memory is dedicated to the app since data can be pulled down from the interwebs or cloud. The downside is users might not be able to access the data if they are in a dead spot or their cell service is poor. No service = no game. No game = sadness.

Native application: A program designed and developed to run independent of a web browser, compiled specifically for an Apple iPod touch, iPhone, or iPad. Native apps load and run faster as the data is resident in the device's memory. The downside is this data can get large (especially art, sound, and video files) and fill up your device's storage quickly. If an app is too big, the user might be compelled to remove it after a while to make room for more Lady Gaga songs. Also, Apple doesn't allow wireless data transfers larger than 50MB: any bigger and it has to be done while the device is connected to the user's computer. Not a huge disadvantage, but you can't get that big game if you aren't next to your computer. Once again, sadness.

---

[9]For a really cool example of how acoustic transducers work, watch http://www.youtube.com/watch?feature=player_embedded&v=2E8vsQB4.

But it's not all rainclouds and pouty faces in mobile gaming land. No matter which way you store the data, the big advantage is that the player can access it (almost) at any time. It is this "on-demand" system that helps make downloadable gaming (using the App Store or the Android Market) so popular. Less than a decade ago, the only option for publishing games for handheld devices was printable media: cartridges and optical media like UMDs (the Playstation Portable's native media). This recent development in downloadable gaming has changed the face of the industry, forcing many hardware developers to adopt online methods of downloading games or risk being left behind. Let's look at the existing handheld gaming systems and see what options they offer:

First up is the Nintendo Dual Screen Portable Gaming System, more commonly known as the **Nintendo DS.** The physical design of the Nintendo DS was inspired by Nintendo's first foray in portable gaming: the **Game & Watch** (Nintendo, 1980) and the extension of the long running line of Nintendo portable game systems: the Game Boy, Game Boy Color, and Game Boy Advance. Game & Watch was a line of charming single-game devices, with gameplay displayed on an LCD screen. In 1982, the line expanded to include dual-screened games that featured famous Nintendo characters such as Donkey Kong,[10] Link (of *Legend of Zelda* fame), and the eternally hapless hero Mr. Game & Watch, the star of Game & Watch titles including *Ball*, *Fire,* and *Oil Panic*.

Nintendo Game & Watch

[10]The Donkey Kong dual-screen Game & Watch was a thing of beauty. My best friend's father bought one for me while in Japan. The game characters were made up of frantic LED-drawn silhouettes that flicked across the screen as you operated the d-pad. The cover of my orange Game & Watch was inlaid with some sort of mysterious metallic material that seemed like it came from outer space, that shimmered and glistened and mesmerized my 12-year-old eyes. Aesthetically and functionally, that Donkey Kong Game & Watch was gorgeous. Sadly, I had to sell mine to pay rent in college. But if anyone wants to send me one care of my publisher, I won't complain!

The Nintendo DS was released in 2004, with more than a few improvements over its ancestor. The Nintendo DS dazzled gamers with its twin color screens, slots for two game cartridges (which supported both Nintendo DS and Game Boy Advance titles), a built-in microphone, Wi-Fi connectivity to allow multiple Nintendo DSs to communicate, and most impressively, a single touchscreen that could be operated by a stylus. Early hits on this system included Nintendo's *Brain Age, Wario Ware Touched!,* and a port of *Mario 64* (*Super Mario 64 DS*). The system exploded, however, with the release of *Nintendogs* (Nintendo, 2005), a real-time Tamgotchi-style game where you played with and trained a virtual dog.

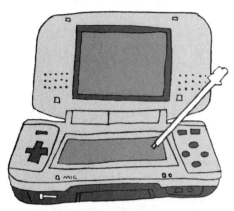

Nintendo DS

The Nintendo DS was popular enough to warrant four significant technology upgrades: The **Nintendo DS Lite** (Nintendo, 2006) featured a larger and clearer screen while slimming down the hardware to fit easily in a pocket. The **Nintendo DSi** (Nintendo, 2008) added built-in memory, dual cameras with image and sound editing tools, and the ability to connect to the **DSiWare shop** (also launched in 2008); an online store with downloadable new and classic games and applications, and share user-created content in programs such as the animation tool *Flipbook*. The **Nintendo DSi XL** added an even bigger display screen. The **Nintendo 3DS** (Nintendo, 2011) introduced a "glasses-free" 3D screen up top, twin cameras that allow gamers to capture true 3D images, an accelerometer, a gyroscope, an analog control pad, and the ability to play built-in augmented reality (or **AR**) games.

Nintendo DS XL

Despite all of these great features, backward compatibility was sacrificed over the evolution of the system. Players could still play their Game Boy Advance titles on the Nintendo DS all the way through to the Nintendo DSXL. But

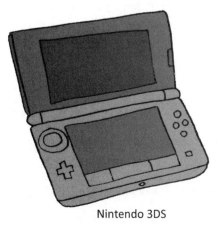

Nintendo 3DS

the functionality was removed for the Nintendo DSi. While the Nintendo 3DS can still play Nintendo DS titles, older systems cannot play new Nintendo 3DS games. Despite this, all five versions of the Nintendo DS have sold more than 146.4 units—impressive numbers when compared to recent "major" gaming consoles: the Playstation 3 and Xbox 360.[11]

At the 2011 Electronic Entertainment Expo, Nintendo revealed its next step in touchscreen gaming, the **Wii U.** The Wii U's "controller" appears to be the oversized love child of the Wii console and the DSi. The Wii U's flat tablet controller features a centrally mounted touchscreen, an accelerometer, and an impressive amount of analog, digital, and trigger controllers. An early advantage to the Wii U controller is that since it works in conjunction with your TV set, the player's hand won't get in the way of

Nintendo Wii U

any on-screen action. We'll just have to wait to see what innovative control and gameplay this brings to the party. Expectations are high, but whether the Wii U ends up as the next Wii or the next **Virtual Boy**[12] remains to be seen.

The **UDraw** (THQ, 2010) is the most traditional drawing tablet available for consoles, similar to those manufactured by Wacom and others. The UDraw is a peripheral for the Nintendo Wii and connects via the console's Wii-Mote controller. Players use the UDraw's stylus to draw, write, and control game characters. Unlike the other gaming devices we've been talking about, though, it has no visual screen of its own. However, many of the game design conventions I talk about in *Swipe This!* still hold true for the UDraw.

UDraw tablet

---

[11]As of 2011, the PS3 had sold 51.8 million units and the Xbox 360 sold 55 million units worldwide.

[12]The Virtual Boy was one of Nintendo's few flops. The 1995 portable gaming system resembled a pair of large red goggles connected to a controller and balanced precariously on a flimsy tripod. The Virtual Boy promised "true 3D" graphics for the player . . . and delivered true 3D all right, but in monochromatic red graphics that induced violent headaches in many users (including yours truly). To no one's surprise, the Virtual Boy was discontinued in less than a year.

Another gaming system that debuted at the 2011 E3 is the **Playstation Vita** (formerly known as the NGP and the PSP2). The system boosts several control options, including analog buttons, control buttons, an accelerometer, and two cameras (one front, one rear). The device supports Bluetooth, Wi-Fi, and 3G connectivity. But the most innovative feature is its twin touchscreens—a front-facing

Playstation Vita

OLED multi-touch capacitive screen facing the player and a rear-facing capacitive touchpad that can be controlled by the user's fingers. This screen has no visual component and is used for game control functions only. Several of Sony's top design teams are creating content for the Vita, and it will be interesting to see how they incorporate this "blind screen" into gameplay. I talk about some gameplay ideas regarding this later on in the book. Stay tuned!

Not all gaming devices start out as gaming devices. Introduced in 2007, the Apple **iPhone** was conceived by then-CEO Steve Jobs as a combination of Apple's wildly popular iPod music player, a mobile phone and an "Internet communicator." The iPhone's large multi-touch touchscreen, with 320-by-480 pixel color resolution combined with Apple's trademark user-friendly, icon-based interface made the iPhone an instant success: Initial shipments sold out in hours, and 1 million units sold within the first 5 days of release. A 2011 report estimates that more than 128 million iPhones have been sold worldwide,[13] making it the second most dominant gaming platform in the world, behind the Nintendo DS.

In 2007, Apple released the **iPod touch,** essentially an iPhone without the phone, or an iPod with a touchscreen (take your pick), which featured similar controls and functions.

iPhone

---

[13]This estimate includes the original iPhone, the iPhone 3G/3GS, and iPhone 4 models.

That touchscreen meant games! Gaming blossomed on the iPod touch, but at first finding and downloading games was another matter. Gaming apps were available on individual publishers' websites, but if you didn't know what you were looking for or how to get them from your computer onto your device, then it could be a confusing and cumbersome process. The breakthrough came a year later. The debut of the iTunes iOS App Store[14] in 2008 transformed Apple's iOS devices into a major gaming platform.

On launch day, around 160 games[15] were available for purchase and the App Store had the secret sauce that few other game stores had: It never closed[16]. Gamers could (relatively) easily find and download games directly onto their iOS devices, and games were sold at prices much lower[17] than console or computer titles. This change in sales strategy (sell low but potentially sell massive volumes) is making a huge impact on the gaming industry: we'll talk about this in Chapter 11. In the meantime, you can find a list of the games available on the opening day of the App Store (and which ones you can still purchase today) in Appendix 1.

The most popular iOS game releases of 2008 included *Crash Bandicoot Nitro Kart 3D* (Activision, 2008), *Super Monkey Ball* (Sega, 2008), *Rolando* (ngmoco, 2008), and *Labyrinth* (Illusion Labs, 2008). These early games focused on one of the iPhone's more popular features: the built-in gyroscope that allowed for tilt control.[18] Soon, games of all genres were available in the App Store.

---

[14]iTunes was established in 2003 to support the Apple iPod digital music player.

[15]http://toucharcade.com/2008/07/10/app-store-to-launch-with-about-160-games

[16]Steam, Valve's online game store was one of the first to the "all-games-all-the-time party" back in 2003.

[17]App Store game prices generally ranged from $.99 to $9.99.

[18]We'll go full tilt on the subject of gyroscopes in Chapter 3.

Gaming on Apple devices got a major boost in 2010 with the release of the **iPad** tablet computer, which featured a 9.7-inch (diagonal) screen with a resolution of 768 × 1024 pixels; coupled with all the functions of the iPod touch and the iPhone (except, of course, the phone), the iPad was perfect for gaming. Even people with enormous fingers (like yours truly) could appreciate content delivered by the App Store.

When Google announced its **Android** operating system (OS) as a competitor to Apple, hardware manufacturers quickly jumped onto the tablet computer bandwagon. In fact in 2009 the Archos 5, the first Android tablet, beat the iPad to market. Tablets like the Samsung **Galaxy Tab,** HP **TouchPad,** and Motorola **Xoom** bear many similarities to Apple's products: large touchscreen, accelerometer, and so forth; a few others, like the Asus **Eee Pad Transformer,** have features like a keyboard dock that distinguish them from their competitors. On the touchscreen mobile phone front, notable examples include the **Palm Pre** (and **Pre Plus** and **Pre 2**) and **Palm Pixi** multimedia smartphones whose **WebOS** offers a Linux-based solution and Accunture's **Symbian** operating system found on many Nokia smartphones. An interesting development on the smartphone front was 2010's introduction of the **Windows Phone 7** OS, which gives players access to Microsoft's Xbox Live! and a direct link to their "full" console experience.

iPad

As you can see, gamers have plenty of exciting hardware options. And by the time you read these words, I'm sure there will have been yet another new and exciting touchscreen system announced. So, how can a game designer stave off the constant march of technology and keep ahead? Can a game designer actually predict the future?[19]

---

[19]No.

Destroy All Humans!

Ah, the future. What will it be like? What is the future of these gaming devices? What if these gaming systems become obsolete? What will replace them? Will the robots eventually destroy us all? What's coming next? These are all good questions that I do not know the answers to. If I did, I'd be running down to the patent office with the designs for the next iPhone[20] rather than writing this!

But, dear reader and fellow human,[21] do not worry—the future is bright! While touchscreen gaming technology is always evolving, the basics of gameplay design remain the same. And this is what we will be learning in the next chapter, so let's get moving before the robots attack!

---

[20]Unfortunately, my time machine only goes backward.

[21]You are human, aren't you?

DEVELOPER INTERVIEW 1

Paul O'Connor

Developer profile: Currently the Brand Manager of **Appy Entertainment,** Paul O'Connor has been described as a "designer's designer." He successfully transitioned from a career as a pen-and-paper game designer to video game designer designing AAA console and tablet games. He helped found Appy Entertainment (*Trucks & Skulls NITRO, FaceFighter*) in 2008.

Last completed/published project: *FaceFighter Ultimate* (iOS)

Company website: www.appyentertainment.com

Previous titles: *Trucks & Skulls NITRO, FaceFighter Ultimate, Candy Rush, Zombie Pizza, Tune Runner* (all available on iTunes Store)

Paul, thanks for talking with us! How did you get into designing touchscreen/tablet games, and what excites you about making games for this platform?

We set up shop as full-time iOS developers on Halloween 2008, after exiting from our V.P. gigs at High Moon Studios following the Vivendi/Activision merger. We had a bit of cash in the bank and were convinced Apple's iOS was the future of gaming (and were equally convinced the incoming Activision administration had no desire to be part of the first wave on this platform).

At High Moon and throughout our careers, my partners and I were original IP guys, but the skyrocketing budgets of console games were creating an increasingly risk-averse environment where innovation was squelched and development was increasingly channeled into "sure things" like annual franchises and movie licenses. Not only was this muzzy thinking on behalf of the console giants—it was also shockingly boring, and we had little desire to spin out our remaining years in service to the same-old same-old. So we hoisted high the Jolly Roger and set sail in search of bluer waters.

What advice can you give to someone who wants to get into designing games for touchscreen/tablet space?

I'd follow Orson Welles's advice about filmmaking, which (roughly paraphrasing) was to either know everything there was to know about filmmaking, or nothing at all. Staggering into this field as a refugee from a failed console studio is to walk into rotating knives. This tech and this field is its own beast and you damn well better respect that. But maybe the best path is to get punched in the nose a time or two (provided you can get back up again).

Think about the tech, embrace it, realize this is a different animal, and please don't give us virtual joystick controls or a cut-down console experience on mobile. Please.

What gameplay and control challenges did you face when designing your touchscreen game?

Well, there's a laundry list, from technology that falls short, to a crap-shoot review process where your game is like Schrödinger's cat, to vexing game players who refuse to recognize the obvious brilliance of our work and tombstone us with shockingly low sales. But if you are asking about tech, well, I find the question boring and will pass on a detailed answer, save to say that the Appy approach involves lots of iteration and shouting, not always in that order.

A common debate among touchscreen game designers is over "direct finger" vs. "virtual interface": which do you prefer?

I prefer the virtual interface, and I'll tell you a story. I used to play ice hockey, and when I bought my first pair of skates, the old Canadian goblin in the skate shop fitted me to the boot without my socks on. I asked him why I should skate without socks, and he growled at me, "Do you make love with a sock on?" and I had to admit, no, that did not seem optimal. "So don't skate with socks on!" growled he, and I took that as the authentic wisdom. Maybe he was having a laugh because I never met anyone else who skated without socks, but that's how I did it through my long and undistinguished amateur hockey career.

Anyway, don't play touch games with a sock on.

In 2011, "freemium" games earned 65% of their profit from in-game stores and monetizing gameplay features. Do you think this model works or will the "freemium" model cause trouble for the gaming industry in the long run?

Freemium is the ONLY method that works for us in the market right now, and we've pivoted our two "premium" titles—*FaceFighter* and *Trucks & Skulls*—to employ this monetization. From this point forward, it will be the only method we employ, until it isn't.

Marketing a tablet game can be a struggle for many developers, yet Appy Entertainment seems to do it successfully. What has worked for you?

We bootstrapped everything. Anyone who tells you that you can sell a 99¢ game by purchasing conventional web banner advertising is delusional—that's always been a mug's game, and never more so than for these inexpensive and high-volume games. Offer walls seemed to work but we were late to that party and never benefited from them before Apple gave the whole idea a curb stomping. Mostly we built up our own little social media presence, went out of our way to be accessible to our fans, and built the kinds of game we thought would be attractive to Apple, hoping they would feature us (and they did, now pause for a second as I bow toward Cupertino). We've kind of jumped up into the air and then held ourselves there. We're near 10 million downloads now and are starting to develop enough of an internal network that we can launch our own stuff, and develop a first-day spike that brings us up the charts enough to be noticed by a wider audience, but it is still a cold and threatening world with few guarantees as you bring your game to market.

There's no place I'd rather be.

chapter 2

Clown-On-A-Unicycle

DO YOU HAVE an idea for a video game? Of course you do[1]. Let's pretend that you have an idea for the BEST. GAME. EVER. A game about a unicycle-riding clown who avoids being mauled by circus tigers while collecting banana cream pies. Genius!

Now, a clown on a unicycle might be a *funny* idea or a *clever* idea, but is it a *good* idea for a game? Making games can take a lot of time, money, and effort. You don't want to spend your time creating something that no one wants to play. (Or worse, something that no one wants to buy![2]) And you sure as heck don't want to spend your hard-earned money making a bad game. But how do you know if your idea is any good? Start with these clues:

- You are genuinely excited about your idea. This doesn't mean you are excited about how much money it will make, or the epic storyline, or the characters that would make great action figures. Rather, it means you are excited to play the actual game! Darn it, why doesn't this game exist yet!? Oh, yeah, because you haven't created it.

- Your mind keeps coming back to the idea. You keep thinking about it even when you are doing something else. Driving, showering, and making other games. And even better, you keep coming up with more and more ideas to improve on that initial idea.

- Other people seem genuinely interested in your idea. Even better, these people tell you that they still really like the idea a few days after you describe it to them.

If these things happen to you, then awesome! You must have a good idea and you should move it to the next step. However, keep in mind that you will encounter people who don't like your ideas. These naysayers will say, "This is a bad idea" or "This is not a good idea" or "This is a game that only a game designer would want to play" or even, as my producer Evan once told me, "This idea sucks[3]." If any of these comments reach your ears, I recommend you NOT do the following:

---

[1]Believe me; *everyone* has an idea for a video game.
[2]Of course, it is possible to have an "unsuccessful" game still make money solely through advertising.
[3]Thanks, Evan.

○ Shout "OH, YEAH!? Where's YOUR game idea, smart guy?"

○ Up-end the table

○ Start punching

While saying "your idea sucked" was pretty jerky for Evan to say,[4] it's more important to find out *why* someone doesn't like your idea. They're not insulting you as a person; they're just criticizing your idea. They might not use much tact or diplomacy, but in their own messed-up way they are trying to help.

I have discovered that people don't often say exactly what they mean; they tend to respond emotionally first, and intellectually second (except for programmers). When they tell you, "Your idea about a clown on a unicycle sucks," it could really mean "I don't care for physics-based platformers," or "I didn't enjoy playing Clown Frenzy 2 so I won't like this game either," or "Clowns scared me as a child." If you can discover the root of the concern, then you can address it. This is especially important if the person who doesn't like your idea is the guy who signs your paycheck[5].

Whatever happens, though, *don't take it personally*. Just suck it up and come up with something else. Besides, ideas are cheap. They're a dime a dozen. They're a whole bunch of other idioms. Why, I'll bet you could come up with five ideas for a game right now! A producer once told me to "not be so dear" about my game ideas. And he was right. Sure, my ego twinged for a minute, but I eventually came up with plenty of other ideas that were better than the first.

Let's Get High (Concept)

I have found there are two types of people: people with a lot of imagination and people with not as much imagination. You will have to present your game idea to both of these types of people. Sometimes people just "don't get it." It isn't that they're dummies. It just may be that your game idea is too complex. Or maybe you aren't clearly communicating your idea. Or maybe your game design has never been made before. New things can weird people out. They get confused when they have nothing to compare your idea to. Stereotypes can help with this. Stereotypes are stereotypes for a reason—they're easy for people to understand.

This is why the **high concept** works so well. A high concept is a concise description of your idea. In Hollywood, this is also called the "elevator pitch" because you only have the time it takes to ride in an elevator to pitch your idea to a prospective buyer. Just like any good pitcher, you need to have several styles of pitches: fastballs, change-ups, sliders. I use three different methods of pitching a high concept.

---

[4]Words can hurt, dude.

[5]I recommend making him or her happy.

The first method uses **similes**[6] where you compare your game idea to something else, usually an existing similar product, but with a twist! Or you can modify an existing game to make your own idea seem new and original. Need some examples?

- ○ It's *Canabalt* but with a flying superhero!
- ○ It's tower defense in the Wild West!
- ○ It's *Plants vs. Zombies* where **you** play the zombies!

The **simile style** lends itself to lots of exclamation points! While it's a perfectly fine way to describe your game, you run two risks when using it: sounding completely unoriginal and sounding completely cheesy. (There's a reason why TV shows and movies make fun of "Hollywood types" who pitch this way.)

However, as any honest-to-gosh Hollywood insider will tell you, keep your pitch as minimal as possible. This allows the listener to fill in the details of the idea however they wish. Everything a designer adds is just an opportunity to add something the listener might not like. The more the listener likes the pitch, the more likely they will be to "green light" your idea. In the case of a pitch, less is more. It's *what you don't say* that gives your idea a chance.

Pitching is hard. Everyone experiences some self-doubt when pitching an idea. Even worse, you might find out about an upcoming or existing game that sounds just like your idea. Nothing takes the wind out of your sails like someone saying, "Oh, that's just like *Trucks and Skulls* meets *Paper Toss*." While people who say things like that might come off as know-it-all jerks, in reality they're just trying to make a connection in their own heads about your game. They're not telling you your idea isn't very original. But then again, maybe they are—even if they don't realize it.

---

[6]A simile is when two unalike ideas are compared to each other. Am I the only person who has trouble remembering third-grade English class?

But here's the thing to remember: It's YOU who makes your game unique. No one is going to make YOUR game like YOU will. I have a dream that when I rule the video game–making universe, I will declare one year where everybody HAS to make . . . let's say . . . a tower defense game. Or DIE! (Okay, I'm kidding about the dying part . . . then again, if I AM the King of the Video Game Universe . . .) Power-fantasies aside, I guarantee you that everyone's tower defense games will come out differently. Some will be science-fiction, some will have zombies, some will have a deep story, and some will break new ground and create some sort of super-amazing new gameplay that I haven't even thought of. And that's cool! So, what does it matter if someone else's game is *kinda* like yours? Your game will be *yours* and your game is going to be better, right?!

My second method of creating a high concept is to combine two existing games. It's pretty easy to do:

○ It's the gameplay of *Bejeweled* meets the world of *Dungeons and Dragons*!

○ It's like *Flick Soccer* combined with *Angry Birds*!

○ Take *Quarrel* and mix it with *Super 7* and *Sid Meier's Pirates*!

The upside to the **combination method** is that it gives the audience an indication of the gameplay. The downside is that it doesn't provide *enough* detail so the audience knows what kind of game this new idea is about. The combination method leaves a lot of room for interpretation. Even worse, it leaves lots of room for *misinterpretation*. If your audience doesn't know the games you're referencing, then your pitch is worthless. It is *No One Can Stop Mr. Domino* meets *Dynamite Heady!* I can see your confused looks from here. The combination method is best appreciated by people with a deep knowledge of video games. But your audience isn't always going to be your fellow nerds. Sometimes they'll just be real people. Stick to references your fellow gamers will know. You don't need to be the winner of the "I know the most obscure game ever" contest.

This brings us to my third (and most preferred) high concept pitching method, which describes the game's **primary action.**

Games are *all about action*. The best game concepts can be described with *one action verb*. (Though sometimes it takes more.) You remember such verbs: a word that shows, well, action or a state of being,[7] like run, jump, shoot, swim, climb, hit, break, match, defend, escape, add, subtract, and so forth. Go ahead: Take that game idea, make it an action verb, and really sell it!

---

[7]This is why you should stay in school.

A verb describes the **primary action** of the gameplay. Pick a verb that describes your game. *Super Monkey Ball* is about rolling, *Flight Control* is about directing, *Bejeweled* is about matching, and *Angry Birds* is about smashing. You get the idea.

You don't need just one verb, either. Several verbs can be used to describe a game. *Super Monkey Ball* isn't just about rolling—it's also about navigating along the floor, balancing to control the ball, and collecting banana collectibles. But all these other verbs are in service to the primary action of rolling. Without rolling, you cannot reach the end of a floor and progress to the next level. Here are some other high concept examples that use the primary action method:

○ Use your finger as a ninja's sword to slice fruit.

○ Build and defend towers from advancing hordes of robots.

○ Use momentum to absorb small orbs while avoiding larger orbs.

○ Direct air traffic to safely land airplanes.

See how all these pitches focus on the primary action? This kind of pitching also brings some other advantages to the party:

○ It sets the game's tone. (Serious? Scary? Funny?)

○ It describes the gameplay genre. (Arcade? Puzzle? Adventure?)

○ It indicates the story genre. (Fantasy? Sci-fi? Horror?)

○ It states the game's victory condition.

There's one other thing this style of pitch does really well—it clearly demonstrates that your idea is "**game-able**." What's that mean? I'm glad you asked.

Yes, But Is It a Game?

If an idea is "game-able," then you can *imagine* it existing as a game and not just as an idea. What the heck does that mean? It means that I hate to be the bearer of bad news, but not all ideas are game-able.[8] Ask yourself honestly if your idea would make a better movie, comic book, toy, board game, novel, or theme park attraction than a game. If the answer is yes, then it shouldn't be a game. Let's say someone tells you they have a "great idea" for a game. They proceed to tell you about the game's character and the richness of the world and all of the feelings of awe and wonder and terror that their game will invoke. But when you ask them "how does it play?" if the answer is "I have no idea" then they don't have an idea for a game, much less a great one. Games are about gameplay first and everything else second. But what is a game? My super-simple definition is this:

○ Playable by at least one person

○ Has rules

○ Has a win/lose (or victory) condition

Now beyond these simple criteria, if you're still not sure whether you have a good idea for a game or not, you can always apply your idea to the test[9]. You can ask yourself questions like:

○ Is this idea something someone can *play* rather than something someone watches?

○ What is the game's primary action? Does it sound like an action that can be played?

○ What are the rules? Will they make the idea challenging? Enjoyable?

○ Is the idea simple and clearly communicated?

○ Will the player know what to do just by looking at the game?

○ Will the game play well on the game platform I'm developing on?

○ Does the idea sound "fun"?

---

[8]Not all ideas are good ideas, like those games where you make a monkey pee. (Sadly, this is a real thing.) Ironically, I always end up really liking something especially when I think it sounds stupid at first. Hmm, maybe stupid ideas = good ideas?

[9]Jesse Schell's *The Art of Game Design: A Book of Lenses* (Morgan Kaufman, 2008) offers several tests which you can apply against your own game ideas.

Some scholars state that a game should also be fun. Personally, I don't consider this a reliable test. There are things such as serious gaming, but that isn't what I'm talking about. I have real issues with the word "fun." Fun is like the terms "sexy" or "scary" or "funny." Fun is like art.[10] You know it when you see it. People find different things fun. Something you might think is fun (like riding a rollercoaster) might make me vomit for an hour in the nearest trash can—which I also don't think is fun. You can think (read: hope) that your game idea *might* be fun. But when you're just starting out making your game (unless it's based on something you already know is fun to do in another game), you're just shooting in the dark. You can start with what may actually be a fun idea, but I've seen many ideas that sounded fun on paper end up not being very fun when made into a game. It's easier to ask if it will make a fun game, aka, is it game-able, than is it solely fun. Knowing if an idea is fun is a gut feeling you develop after many years, but you can quickly determine if an idea will make a playable game if it's game-able.

Before I forget, I keep a notebook (and more recently a voice recorder) with me at all times. Why? Because I never know when a good idea is going to come along. The first step to a great game is a great idea. Don't lose that great idea. Make sure you *write it down!*

You'll need a reminder because as you design your game, details such as story, characters, mechanics, cinematics, controls, and so forth, will distract you from remembering your game's primary action. If you forget it, you could lose sight of the heart of your game design—and this will cause trouble in the long run. To help you remember, I have created a very special document I call the ***one-sheet.***

Really Quick Guide to the One-Sheet

If you've read my previous book, *Level Up! The Guide to Great Video Game Design,* then you should already know how to create a one-sheet. If so, feel free to jump ahead to the next section. However, if you haven't read that book yet or your brain is jammed up with other things such as all the names and professions of the creatures in the Star Wars Cantina or the names of every suduko game in the Apple App Store, then here's a quick refresher.

The one-sheet is the paper equivalent of the high concept pitch. It's a simple overview of your game which will be read by a variety of people: teammates, prospective investors, marketing people, and most of all, you! It should be short, interesting, informative, and short! Most importantly, it's just *one sheet of paper*. Here's what you should put on it:

- ○ Your game's title
- ○ The game's intended platform
- ○ The primary action(s) of the gameplay

---

[10]Don't get me started on whether I think games are "art."

○ A short description of the controls

○ A brief summary of the story (beginning, middle, and end)

○ Any cool and unique mechanics, controls, and puzzle ideas

You can find a more detailed template for writing a one-sheet in Appendix 2 of this book.[11]

The one-sheet is a pre-production tool and your constant reminder of what's important in your game. After you create it, every team member should own a copy. The one-sheet is their blueprint, their manifesto, and their guidelines to making decisions during production[12]. If all goes well, there will come a moment when you come up with a new game feature and your teammate replies, "Wait a second. That feature clearly violates what is on the one-sheet!" And you know what? They are right! You know they're right, and you're going to have to come up with a new idea. (Don't worry, ideas are cheap, remember?) You should celebrate because you have won a moral victory! Someone else finally understands your game idea!

Form Follows Function

So you've got your idea. You've got your primary action. What now? When you are designing *anything* in a game, you must decide **what it does** first. Let's say your enemy walks and shoots. Determining *how* it walks and *how* it shoots can inform what it looks like. For example, if you have an enemy that walks mindlessly back and forth and shoots straight ahead, it could be any of the following:

○ A laser-shooting robot:

---

[11]Convenient, eh?

[12]Keep in mind that the one-sheet is not a replacement for a game design document. It is simply the first step toward that more detailed game design.

○ An enemy soldier who marches back and forth:

○ Some sort of goo-spitting plant monster:

It's the **story genre** (like horror, sci-fi, western, and so forth) that will influence what your character looks like, but how it acts determines the gameplay. And the gameplay comes first, remember? However, I know it's very easy to get engrossed with what something looks like. I started my career as an artist, so I know how much fun it is to design monsters and other baddies—but if you start your design with a visual instead of the gameplay, you will be stuck with something that doesn't make for good gameplay. This is true for anything: mechanics, level design, HUD elements, and game options and save screens. Worry about what it looks like later. Design first, visuals second. Form follows function.

Function Follows Form

Okay, you know how I just lectured on how form follows function? Well, sometimes there are exceptions to the rule. Sometimes a game idea starts with a character instead of the primary action. Sometimes that game is the biggest selling game in touchscreen history: *Angry Birds* (Rovio Mobile Ltd., 2011).

The game was built around the characters that Jaakko Iisalo, our game designer, came up with. The original idea was very different, but everybody loved the birds, so it was decided to build a game around the birds. Over the next 8 months Angry Birds became the game we know today.

Peter Vesterbacka[13]—the Mighty Eagle of Rovio Mobile Ltd.

Thanks for making me look bad, *Angry Birds*[14]. The original *Angry Birds* game design involved the colored birds flying against corresponding colored blocks[15] but the team didn't think the design made sense. Instead, they looked to other popular physics-based flash games (like *Crush the Castle*) for inspiration. In the end, while the game was inspired by the form of the flightless birds, the function had to make sense for the form they liked.

Length Matters

While we're on the topic of "very simple rules game designers forget about," remember that **tablet gamers are mobile gamers.** This might seem like a no-brainer, but there's a big difference between the way someone plays a tablet game and a console/computer game. A console/computer game is usually played on a television screen or at a desk. Players hunker down in a darkened living room or man-cave for a marathon session of *Call of Duty: Modern Warfare 3*, or for hours building a monument to their favorite 8-bit character in *Minecraft*. These console

players have *time*: Time to "get into" a game, time to develop a character, time to get engrossed in the story, time to play through hours of content[16]. Their play experience is very different than those who play mobile games.

---

[13]http://technmarketing.com/2010/12/peter-vesterbacka-maker-of-angry-birds-talks-about-the-birds-apple-android-nokia-and-palmhp/

[14]Now I know why those pigs are so angry at those birds.

[15]You can watch a movie about that original pitch here: http://mailchimp.com/about/customer-stories/angry-birds/

[16]Once again, there are exceptions to the rule. The Nintendo Wii became popular because many of its players were casual gamers who played for shorter periods than the stereotypical gamer previously mentioned.

According to a 2011 Localytics study,[17] iPad users only played games for 75% of their average session length[18] (use of news and music apps were well past the 200% range), but games have the highest percentage of play sessions a month (13 sessions). This means mobile players are playing shorter games, but playing them more often. It isn't really a big revelation, it just confirms what most people already know: "Bite-sized" play sessions work best for mobile gamers, not epic quests or involved storylines. I'll teach you how to design for shorter experiences later, but for now, let's start with my TOP SECRET basic rules of tablet game design:

- ○ The average play session will last 2 to 5 minutes.
- ○ The overall game length should only be a few hours.[19]
- ○ Develop gameplay in terms of depth, not length.
- ○ Emphasize repeatability over content.
- ○ Create natural play breaks over the course of the game.

Let's look at each of these rules more closely.

---

[18]The session length equals the time the user spends in an app once it is opened.

[19]This is in sharp contrast to console games, where the average overall gameplay time is 8 to 10 hours, and PC games, where sometimes this is measured in months or even years!

The Average Play Session Will Last 2 to 5 Minutes

Why 2 to 5 minutes? Well, it doesn't have to be 2 minutes. It can be 30 seconds. It doesn't have to be 5 minutes. It can be 6 minutes. Keep in mind that 2 to 5 minutes is a target time length and not always the case depending on the game, the player, and the situation. Some players play longer on their iPad or their Nintendo DS than they would on their Android phone. But don't forget that *tablet gamers are mobile gamers.* Consider how long it takes to wait for that movie to start or for that line at the ATM to move. Look at other games and see how long a play session lasts for some of your favorite games. Do your own field research to determine the optimal play time for your game. Ultimately, the experience needs to be short, intense, and fun. A level in *Cut the Rope* only takes 20 to 30 seconds to beat, but launching the next level takes less effort than turning off the phone. Your audience just doesn't have the time or patience for anything longer.

The Overall Game Length Should Only Be a Few Hours

How do you determine the overall length if your game hasn't been created yet? *Use your imagination.* Pretend you are holding a tablet computer in your hand. Now imagine your finger touching the screen. On that screen is a little spaceship. (It could be a glittering column of jewels, a ninja running infinitely across the screen, a row of word tiles . . . whatever you can imagine!) Would it help if you draw a picture? Turn to the tablet screen template in Appendix 3, photocopy it, and draw what the player will manipulate.[20]

---

[20]You can use a notebook, a tabletop, a tablet computer, or the cover of this book! Any flat surface will do!

See? I drew a clown on a unicycle. Go ahead and move your finger around, imagining you are playing the game. In my imagination, as I poke at the clown, his unicycle moves forward or back, depending on the direction I poke him in. What does he do in yours?

How fast does that unicycle roll in your imagination? How many times do you have to poke him to move him all the way to one side of the screen? Is one poke not enough? Are five pokes too many? Maybe a swipe will feel more natural than poking the clown. I like that better because it feels more like I'm pushing him along. Swipe him again. How many swipes did it take? How long did it take that clown to roll to the edge of the screen? Three seconds? Four seconds?

Now imagine what the player will be doing over one level or session of gameplay. Let's pretend that our clown rolls along a continuously scrolling landscape. Anvils drop out of the sky and the player has to push the clown in a direction to avoid getting smashed. We can poke the clown to make him jump. With this jump he can hop over anvils that have smashed into the ground. Make believe you are playing this game . . . swiping at the clown to make him roll, avoiding the anvils as they thud into the ground, poking the clown to make him jump, collecting pies along the way.

How long did it take to play that game in your imagination? Now be honest with yourself: How long do you think it would take before a player got bored doing this? Add some new challenges to your imaginary gameplay. How many new challenges or twists do you need to add to keep things interesting? How long did it take to get through all these challenges and reach the end of the current level? Did it take you two minutes? Three minutes? How many levels do you think the player would want to play back to back? How many levels *do you want* the player to play? How many levels can you design before you exhaust all your good ideas? How long until the player gets bored and stops playing? Don't create just to create. If something feels too long or too boring, then it is. How long until the player finishes playing your imaginary game? *That's* how you determine the overall length of your game.

I call this exercise ***pacing out the game.*** This process gives you a basic idea of what the game should feel like without writing a single line of code or drawing a single pixel. You might not hit this target once you start getting the game up and running, but it provides a good starting point to aim for.

Another way to pace out a game is to pick some music and make the gameplay last as long as the song. I pick something that fits the "feeling" of the gameplay: fast-paced music for action games, slightly slower for exploration or puzzle games. When the song ends, did the game-playing in my imagination feel too long? Too short? Just right? I always say that a game should last as long as it feels right to play. It's an instinct that you will have to develop over the course of your game. It will also help you create the "**flow**" of the game.

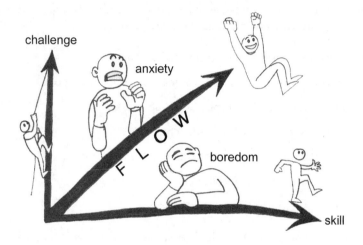

The preceding chart is from the work of psychologist Mihaly Csikszentmihalyi[21]. He coined the term "flow" and described it as a creative or active state where time feels temporarily suspended, focus is intensified, the impossible seems possible, and a sense of pleasure is derived from performing the activity. Flow is the state that exists between boredom and mastery. Some call it "being in the zone." A game designer's goal is to keep the player in the flow for as long as possible by using two techniques: **challenge** and **skill.**

If a game isn't challenging enough, then the player will get bored and stop playing. If the player fails to master the skills of playing the game, either by solving puzzles or quick reflexes, then the player will get frustrated and "drop out" of the flow.

---

[21]Want to learn more? Start with Csikszentmihalyi's *Flow: The Psychology of Optimal Experience* (Harper Perennial Modern Classics, 2008).

Develop Gameplay in Terms of Depth, Not Length

I know this rule seems contradictory since we've just spent two pages talking about game length, but you always want to think about how your game can get increasingly more complex and interesting to the player. Adding complexity doesn't mean adding more elements. It just means combining your elements in a simple, logical way. You don't even need many game design elements to create a compelling game. I find it better to work from a limited palette. It forces you to be more creative, and creative is good. For example, Firemint's *Flight Control* is a great game with a very limited game design palette:

- ○ Colored airplanes must land at matching colored airstrips.
- ○ Slower moving helicopters must land at matching colored heliports.
- ○ Players draw lines that direct airplanes and helicopters.
- ○ Players have the ability to redraw/redirect traffic.
- ○ Players have the ability to speed up traffic.
- ○ A radar warns of an imminent collision.
- ○ Traffic increases as the game progresses.

Seven game design elements, that's it! And yet, it's an engaging game that has sold almost 4 million copies.[22] You don't need too many design elements to make a great game, just the right elements. Quality, not quantity, prevails. Pick the right elements that will allow you to craft varied, deep gameplay. These elements are going to vary depending on the game genre. There are so many different game genres available on tablets and mobile devices that we'll be looking at them individually. For now, let's just stick with *simple is always best*.

Emphasize Repeatability Over Content

Continuing this train of thought, *Flight Control* really hooks the player to give it "just one more try." Because the game is very simple to play and the play sessions are so short, the player is encouraged to try again. This is a great goal for mobile gamers as games are played in short bursts. By keeping the play experiences short, interesting, and exciting, the game won't feel stale. Each play session/level/chapter will act as a natural break, and the player won't feel guilty stepping away from the game for a while. But your addictive gameplay will keep bringing them back. And that brings us to . . .

---

[22]www.gamasutra.com/view/news/32548/Firemint_IPhone_Flight_Control_Sell_39M_Units.php

Create Natural Play Breaks Over the Course of the Game

It isn't a bad thing to let players take a break. If your game is compelling, they'll return. You might even want to encourage them to take a break. Get on with their lives for a while. The game will be waiting for them. *Superbrothers: Sword and Sworcery* does this very cleverly without breaking character: The game's narrator encourages the player to stop playing, go outside and experience life for a little while. Structuring your game progression by chapters, sections, or components not only will keep things short and peppy, but also foster progress. The higher the number players get to, the more they'll feel like they've progressed and achieved. There are plenty of gameplay tricks you can use to make players want to play: High score and leaderboards promote competitive behavior in players, or the "must improve" addiction that players often experience in puzzle and arcade games. You learn more about these later in the book.

Emergent Eschmergent

The best thing to keep players playing is that spice called *variety*. Gamers love variety. Players love it when something changes: a new level, new enemies, a change in AI behavior, or the drop speed of a jewel. It's cool when things get subtly harder but players can still succeed. They love it when they earn a new weapon or have to use a new strategy to defeat an enemy.

Gamers also love *surprise*. Surprise is just variety that the player doesn't expect. The irony is that surprise shouldn't be a surprise to the game designer. You can build surprise into your gameplay just like anything else. I use a very handy tool called a ***beat chart*** to help plan out everything that comprises your game, from story, levels, mechanics, color design, time of day, rewards, progression . . . everything! *Level Up!* covers beat charts pretty thoroughly, but since you aren't reading that book, I have included how to create a beat chart in Chapter 7 of this book, too. I like to cover all the bases!

As you will learn when you create your own beat chart, even surprises must be planned. However, some people believe that surprise happens by itself; they refer to it as ***emergent gameplay.*** And I call baloney on this. There are two types of emergent gameplay: The first can develop while designing AI and physics. These types of interactions have just enough randomness in them to create fun and unexpected interactions. Entire gameplay modes can be inspired by these happy accidents. The second type is when a designer puts several elements into an environment and thinks fun and good gameplay *will just happen*. I'm sorry, but this is just dumb.

To illustrate this idea, let's look at *Scribblenauts Remix* (5th Cell, 2010). *Scribblenauts Remix* has a vocabulary of around 35,000 words that can be used to create objects in the game. Each word has several attributes linked to it. For example, a "policeman" is designated as a male, a person, and a walking character. He will fight someone who is marked as a "criminal" and try to eat anything marked as a "donut." The game's designers know all the attributes that have been assigned (designed) to

the policeman. They also know all the attributes of a zyzzyva; a genus of tropical American weevil often found in association with palms. It will eat plants and hop around. Now it might not be the designer's first thought to put a zyzzyva next to a policeman, but based on each character's attributes, the game designer can predict what will happen when these two encounter each other[23]. Some might say that is emergent gameplay; I say they just haven't thought the interactions out far enough.

To me, thinking about gameplay interactions is like sonar. If your "ping" is strong enough, you will be able to see very far. If your ping isn't very strong, you will only be able to see a short distance from your starting point. That doesn't mean that the things that exist outside of your radius aren't there; they just aren't on your radar. The goal is to create the widest ping possible. Hey, it's my metaphor, and it works for me.

---

[23]Spoiler alert: The Policeman will ignore the zyzzyva . . . unless you make it a gigantic murderous zyzzyva!

I Want to Be Rich and Powerful

As I see the end of this chapter coming up fast, let me toss out a few more basic game design grenades:

- ○ Beware of **designer blinders!**
- ○ The **Theory of Unfun!**
- ○ All games are **wish fulfillment!**

Designer blinders are insidious things that latch onto all game designers. They sneak up on you when you least expect it, when you have played your game for the thousandth time and it's no longer fresh and exciting. You are so tired of playing your game that all you care about is finishing it. You are so relieved that your gameplay isn't broken. You are so used to those clunky placeholder controls and the sticky camera that doesn't show off the best angle for gameplay that you don't care, or you don't mind that cheesy-looking artwork. This is when you need to rip off those designer blinders and walk around in the shoes of the first-time player.

You need to put your best foot forward and *be* that new player. Use your imagination and play your game for the first time again. Rediscovering your inner first-time player is harder to do than you might think, but it's totally worth it in the end. Look at your game with a critical eye. A hyper-critical eye. If you need some help, rely on your teammates, mentors, friends, and family. They'll help you discover truths about your game. For example, if people say your game is too hard, then it probably is. If people say your game is too boring, then it probably is. Fix that bad camera, remove those clunky controls, and update that ugly art. Apply what I call the **Theory of Unfun:** Remove all the "unfun" from your game. When you have removed it all, then all that should be left is the fun! Simple, right?

Tim Schaefer, who designed *Costume Quest* and the *Monkey Island* series and a million other awesome games, said something really smart that helps remember how to get into the mind of the first-time player. He said, "All games are **wish fulfillment**" (my emphasis). Players want to be something they (likely) aren't: smart, rich, powerful, clever, magical, evil, successful, sexy, and brave, and they're looking to your game to give them that, even if it's just for a short time. They've paid their hard-earned money to play YOUR game! They don't know how hard it was to make your game, to get that enemy encounter to work, or how the original art was so much better until you ran out of RAM—and frankly, they don't care. They just want to play something cool. They need a break from the real world, and they think your game can deliver that relief. They are your friend. Who knows, maybe they'll really like your clown-riding-a-unicycle game?

GAME DESIGN SPOTLIGHT 1

Fruit Ninja HD

Format: iOS (available in regular, lite, and HD versions)

Developer: Halfbrick Games

Designer: Luke Muscat

Fruit Ninja is a juicy action game with squishy, splatty, and satisfying fruit carnage! Become the ultimate bringer of sweet, tasty destruction with every slash.

The action arcade game *Fruit Ninja* boasts a "why didn't I think of that?" premise that show-cases the touchscreen better than any other iOS game around. Often, a simple and great control scheme is all you need to make a great game, but the Halfbrick team didn't rest on their laurels with that victory. *Fruit Ninja* dedicates everything in the game completely to its primary action: slicing things in half with an imaginary ninja sword. You don't do anything else, and you don't need to do anything else to have fun.

It's interesting that *Fruit Ninja,* despite its somewhat silly premise of dicing up fruit with a ninja sword, never dips into parody or irony where it easily could have done so. Its tone is somewhat reverential to the Zen aspects of Japan in general and Japanese martial arts in particular, which are especially reflected in the game's backgrounds that feature images of a yin-yang symbol and Hokusai's *Great Wave Off Kanagawa.* Between these images and the

Japanese influenced soundtrack, there's just enough culture to provide theming, but not so much that it feels singularly Japanese[1] (compared to Sega's *Samurai Bloodshow*, for example).

The best way to describe *Fruit Ninja*'s visuals is cute, but not what I'd call cloyingly cutesy. The fruit and bomb objects are graphic to the point of being cartoony. But that isn't a bad thing. They're just detailed enough to make slicing them feel satisfying but not so realistic that it comes off as too . . . gross. And color-wise, they are distinct enough to be able to tell them apart as they come shooting up into the playfield. The Sensei, the only visible character in the game[2], is depicted as a gentle Mr. Miyagi type of character, dispensing encouragement and fruit-related trivia in equal measure.

The game's selection screen is colorful and alive with motion. Five different fruits representing the player's five selection choices rotate within spinning colored circles. Each fruit is different enough in color to prevent mistaking one for another. The size of the fruit represents the player's priority in choices. Want to get right into the game? Slice the watermelon, the largest fruit. The multiplayer strawberry (with a big green VS on it) is the next largest. The bright yellow mango is the dojo selection, and the achievements and more games choices are off to the side because they aren't used as often by the player. A gloved hand periodically swipes past the "new game" option—not so subtlety informing the player what to do to get started. If that weren't a big enough clue, a sign reading "slice fruit to begin" is also displayed. I'm a big believer in "the more information for the player, the better," and this screen is a fine example.

---

[1] I might add that Halfbrick is an Australian development studio.

[2] An unnamed narrator informs us that "ninjas hate fruit." Perhaps scurvy will be the common ground that will finally bring ninjas and pirates together.

Like I said before, *Fruit Ninja*'s control scheme is where the game really shines. All the player has to do is slice. Selecting a new game? Slice the fruit. Select multiplayer? Slice the fruit. Visit the dojo screen? Slice the fruit. Return to the main menu? Slice the bomb. The theme logic is extremely strong. All games should be this clear. Even when new players try to "tap" or "push" a fruit to start the game and fail, they have that "a-ha" moment and realize they just need to slice. *Fruit Ninja* supports up to eight fingers, allowing many participants to slice at once or a single player to use many digits. This feature is probably there to support the game's multiplayer mode, and it's interesting that Halfbrick didn't disable it for the single player mode. The tradeoff is, you can use many fingers to cut more fruit at once, but also risk striking a bomb, which results in game over.

Gameplay in *Fruit Ninja* is exceedingly simple. Fruits (including pineapples, apples, mangos, bananas, watermelons, kiwis, and coconuts) are tossed into the air for the player to slice in half. When sliced, the fruits squelch and spray juice against the background, satisfying the player's "bloodlust" for slaughtering fruit. Coconuts make a nice clunk when cut in half. Fizzing bombs are also tossed up (their launch sound effect gives the player one more cue when one is coming), and explode if cut. This has a different result depending on the game mode. Critical hits (that award more points) can be earned with well-placed cuts, too. My only complaint about the game is you can't cut the fruit into anything more than halves. The bananas alone are begging to be diced up into little discs!

Classic mode has the player slice fruit until either three fruits are missed or a bomb is sliced. The goal is to obtain the best high score, with combos (multiples of three or more fruit sliced) adding to the overall score. Occasionally, a slo-mo pomegranate sails by; the player can furiously slice it for a combo bonus. This change of pace from precise slices to a frantic "cut as fast as you can" motion breaks up the play nicely.

In arcade mode, the player cuts as many fruit as she can within a time limit. Players aren't penalized for missing fruit but they are if they cut a bomb, which takes 10 points off the overall total. In this mode, three varieties of bananas appear: one that doubles points for a short period of time, a frozen banana that slows time making it easier to cut fruit, and the frenzy banana that unleashes a furious flow of fruit for the player to "go bananas" with[3].

Zen mode removes the bombs and the special fruits, allowing the player to just enjoy cutting apart produce within a time limit. It's a good way to practice for the other modes without having a nerfed training mode.

Multiplayer mode gives the player a choice between local two-player/one-screen classic attack and Zen duel as well as an online battle mode. Two players on one screen is particularly fun, and gets even more hectic if one player decides to intrude into the other player's screen.

Although it doesn't impact gameplay too much, there are also achievements that the player can perform to unlock new "blades" (really slicing effects with particles) and backgrounds. They don't contribute too much to the game other than the "where did you get that?" factor when showing your game off to others. I believe that you can never have enough particles, and the *Fruit Ninja* team members obviously agree. Fruit juice splatters against the background. Different blades emit sparks, puffs of shadows, or butterflies. The bombs sputter smoke as they are lobbed up. The pomegranate explodes like the Death Star at the end of *Star Wars* after the player has assaulted it. Confetti showers down when players beat their high score. *Fruit Ninja* is ultimately about pleasurable feedback, which makes it a pleasure to play.

So why is *Fruit Ninja* so good? I chalk it up to the following:

- ○ A single primary action that is used for everything in the game.
- ○ Satisfying feedback for every action.
- ○ A gentle yet fun tone that touches every aspect of the game's theming.
- ○ Simple yet compelling gameplay with just enough achievements and rewards to keep the player engaged.

Fruit Ninja is available on iTunes.

---

[3]Sorry.

chapter **3**

Finger Fu!

I'VE FOUND THAT game designers think a lot about how their games are going to play, but don't always think about how their games are *going to be played*. Although it's a subtle difference, it's an important one to consider when designing touchscreen games. As fingers and hands are integral to playing a touchscreen game, *how you want your game to be played* is one of the first things you should decide. In order to do that, you need to know about **ergonomics.**

> *Ergonomics (n): The applied science of equipment design, as for the workplace, intended to maximize productivity by reducing operator fatigue and discomfort.*

Ergonomics' most important contribution to humanity is U.S. patent #5,566,997: little corn-cob-shaped skewers that prevent your hands from getting buttery. Ergonomics' second most important contribution is assisting developers in creating awesome touchscreen gameplay design. The correct use of ergonomics can influence your controls, **user interface (UI)** design, and game length as well as your gameplay design. It's only a slight exaggeration to say that ergonomics can be critical to the successful design of a handheld game. Raise your hand if you know what stands (well, flops) in the way of that success?

Exactly! Your hand is the enemy! Wait! Stop! Don't lop off your hands! You will still need them later. Right now, I want you to look at your hand. Right there at the end of your arm. Turn it over, stretch out those fingers. Wiggle them around, give 'em a good flexing. Unless you are a pirate captain with a vendetta against a flying 8-year-old boy or a high school woodshop teacher, you should still have five fingers on that hand. Believe it or not, once upon a time, early (non-video) games were played with these things. Hands with fingers. Fingers that moved Mankala stones. Fingers that drew tic-tac-toe boards in the sand. Fingers that played that millennium-old game, "Dad! He's poking me!" Eventually fingers became stand-ins for other things: a pistol for "cops and robbers," a freeze ray for "freeze tag," a spider for "itsy bitsy spider." Fingers were all the rage.

As humanity evolved, humans realized they could play games using their *whole hand*. New games emerged: handball, basketball, football[1], Aussie rules football, bowling, dodge ball, ultimate Frisbee, "rock, paper, scissors," Jarts, and whatever the heck bocce ball is supposed to be.

In the 1970s, gaming became digital and kids immediately stopped playing outside[2]. Technology took over the world, we all became cyborgs, and video game controllers became stand-ins for human limbs. What you once were using your finger for, you could now use a multi-button, multi-stick, D-pad, analog controller.

Thankfully, the robot wars are over, and technology has flipped back around 360 degrees. We're back to playing games with our fingers, humans can easily pretend that a finger is a stand-in for a sword, a joystick, a slingshot, a press button, a gun sight, a marker, a laser pointer, a hand, and even . . . a finger.

Thank goodness players can use their imagination. It makes our job as game designers so much easier. If we are making, let's say, a golf game, it's no big deal for players to visualize their finger as a very tiny golf club.

Think of all the actions a golf club can do. (HINT: There aren't many.) This list will help us determine our game's **primary action**[3]. (SPOILER: It is swinging a golf club, unless this is one of those "Tower Defense Golf" games that will probably be all the rage after this book comes out.) Once you've made your choices, select the proper finger motions to these actions. Voilà! You have your initial control scheme! What? You don't know about finger motions? Not to worry. Like a naturalist crouching in the bushes and watching gamers in the wild, I have classified 22 distinct finger motions. To help you select the appropriate motion to represent your primary action, I present to you, in poetry form, the **Fantabulous Folio of Facile Fingering.**

---

[1] I mean American football, not soccer football, in which you mostly don't use your hands.

[2] According to your mother.

[3] Remember primary actions from the last chapter?

The Fabulous Folio of Facile Fingering

Come and read my folio,

my rhyme to you is true.

When it comes to finger motions,

I have found there's twenty-two.

A simple *tap's* quite useful

for rapid activation:

selection and detection, and

smart bomb detonation.

I suggest a *double tap*

to make your selection,

to open and to close windows

or indicate direction.

A *timed poke* makes for suspense:

When will I need to press?

Now? Or now? Or how 'bout now?

(My heart can't take this stress!)

In music games ***staccato pokes***

will make you keep the beat.

On a pad your fingers dance,

like little tiny feet.

Pecking on a tablet,

just causes me to gripe.

A keyboard that is virtual

is really not my type.

Touch and hold will always work

to keep things in their place,

so they don't run around the screen

or float off into space.

When moving items into

inventory or the trash,

use the ***hold and drag*** technique

to move it in a flash.

Fling away invaders,

shoot pucks without a stick,

soccer balls and marbles can be

flung with just a ***flick.***

Fig. I

Paging up and down is no different than a "flick," but no motion gets you through menus quite as quick.

Pull and release is favored by all the gaming nerds, just a backward flick is used to launch those angry birds.

Fig. J

Fig. K

Another motion I find good is what I call **'scrubbing'.** for removing any obstacles with just a little rubbing.

For making large movements,

a *swipe* is one that's vital:

swipe up, swipe down, or swipe across.

(Hey, now I get the title!)

Fig. L
*ce n'est pas le fait de
piquer passant une tablette*

Fig. M
*un cercle ressemble à un
donut autour de votre cœur*

A *circle* with a finger drawn

can rope a meteorite;

create a rolling wheel

or shield against a knight.

Wario can create boxes

by merely drawing *squares.*

Useful for materializing

doorways, chests, and stairs.

Fig. N
*oui j'ai juste copié la même
image du dernier*

Fig. O

c'est ça, je l'ai fait de nouveau – qu'allez-vous faire avec cela ?

Motion like a ***triangle***

will always have a sine;

Don't stop or else your code

will mistake it for a line.

Scribblenauts use advanced

handwriting detection

for ***writing numbers and letters.***

(More on this in another section!)

Fig. P

j'ai été à bout des choses amusantes à écrire dans le français

Fig. Q

voyez la ligne serpentine qui se dégage comme un ver

Avoid drawing too elaborate shapes;

keyholes? Squiggles? Enough!

I've heard that it's hard to code

detection for that stuff.

The **zig zag** is the best for making zippy motions, scribbling over pictures or drawing waves on oceans.

Fig. R

ceuxci la photo a fait des achats des images sûres me souvent alot de tirer le temps

Fig. S

déplaces les deux doigts simultanément pour l'effet maximum

Pinch open to scale it up and see your dungeon map. **Pinch closed** to scale it down. Ah ha! You've found a trap!

Rotate your target by drawing in a **swirl**. The spin you get is loose or tight, depending on the curl.

Fig. T

la spirale tourne autour de l'eau pareille tournant autour en bas de la canalisati

Fig. U

l'homme stupéfié en bas les pas comme un zombi

The angled ***stair step*** motion

is this list's last entry.

(Hey! I made my folio

without mentioning a zombie!)

Twenty-two moves are now complete,

folio's back on the shelf.

If you didn't like my poetry

then go write some yourself!

Twenty-two might sound a pretty limited number of finger moves, but they are plenty to make a wide variety of games. I guarantee you won't even end up using all of them in your game. Heck, if you are clever enough, you will only use one.

> *"One of our core design philosophies was that the whole game had to be playable with one finger."*
>
> *Donald Mustard, Co-founder, ChAIR Entertainment*

At the 2011 Game Developers Conference, Donald Mustard of ChAIR Entertainment (creators of *Infinity Blade*) offered an intriguing challenge to touchscreen game designers: Can your game be designed to be played with just one finger? Well, of course it can. But the idea Mr. Mustard was trying to get across was just because you have 10 fingers, it doesn't mean you have to use them all. (You actually can't use them all at once, but we'll get to that in a moment.) The question is, how do you design a one-finger game? There are plenty of examples. Take *Fruit Ninja HD* (Halfbrick, 2010), for which the player uses one finger to perform a basic swipe. That swipe is used to . . .

- ○ Cut horizontally
- ○ Cut vertically
- ○ Cut diagonally
- ○ Cut in a zig-zag
- ○ Cut several fruits at once
- ○ Cut a bomb (results in a negative score or game over)
- ○ Multi-cut time attack
- ○ Cut to select option/modes

One motion for eight different functions! Efficient! Good game design! The game fosters the "fantasy" of being a fruit-slicing ninja in many ways. A "sword-trail" (that creates the "path" of a blade) follows the player's finger movement. A "whoosh" sound effect plays whenever a swipe is made. All the selections are made by slicing rather than tapping. I say anything you can do to enhance the player's primary action will make the game feel more immersive and more . . . dare I say it . . . fun!

While it's easy to get caught up in the fun of designing functionality, fight the urge to layer in too many primary actions. In his GDC talk, Mr. Mustard revealed that his team considered arrow shooting and grappling hook throwing mini-games for *Infinity Blade*, but since the game's primary action is sword combat, these ideas were discarded. They distracted from the game's primary action.

You Only Have Two (to Four) Fingers

Now that we've spent almost three chapters together, I feel like I can confide in you. Don't tell anyone else, but my darkest secret is that I have pretty large fingers. Not ginormous, bratwurst-sausage-sized fingers, more like two Slim Jims held together-sized fingers. When I first started using the iPod touch in 2007, I had trouble using the touchscreen because of my oversized digits. This got me thinking about how to make games playable for people with all-sizes of fingers. The result? These rules of . . . finger . . . er . . . hand . . . er . . . thumb:

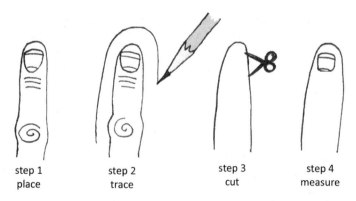

step 1
place

step 2
trace

step 3
cut

step 4
measure

○ Create a "finger gauge" for your game's layout. Use this "finger ruler" to gauge screen layouts and in-game distances for controls.

○ Buttons and on-screen controls should be big enough to be viewable even when a finger is over them. If the player's finger completely obscures a selection button, then the image is too small.

○ Don't place "opposite" user-interface elements next to each other. For example, if the Continue button is placed too close to the End Game button, the user might accidentally make the wrong selection (trust me, it happens). Separate these buttons using your finger gauge.

○ Thicker fingers make wider lines. For example, in *Sr. Mistu* (We Choose Fun, 2010), drawing a swirl is a tactic used to delay the constantly moving lead character from colliding with hazards. The radius of the swirl determines how long that delay lasts. I have found that a thicker finger draws a looser swirl than a smaller one, which affects gameplay. Account for differences in finger widths when designing gameplay. You can do this by considering the distances as you place gameplay and navigation screen elements. Be a little more generous with your spacing to compensate for your thick-fingered friends.

○ Does the player need to "lift and drop" a finger during the course of gameplay? Anticipation can play a big part in the action and rhythm of a game.

○ Be aware of where and how players position their hands and fingers on the screen in order to play the game. Remember, it's a video game, not a game of Twister. (Unless it's a touchscreen game of Twister!)

○ Hands can obscure UI elements at the bottom and sides of screens. Move those elements toward the center of the game screen or find another way to represent the information: This can be a flashing visual, sound effect, or text alert . . . preferably all three! Whatever you do, don't obscure characters, enemies, and other important game elements!

○ As the player's attention is usually fixated at the center of the screen or the tip of their finger, try to have the most important information communicated there first. All information should be placed slightly above where you want the player to touch so it's not obscured by those meaty Slim Jims of theirs.

○ Hand widths vary. A child's hand can't stretch as far as an adult's. Unless players are meant to use two hands to play your game, don't rely on them to extend their hand to touch two things at once.

○ Precise navigation while using a finger for control may be hampered by the build-up of sebaceous oils on the touchscreen's surface[4]. Because of this, allow a little "give" in the player's controls and physics; don't expect a finger-flinging gamer to pull off pixel-perfect moves.

---

[4]Which is about as gross as it sounds.

Of course, user hand size and use might make some of these rules less important than others. You'll just have to be the judge of what works best. What's the most important rule? Always give the player a "hand" when designing for hands.

Hands Solo

The average human has 10 fingers but the average touchscreen gaming human only uses 2 or 4 of them. What are the rest doing? Signing? Rolling pennies? Thumb wrestling? No. They have an important job too: stabilizing the gaming device. Consider how the player holds the gaming device. For example, a player holds the Sony Vita with two hands, thumbs extended to operate thumb sticks and index fingers placed on shoulder buttons or poised over or behind the touchscreens, like so:

Compare that to how someone holds an iPhone: like a waiter waiting for an order, the device cradled in one hand and the other hand poised with the thumb and finger extended for quick poking or pinching. Note how the middle, ring, and pinkie fingers curl up like some sort of a dead Alien face-hugger. Why does *that* happen? I don't know, but it does. Watch someone playing a touchscreen game sometime. They might hold the iPhone in a death-grip with both hands; thumbs furiously working a virtual joystick, button controls, or keyboard like a teenager texting that she's just seen Katie at the mall, hanging out with *Cooper*! OMGWTFBBQ indeed!!

Acknowledging how the player holds the device is not just important for determining the placement of controls. Take into account the time it takes the player to use those controls. Programmers may need to make allowances for the time and distance it takes the player to activate controls by slowing down required reaction times, adjust enemy attack

speeds, or the rate of displaying quick timer events. Or you can also capitalize on this player clumsiness to create tension in your gameplay. Both *Enviro-Bear 2000* (Blinkbat Games, 2009) and *Dead Space* (EA, 2011) use awkward controls to create different gameplay feelings — one for humor, the other for horror.

Game designer Charley Price offers some good advice: "Know your devices backward and forward. Get them in your hands and use them as much as possible where and when your target audience will use them. Use them in line at the store, use them in the bathroom, use them in places where sound isn't an option, or where sunlight causes awkward glare and constrains how the player can look at the screen. The reality of these devices is that they are often used in non-ideal gaming scenarios: when a person can be interrupted by a phone call at any moment or potentially distracted or further constrained by being in a public environment. The more multi-scenario friendly your game is, the more likely your player will use it."

Good advice, Charley! And even if you aren't a "hardware guy," knowing what a device can do is just a smart idea. You might not use all of a device's functionalities; a little-used feature might provide inspiration for a new type of gameplay. Take **multi-touch,** for example. Many touchscreen devices allow for multiple inputs. Designing for multi-touch can completely change your game's controls and gameplay. What's the design advantage of multi-touch? Well, you can connect three things together. You can hold an enemy in place while materializing a hammer to whack him on the head. You can open an inventory screen and scroll through the options. You can rake the screen with multiple fingers, decimating several enemies at once. The options are endless! Some current multi-touch screens can support up to 11 touch points, which is great if you are playing with several friends or are a giant squid.

Several of iOS5's functions in the iPad are multi-finger based, such as shutting down or switching apps. That's not going to be very popular mid-game! Since you can't use 11 figures AND hold a gaming tablet at the same time, I have found that many multi-touch games are best played by setting the tablet flat on a table. Other options include but are not limited to a player's lap, the back of a pack animal/small child, or some other horizontal surface. Designing controls for multiple fingers can be challenging. I recommend you don't count on a player using more than four fingers at once, unless you are creating an extremely unique control

scheme. It's just too hard for players to react to 11 different events. Humans can't even multi-task, according to a 2008 University of Michigan study[5].

According to the study, the part of the brain that handles multiple inputs is called the "executive system," and it acts like a conductor signaling parts of an orchestra to play rather than commanding them to all play at once. During their tests, they flashed digits to test subjects. "If the two digits are one color—say, red—the subject decides which digit is numerically larger," says neuroscientist Daniel Weissman. "On the other hand, if the digits are a different color—say, green—then the subject decides which digit is actually printed in a larger font size." But if the test subject has to go from determining red information to determining green information, then his brain actually pauses before responding. The brain has to literally switch gears to process the green information. And if the subject has to switch between three colors, the brain has to keep swapping to process red to process green to process blue. The executive system can't process the data simultaneously.

In my own studies, I've observed that players usually concentrate on their fingertip first, their immediate periphery next, and anything else (usually the sides of the screen) last. Essentially, no matter how large or small the screen, the user develops tunnel vision to maximize concentration. This results in the player failing to see everything going on at once[6]. I've experienced games where I was so hyper-focused that I failed to see a slow-moving threat coming my way UNTIL IT WAS TOO LATE.

Okay, so we shouldn't design for one player to do 11 things, but how about four players doing two and a half things[7]? I'm talking about multiplayer touchscreen games. There's something very old-school about huddling around an iPad, like a high-tech board game. In fact, many multiplayer tablet games are based on their board and card game counterparts: *Scrabble, Chess, Monopoly, Catan, Small World, Uno,* and *Bang!* just to name a few. These games are played the old-fashioned way: featuring ***asynchronous play,*** where a player takes a turn and then waits for the next player to take his turn. However, as anyone who has attended a game night knows, there's nothing worse than waiting around for Aunt Judy to take her turn.

---

[5]"Think you're multi-tasking? Think again." www.NPR.com (http://www.npr.org/templates/story/story.php?storyId=95256794)

[6]Psychologists Simon and Chabris conducted a famous study about attention blindness in 1999. Watch a great example of attention blindness in action at http://www.youtube.com/watch?v=vJG698U2Mvo.

[7]Actually 2 and 3/4th things if you do the math.

As a game designer, I would rather let players play all the time and give them something to do even when it isn't their turn. In
Quarrel HD (Ignition Entertainment,
2011), players assemble words even when
it isn't their turn. If they successfully spell a
word, then they earn points that give them
an advantage when it's finally their turn.
That's good game design! Of course, if your
game play is sufficiently nerve-wracking enough, then it's only fair to give your players a rest.

Another way to let everyone play together is to let everyone play together. Thanks to Wi-Fi,
simultaneous multiplayer is the most common way to play together on the Nintendo DS
and other mobile devices. Some Nintendo DS games require an additional cartridge to play
multiplayer, while others allow for a limited number of players using one cartridge via the **DS
Download Play.** DS multiplayer standouts include *Namco Museum's Pac-Man Vs.* (Namco,
2007), *Dragon Quest Heroes: Rocket Slime's Tank Battle Mode* (Square Enix, 2005), and *Advance
Wars: Days of Ruin* (Intelligent Systems, 2008), as well as that old stand-by *Mario Kart DS*
(Nintendo, 2005).

Although **peer-to-peer multiplayer** gameplay is common on the Nintendo DS, only a few
games were available on early iOS devices (*EUIPong*, EUI, 2008, being an example). It wasn't
until the introduction of Bluetooth that peer-to-peer gameplay blossomed. *Flight Control HD*
and *Bluetooth Hot Potato* (Nathan Peterson and Edwin Calo, 2009) both allow players to send
game elements off-screen, which appear on another player's device. Both DS Download Play
and Bluetooth are great for multiplay, but the range is limited. In most cases, all of the players need to be in the same room together.

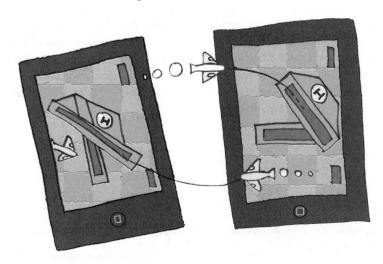

Fruit Ninja HD and *Mirror's Edge* (EA, 2009) have added **head-to-head competition** modes. *Air Hockey Gold* (Acceleroto, 2008), *Shot Shot Shoot* (Erik Svedang, 2011), and *Omium – 2 player shooter* (NimbleBit, 2010) have been designed specifically for head-to-head play. This works out particularly well on tablet platforms because each player can comfortably play from their "side" of the tablet. A precious few games have been specifically designed for more than two players; *Gurlz VS Robots* (Sticks+Stones Games, 2010) and *Semi-Automatic* (Samuel Farmer and Asher Vollmer, 2011) revel in the chaos that four sets of fingers all poking, swiping, and pinching at once creates.

Designing for four players not enough of a challenge? Then try adding a **stylus.** Specific stylus-using systems like the Nintendo DS and the UDraw rely on a stylus for player interaction with the touchscreen. Although a finger might act like a stylus, a stylus is definitely not a finger. A stylus fails to provide a tactile connection to the game screen that a finger provides and . . . it's a lot harder to lose a finger than a stylus[8].

Instead of a D-pad or analog stick, many touchscreen games use a stylus to move the character around. Cole Phillips, designer on *Drawn to Life* (THQ, 2007), offers this advice: "Don't. Using a stylus to click and drag, swipe and slash, or write or draw is great! Using a stylus to move a character is much more difficult . . . . Ideally I try to avoid situations where the player has to holster and draw his stylus often. A player doesn't mind holding the stylus if he's constantly using it, but having to switch back and forth is just no fun."

If your gameplay absolutely has to switch between traditional controls and a stylus, then strive to create opportunities for the player to comfortably physically swap the D-pad and the stylus. This swap can't occur in "panic" situations that could result in stylus fumbling and in-game death. At least display a "now pull out your stylus" screen, or provide an in-game moment to allow for this real-world interaction to happen. By considering the ergonomics, you will create a better play experience.

---

[8]Needless to say, I've lost many styli. However, when you've run out of losing styli you can at least replace them with fingers. The reverse doesn't work so well.

Virtual Joysticks Suck . . . or Do They?

"You know what the iPad doesn't come with? It doesn't come with a joystick."

Graeme Devine, Founder, GRL Games

A **virtual joystick** is a HUD graphic displayed on the screen. Players move a character (or whatever) by "pushing" the stick in the desired direction. Most commonly used for arcade-style games, they come in two varieties: single stick as used in *Ultimate Spider-Man: Total Mayhem* (Gameloft, 2010), *Predators* (Fox Entertainment, 2010), and *Death Rally* (Remedy Entertainment, 2011), and twin "thumb-sticks" like in *Simpsons Arcade* (EA, 2009), *Minigore* (Mountain Sheep, 2010), and *Solomon's Boneyard* (Raptisoft, 2010).

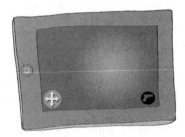 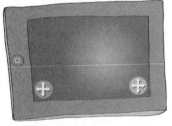

Single virtual stick   Dual virtual stick

A single virtual joystick is usually found in the lower left corner of the screen and attempts to match the feel of an analog arcade stick. They are often accompanied with button controls used for combat, jumping, and other actions, but variations on these schemes do exist. The *Modern Combat* series (Gameloft, 2009) uses a combination of virtual joystick and swipe controls to aim and shoot, while *Conan: Tower of the Elephant* (Paradox Entertainment, 2011) has an area in which the player draws sword swipes. Remember to give left-handed players the option to reverse these control schemes. Just because most games don't offer the option doesn't mean your game shouldn't.

Twin virtual joysticks are usually positioned at the bottom on the screen: one stick to the left and the other to the right. More often than not, the left stick is used for movement and the right stick is used for shooting—a control scheme first seen in the arcade game *Robotron: 2084* (Williams, 1982). Sometimes these sticks are invisible to the player, making for a less-intrusive control experience.

Despite all these features, the truth is that virtual joysticks are pretty reviled among the touchscreen community, who are split into two camps: those who don't like virtual joysticks and those who *really* don't like them. Okay, I'm kidding[9], but as Mr. Devine argues, why would you want to add a layer of interference between the elegance of direct control on a touchscreen? Virtual joysticks are an attempt to imitate a "real" joystick controller[10], but they can suffer from a range of problems:

Problem: You've designed your joystick as a series of directional arrows rather than a true joystick.

Solution: If you have joystick functionality, then take the time to design a true joystick which will reduce screen real estate. In the case of an eight-directional stick, a clear delineation of the selected direction is a must.

Problem: Without the tactile feedback of a physical stick, a finger can drift off the joystick's position.

Solution: Solve this by having the joystick snap back to the center position if the player loses contact with it. The player will quickly learn to reorient back to the center of the control area.

Problem: Sometimes the player tries to grab the joystick and just misses it.

Solution: Make the collision radius a little bigger than the graphic of the area it represents. Allow for those thicker fingers!

Problem: The player's finger drags off the joystick's position.

Solution: What!? This happened again? You can always have the joystick move with the player's finger or draw the joystick under the player if it leaves the original radius. Be careful that this doesn't result in the player "chasing" the joystick around the screen.

Problem: Player moves in a random direction when your finger is lifted and replaced on the joystick.

Solution: The joystick's center should be a "dead zone" so nothing happens until the stick is pushed in a direction.

---

[9]Somewhat.

[10]Not ironically, several companies have found a way to make lemons into lemonade and are manufacturing physical joysticks and mini-arcade cabinets that you can dock into or suction-cup onto your gaming tablet to compensate for the lack of a physical joystick.

Problem: Player movements feel too slow.

Solution: You might have made the visuals too large. Design a smaller joystick image with a tighter radius.

Problem: The player's hand ends up covering part of the game screen.

Solution: Keep UI elements away from corners and sides of the screen.

Problem: Players have trouble determining how far their finger can travel away from the joystick before losing contact.

Solution: Many virtual joysticks show the radius of the stick's movement. Not a bad solution, but it results in a large circle graphic chewing screen space. Lessen this problem by making the visual semi-transparent.

Another solution is to segment off-screen real estate. Games like *Bring Me Sandwiches!!* (adult swim, 2011) and *Don't Run with a Plasma Sword* (XperimentalZ Games, 2011) divide the player space into "areas of movement" and "areas of action" (such as a jump or sword swing). This allows the player to touch anywhere within the designated area and successfully perform the action without worrying about precisely touching a virtual stick or button. Just make sure the player doesn't cover-up important visuals with his fingers.

Hands Get Their Revenge

Not all touchscreen games need finger-based controls. Many handheld gaming devices have an arsenal of creative control options, including GPS and internal compass, built-in microphone, and still and video cameras. Even the hinge of the Nintendo's DS can be used for gameplay! We'll get to these other control schemes when applicable[11], but as we finish up, let's look at one of tablet gaming's most signature features: the ***accelerometer.***

Accelerometers detect the position of the device in space and provide that data to a game's code. By measuring weight, the accelerometer determines the free-fall inertia relative to itself. Accelerometers have limitations to how quickly they respond to changes in acceleration and cannot respond to changes above a certain frequency or extreme angle, which is why they sometimes feel sloppy and imprecise.

---

[11]Read: when I feel like it.

An accelerometer allows the player to speed up or slow down a character (or metal ball or pirate ship or cat-creature . . .) by tilting the gaming device. Tilting can be subtle or severe, depending on the gameplay. Tilt controls bring a level of realism that touchscreen controls can often lack. Accelerometer controls are often used to simulate real-world controllers like steering wheels, or labyrinth-style tilt-puzzles. Accelerometers are commonly used in conjunction with a built-in camera and **augmented reality** games such as *Star Wars: Falcon Gunner* (THQ, 2010) and *UFO On Tape* (Revolutionary Concepts, 2010).

However, despite having a full 360 degrees of rotation for controls, few games currently take advantage of this range of motion. Tilting gameplay trends toward finessing the tablet rather than making broad motions, usually resulting in spin-outs and other disasters. Do a quick and big tilt in both *Labyrinth* (Carl Loodberg, 2008) and *Plunderland* (Johnny Two Shoes, 2010) and watch the difference. All I'm saying is to cater the tilting to the game. Poorly designed tilt controls can be a source of frustration for the player. Avoid this by considering the following:

○ Account for the player's inertia by putting extra space between mechanics, hazards, geometry, and enemies.

○ Accelerometer-controlled character can't "stop on a dime" unless you specifically create controls to do so.

○ Give players the opportunity to change direction, jump, or correct their course.

○ When panicked, players will overcorrect, causing them to lose control. You can make this behavior a part of gameplay, but if it happens too frequently, players will just get frustrated.

○ If things get too hectic, give the player an opportunity to "level-out" the character's movement. In many games, this means immediately stopping the character's movement with a button or stabilizing a horizontal playfield by laying the tablet flat.

Naught (Blue Shadow Games, 2011) flips tilt controls around (pun intended) where the player rotates the world rather than the game's cat-hero. When the world is the controllable element, it helps to keep the player character locked to the center of the screen. By giving the player a stable point to visually fixate onto, the illusion of motion created by the rotating world increases[12].

Players can also "shake" the accelerometer in the mobile device to create gameplay. *Motion X Poker* (Full Power Technologies, 2008) and *Shake and Spell* (SocialDeck, 2009) let players shake to jumble dice and word tiles. *High Noon* (Happylatte, 2011) has its gun-slinging player draw their mobile device like a six-shooter. *Xhake Shake Graffiti's* (Cross Discipline Technologies, 2009) has the player shake, flip over, and even *not move* for gameplay[13]. Just be careful when designing these motions. A shake that goes on too long or a motion that is too fast or broad could have a player drop and break their device if it slips from their hands!

KRASH!

---

[12]The visual effect in *Naught* reminds me of the "goat trick" you can experience at Disneyland's Big Thunder Mountain. As you ride the rollercoaster, the runaway train passes a dynamite-chewing goat. If you focus your attention on the goat as the train speeds down and around a tight corner, you experience what feels like increased acceleration. In reality, it is caused when a person's head (and the ear's semicircular canal, which helps regulate balance) rotates while the ear's endolymph stays stationary. Fluid in the ear canal pushes against the cochlear cupula, which creates a sensation of accelerated turning in the opposite direction, hence the spatial distortion. Who says you can't learn anything from video games?

[13]Normally, I don't condone "not moving" as gameplay, but in the case of *Xhake Shake Graffiti*, it actually works.

As we have seen, good game designers are familiar with all the tools available to them—from knowing their devices to what the players can do with their hands and fingers. It all boils down to these three simple questions:

1. How do I want the player to play the game?

2. Is the game's primary action supported by the controls?

3. What motions work best for my game?

Now that we've examined controls, let's start designing some games we can use 'em in!

DEVELOPER INTERVIEW 2

Andy Ashcraft

Developer profile: After many years as a designer with AAA companies, including Visual Concepts, SCEA, and THQ, Andy Ashcraft struck out on his own to form **Giantsdance Games,** an independent developer of mobile games.

Last completed/published project: *Disney Pixar Cars 2:* AppMATes (iOS)

Company website: www.giantsdancegames.com

Previous titles: *Lock's Quest* (Nintendo DS), *TRON, Jellycar 2* (iTunes Store)

Hey Andy, thanks for talking with *Swipe This!* What would you say excites you the most about designing games for devices with touchscreens?

What I like about touchscreen devices is just how immediate the player's input can be. You can tap on your guy (or whatever) and drag him where you want him. When playing a traditional console game, I have to remember an arcane set of finger and thumb twitches to do that same thing. Not all player input can be that immediate, of course, and touchscreen devices also have other inputs as well: tilt and motion, microphones, cameras, buttons, and even GPS that work in tandem with the touchscreen. Between touchscreens and motion input, I like that we're re-thinking how the player gives commands to the game.

What advice can you give to someone who wants to get into designing games for touchscreen/tablet space?

Okay, my advice to anyone designing touchscreen games: Fer heaven's sake, please don't use *Angry Birds* as your model for success. *Angry Birds* is a cute, good little game, but is not excellent **except** in its performance in the marketplace, and that is a fluke of timing and won't be repeated. The last game to have this kind of success was *MYST* in 1993. *MYST* was the game everyone HAD to own when he or she bought his or her first computer and CD-ROM drive. Everyone bought it, but very few people finished it and went on to buy more games. That was a win for Cyan, the publisher, but an enormous failure for the industry. I predict that *Angry Birds* will stay at the top of the charts until the next piece of hardware has the kind of explosive growth that the CD-ROM had and that iPhone has currently.

What gameplay and control challenges did you face when designing your touchscreen game? How did you overcome them?

The biggest challenge that the touchscreen offers is the lack of a "mouse-over" function. That is, you can't select a UI element without actually touching it and activating it. On other game machines, you can select something, find out about it, and then press a button to commit your choice. The biggest challenge to ANY game design is how it communicates to the player, so a feature like this is sorely missed. There are other ways to explain the game features: tutorials, VO, pop-up screens, but none are as elegant as the basic mouse-over.

Which do you prefer? A "direct finger" interface or a "virtual joystick" style interface?

I think I'm a "direct finger" man. Wait, that sounds dirty. I mean that I have never met a virtual joystick that I liked. At best, they are only semi-successful. The biggest problem is the lack of tactile feedback. On an actual joystick, you know without looking which way your thumb is pressed by the rotation of the stick under it. You can feel that. On a virtual joystick, if the game doesn't react the way that you think it should, you have to look away from the action to see where you're touching. You lose your sense of feel, and have to make up for it with either audio that can get repetitively annoying, or visuals that clutter up the screen and can be hidden by your thumbs anyway.

What are some of your favorite touchscreen/tablet games?

My favorite touchscreen game is *Trainyard* (iOS) by Matt Rix at Magicule. *Trainyard* does an excellent job of making me feel clever, provides a series of short gameplay experiences that are good for mobile play-patterns, AND it avoids a major pitfall of other touchscreen games: Your hand gets in the way. The solution was to make the controls asynchronous to the action: That is, you draw the paths and then press "go" to see if you were correct. Your fingers never hide the action.

What advice do you have for those designing for augmented reality (AR) games?

AR games are still in their creative infancy, but I see two major types emerging: games that know where you are (location based) and games that can see what you see (camera based). Naturally, some games will use both, but that limits the audience by hardware. There are very successful AR games out there now, but they don't feel like "games" in the traditional sense, like *Foursquare*. I have not yet seen an AR game (in the traditional sense) that was very compelling. I can see a future where a great AR game sweeps the public off their feet and reaches the level of mainstream hobby.

What are your thoughts on the "freemium" model of distributing games? Is it good for the industry, or will it cause trouble in the long run?

I've heard designers complain that a financial model that relies on in-game purchasing turns their job into a marketing job. My response: "Yes, and . . .?" As designers, we have always been marketers: We need to know what our audience wants and how much they are willing to pay for it. Only then should we bother to figure out how to make it work as a game. We abdicate the responsibility of knowing our market, and then complain about the marketers who try to do that for us, but can't see what we know about our games. The "freemium" business model simply forces us to own what should be ours to begin with.

chapter 4

GenreBusters

LET'S FIND A game on the iTunes App Store. Take a look at how those games are classified: Action, Adventure, Arcade, Board, Card, Casino . . . . They are listed by **genres.** According to the dictionary, genre is "a class or category of artistic endeavor having a particular form, content, technique."

Stories also have genres: Action, Adventure, Crime, Comedy, Drama . . . . Wait a second! You said "Action" and "Adventure" twice! Are you getting senile? Is Action and Adventure a story genre or a game genre? Make up your mind!

Here's where terminology gets a little screwy. You see, video game developers have a bad habit of using the same word for different things. Map. Level. Ghost. Farming. Genre is one of those words. To help us tell the difference, I will be using **game genre** and **story genre.**

Game genre refers to type of gameplay the player experiences. There are lots and lots of different game genres. Here's how the Apple iTunes Store classifies games by using game genres:

○ Action   ○ Music

○ Adventure   ○ Puzzle

○ Arcade   ○ Racing

○ Board   ○ Role-Playing

○ Card   ○ Simulation

○ Casino   ○ Sports

○ Dice   ○ Strategy

○ Educational   ○ Trivia

○ Family   ○ Word

○ Kids

Within these genres, we can find subgenres. Action-adventure, survival horror, physics puzzle, rhythm game. Later in the book, I break these game genres down into more specific styles of games, especially those that have become really popular on touchscreen and tablet systems.

Using genre to describe your game helps other people understand quickly what your game is about. It also sets player expectations. If a game is advertised as a role-playing game (RPG), I would expect there would be a customizable character, leveling up, an inventory system, maybe even a weapon upgrade system. If the game is an arcade game, play should happen in short bursts with frantic action, scoring, quick reflex gameplay, and maybe a charming player character. If you deliver content contrary to these expectations, you risk turning players off, making them sad and confused. Players don't like to think a game is one thing only to learn it's something else.

The other genre, the **_story genre,_** describes setting, mood, theme, and topic. Remember going to video stores before so many of them went out of business? Do you recall how all the movies were organized on the shelves by genre to make it easier to choose what to watch? Remember how the movie you went to the store to get was always the one movie that was checked out? That sucked. No wonder so many video stores have disappeared. Anyway, in case you've forgotten what movie genres are, they include:

○ Action   ○ Film Noir

○ Adventure   ○ Horror

○ Comedy   ○ Mystery

○ Comic Book   ○ Science Fiction

○ Crime   ○ Sport

○ Drama   ○ War

○ Fantasy   ○ Western

Story genres are a great way for someone to quickly "get" what your game is about, or at least what it will look like. I say "Horror" and you are going to expect specific things, right?

But if I say "Horror" and my game looks like this:

Then you are going to say "What the heck!? That's not a horror game!" You see, the story genre provides a preset "flavor" that the player likes and presumably meets her expectations. This is why fast-food restaurants are popular. Customers expect the same (if not similar) things every time they visit. Have you ever seen someone discover that his favorite item is taken off the menu? Believe me, it's not pretty.

Story genre can make things easier when you are writing a story. A western is going to have a different type of protagonist than a comedy. The antagonist in a fantasy game might be different than one in a puzzle game (then again, maybe not!). Genre can help you determine weapons and equipment, vehicles and locations, even music and lighting! And then there's the power of genre-loyalty! Many devoted gamers will try a game just because of its genre[1]! If you are smart (and I know you are), you will harness the power of genre!

---

[1]You should find out what that genre is and make a game in that genre immediately.

When determining your game genre and story genre, remember that the two don't have to be identical. You can have a horror puzzle game, an action science-fiction game, a comedy role-playing game. In fact, the more unusual the combination is, the more original your game might be. I say "might be" because of the **Triangle of Weirdness.**

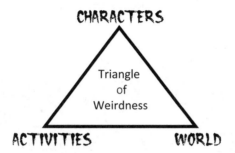

Now remember when I said I "don't do theories"? Okay, I lied . . . but just a little. The Triangle of Weirdness is my theory that states that there are three aspects to a game: character, world, and motivations. But only one of these aspects can be weird. Examples:

The characters in *The Wizard of Oz* are weird—a living scarecrow, a robot woodcutter, and a talking lion—but a fairy-tale world was pretty commonplace to readers in 1900 when the book was first published. The heroes had very relatable motivations: They just wanted to be brave, smarter, more loving.

Contrast the *Wizard of Oz* with *Star Wars*. The characters in *Star Wars* are pretty conventional: a farm boy, a princess, a smuggler. Their motivations are pretty boilerplate: Luke wants to be a hero, Princess Leia wants to defeat the Empire, and Han just wants to get paid. But the world they live in, with hyperspace travel and death stars and Wookies and Jawas and cantinas filled with intergalactic weirdos is a pretty strange place to live.

In the TV show *Family Guy*, the Griffins are your average (if dysfunctional) American family living in their completely average town of Quahog, Rhode Island. However, if knock-down fist fights with sport team mascots, a human dating the family dog, or Wilford Brimley on a murderous rampage aren't bizarre, I don't know what is. As you can see, none of these three popular (and successful) movies, TV shows, and books violate the Triangle of Weirdness.

By applying the Triangle of Weirdness, you can give your story *just enough* weirdness to make it memorable and original, but you can have too much of a "weird" thing, too. Don't risk alienating your audience. Play it safe. Stick with one weird element.

Now that you're champing at the bit to write a story full of interesting characters, I recommend that you first choose your game genre *before* selecting your story genre. Just like the primary action determines your game's controls, the game genre determines the gameplay your game will have.

And gameplay should always come before story. But something else comes before creating a story, too.

Making a Name

Every story needs a **name.** It's the first thing anyone sees of your game. And while you can't judge an iPad game by its cover[2], you can judge a game by its name: so you'd better come up with a good one! But what's a good name? That is up to you, but here are a few ways to name your game:

A **literal title** is what the game is literally about. LITERALLY. *Cut the Rope. Words with Friends. Swing the Bat. Save the Sheep.* You would have to be pretty dense not to understand what these games are about. Literal titles are usually three words long, which has been something of a fad since *Cut the Rope* came out. *Something the Something.* That seems easy enough. Let's try coming up with a few of our own:

- ○ Swat the Fly
- ○ Kick the Monkey
- ○ Poke the Zombie
- ○ Stab the Pirate
- ○ Destroy the Universe

Hey! That was pretty easy. If I can come up with five completely original (if not awesome) game titles in, like, 5 seconds, then I'm sure you can come up with a really cool literal title of your own. Give it a try!

My game is called: _____

---

[2]Because it doesn't have a cover! The saying will have to be changed to "You can't judge a game by its icon."

Couldn't do it? That's okay. Go ahead and create an **action/cool title** instead. These are names that just sound cool. The name might give you an idea of what the gameplay might be about, but you can never be entirely sure. *Rage, Aurora Feint, Mirror's Edge, Zombie Gunship, Vertex Blaster, Semi-Automatic, Infinity Blade.* All cool-sounding names but at first glance, I really don't have any idea what the games are about. Sure, *Rage* is about being really mad, but who am I supposed to be mad at? Just how mad am I? Mad enough to kill someone or just mad enough to kick them in the shins? Fortunately, the action/cool title names make sense once you actually play the game.

Is an action/cool title too generic? Then how about a **purple cow title?** It's a title that is so crazy and memorable that it gets people's attention all on its own. *Get out of my Galaxy! No, Human. Blork. Gesundheit!* Like an action/cool title, the purple cow title makes more sense once you've played the game. Sometimes.

If you are really clever, you can come up with a **punny title** for your game. Sadly, punny game names aren't as common in mobile games as they are in, say, movies[3]. To create a punny title, you need to come up with a play on words. Or, if you are less clever, you can name your game after a famous game . . . but with a twist. See? It's funny (chuckle) because it's not really the name (heh heh) of the original game . . . (Bwa-haha!). Never mind. Punny names take thought and, IMHO, aren't that easy to create. That said, here are a few that I think are pretty good: *Plunderland. Corpse Craft. King Cashing.*

Or if puns aren't your game, how about an **ironic title** instead? *Bumpy Road, Don't Run with a Plasma Sword* or the inappropriately named *Justin Smith's Realistic Summer Sports Simulator.*

Brain hurting from all the effort? Not feeling very clever or creative? You can always rely on the **hero name.** This is probably the easiest way to name a game. Q: What's the name of your hero? Super Dude? Mighty Bedbug? Furious Squirrel? Then that's the name of your game! Done and done. If it's good enough for *Pac-Man, Dig-Dug, Sr. Mitsu, Pizza Boy,* and freakin' *Spider-Man,* then it's good enough for you.

---

[3]Read: pornographic movies.

Did you come up with a title yet? Well, you'd better double-check whether you can use it first. The iTunes App Store has more than 450 bazillion; there's a good chance that your name has already been taken. When naming a game, keep in mind that the iTunes App Store only allows for names no longer than 14 characters. This *includes* spaces and punctuation. If you go over, the rest of your title gets condensed down with ellipses. Your action game *BigFastRedTrucks* becomes known to the world as *BigFas...ucks,* which would not be good (though clearly, could be worse). If your game title isn't short, then I suggest trying to keep in the 8 to 10 characters range. If you go over that length, the name starts to "slop out" from under the icon. I don't know about you, but I think it looks a little sloppy when the name runs over like that.

Do your homework. Get to know naming conventions and trends in games. Popular games spark trends in game names. When the App Store first opened, many games used "touch" and "tap" in the title[4]. Here's some data you might not know:

- ○ 329 games start with the word "Zombie"

- ○ 283 games use the word "Touch" in the name

- ○ 185 games use the lowercase letter "i" as the prefix of the name

- ○ 175 games start with the word "Angry"

When you do come up with a really good name, then congratulations! Everyone else will end up naming his or her knockoff after yours. You could employ this strategy yourself, but I think

Kingdomof...lame

this is a pretty sleazy way to go about naming a game. Sure, you might get some hits if someone mistakes your game for a more popular one, but this strategy will probably backfire against you. I don't recommend it.

---

[4]Remember, like, a few years ago, every other boy was named Jason, and the girls were all named Brittany?

You could also try the "telephone book" strategy: The first letter of your name starts with either an "A" or a "Z." The hope is that someone browsing the store shelf or the App Store will start at the beginning of the list or jump to the end and work backward.

The best rule is to give your game the most appropriate name. Ultimately, people will fall in love with a game no matter how clever or memorable or stupid or punny the name is.

Games Need Story . . . or Do They?

Once upon a time, games didn't have a story . . . but no one seemed to mind. Players were too busy pushing stones around to notice. Over time, the players gave these stones individual gameplay capabilities; as a result, titles were given to the game pieces to match their "person-alities." The pieces became stand-ins for real world activities like racing and warfare. Even the gameplay boards had theming; a moral path to follow or a neighborhood to own.

Eventually these themes expanded into story genres as they attempted to replicate the plots of movies, TV shows, and comic strips. Here's where video games enter the story. Early video games were simple, but they were flavored with story genres to add character, mood, and a sense of place, or at the very least, an excuse for sporting some bitchin' artwork on the cabinet!

As games got longer and more involved, designers realized they could tell real stories. They unleashed their inner screenwriters and wrote spectacles that could rival the most blockbustery of Hollywood's endeavors. And here's where we are today.

Before writing a blockbuster of your own, you might want to ask yourself a few questions to help determine the kind of story you want to tell:

1. What is the **theme** of your story? The theme is a broad message, idea, or moral of your story. Will it be that "Crime never pays?" or "True love conquers all?" or "No good deed goes unpunished?" Your theme doesn't have to be very high-minded, but knowing what the theme is will help when you create situations and motivations for your heroes.

2. Who is your game's **audience?** Casual gamers? Moms? Kids? Hardcore gamers? Knowing who is meant to play your game helps you determine many things, from who the hero is (usually kids are the heroes of games aimed at kids) to the level of violence featured in your game (parent groups frown on decapitations). But never dumb things down for the sake of your audience—especially kids. They can deal with far more complex stories and gameplay than many adults can!

3. What is the **mood** of your story? Mario's creator, Shigeru Miyamoto, says you should determine the feeling you want the player to experience while playing the game. Is it wonder? Fear? Excitement? As you write your story, support these emotions with scenes and situations that will make players experience them. Read books, watch movies, look at other games, and dissect what makes them work and how to create these emotions for your game. (It's not called "ripping off," it's called paying homage.) It's not always easy to achieve emotions[5], but it's totally worth the effort.

4. What is the **premise** of your story? The premise is a fundamental concept that drives the plot. Many classic arcade games didn't have stories, but they still had premises to define the action.

Some designers insist that video games are a storytelling medium. Stories transport players to lives they'll never live and worlds they'll never experience.

Other designers believe that games are just meant to be pure entertainment, more sport than story. Since games are an interactive medium, I'm letting YOU choose your own answer to this debate!

---

[5]Publisher Electronic Arts' original mission statement was to create a game that "made players cry." Sadly, they never achieved that goal, unless you count the time I accidentally erased my *Archon* save file.

ANSWER 1: I absolutely, positively believe that story should be emphasized! Here's why:

- ○ **Stories provide a reason for players to keep playing: to find out the end of the story.** Players are often driven by curiosity. They want to know what happens next, and a story provides the excuse to keep them engrossed. Gamers will put up with some heinous gameplay just to find out how the story ends. Do them a favor and make sure the conclusion of your story is worth reaching; otherwise, you'll just disappoint everyone.

- ○ **Stories give designers a way to communicate big ideas.** Games, like any other artistic or entertainment medium, can speak to the human condition and offer insight into other people's lives. They can make statements about social issues using the guise of science fiction or fantasy. They can offer the player moral choices that they might never have to wrestle with in their own lives. They might even change a mind on an issue or at least get the player to consider another point of view. Just don't get too preachy with your message. A good writer will slip his message into the game without the player realizing it. Strive to teach without preaching.

- ○ **Stories give players characters to care about.** Characters offer the player an opportunity to step into the shoes of another person. Characters allow players to be everything they aren't in the real world: strong, rich, smart, bad, pious, magical, an expert at something—or at everything. Games are all about wish fulfillment. Being another character allows the player to experience anxiety, fear, despair, and sadness at a safe distance. After all, it's the character experiencing these emotions, not me, right? (*Sob!*)

- ○ **Stories provide structure on which to build a world.** World building begins with characters and their stories. Who lives in this world? Where do they live? What kind of action happens in these places? How is this action represented in the game? Now you're creating gameplay! The more you know about your fictitious world, the easier it will be for you to create believable locations and situations. Develop rules for your universe. For example, did you know that there's no paper in the *Star Wars* Universe? It's a small detail, but one with big ramifications to delivering story details: You can't discover a distress letter from the princess, but you can watch her holographic cry for help. Although it's great to create all these details, you don't need to explicitly tell them to your players. They'll figure it out. Be careful not to get too carried away with over-explaining your world to players. Let them experience it through locations and action rather than dialogue, or even worse, monologues.

○ **Interactive games can create stories with multiple endings.** There's one question that we humans will never answer, and that's "What if?" Games, on the other hand, can attempt to answer that rhetorical query with multiple endings. But don't get carried away with variations. Remember that each ending has to be designed, written, animated, and have music . . . that's a lot of effort for something the player might never see. Make sure you weigh the cost to your production before creating more than one ending.

Speaking of endings, did you know that every story needs three things: a **beginning, middle, and end?** It's true. And it's very important. The beginning is where you introduce the audience to the characters, the world, the desires of the main character, the conflict that the main character is going to have to face. And the beginning (or the **first act**) always ends with a situation that propels the hero into action. The middle (or the **second act**) throws complications at the hero. After it looks like he's licked a problem, a new one arises. These problems get harder for the hero as the story progresses, much like difficulty in a video game. You have to be careful when writing a story and designing a game; this is the part of the game where you might want to spend the most time creating. The ending, or **third act,** is where everything pays off. The situation comes to a head and the stakes are highest. It's life or death at this point. Even if your game isn't about life or death, it's still got to feel this way to the players who invested lots of time and effort to stick with the story.

Sometimes you want to add a **coda** or **denouement** to your story. This is a bit after the ending that tells a little bit more of the story and brings it to a satisfactory close. Often a coda takes place days, weeks, or years after the events of the ending. Whatever you do at the end, do not neglect the beginning or rush past the climax of your story. All three main parts are equally important to telling a story, even if your story is short. Just because tablet games are meant to be played in short bursts doesn't mean you still can't create an epic story; you only need to hit eight story beats:

1. **The hero has a desire.** The love of a princess. The need for a friend. Lusting for a hot car. Show that desire, don't just tell us. Actions speak louder than words! Show us why those birds are so angry, or why Barry Steakfries needs to steal that jetpack.

2. **An event happens that blocks the hero from his desire.** The princess is kidnapped by the black knight! Aliens arrive on Earth! Someone else buys the car! This is the first salvo thrown against the hero. Despite these problems, the hero's desire should still seem achievable. In the game, this is where the player encounters the first bit of gameplay. Enemies and simple hazards show up here.

3. **The hero attempts to overcome the problem, but he fails.** The hero storms the castle and is captured. The hero contacts the aliens and is misunderstood. The car's owner refuses to sell so the hero steals it. Writers have a saying: "Chase your hero up a tree and then throw rocks at him." Here's where you start throwing rocks. I don't advocate making a player lose to get them to realize a game is challenging, but here's where the player realizes things aren't going to be a cake walk.

4. **There is a reversal of fortune in which the hero's problem becomes more complicated.** The hero is thrown into the dungeon! The aliens abduct the hero's entire neighborhood! The hero discovers the car trunk is filled with drugs—he just stole from a crime lord! Usually this is where a twist in the plot comes into play. Do something unexpected to grab the viewer's attention and to escalate the danger, drama, and tension to the next level. Now that the player has tasted some success with the methods they've been using, it's time to change the controls, flip the mechanics on their head, or adjust the rules.

5. **An even greater problem puts the hero at risk.** The black knight challenges the hero to a duel! The aliens are going to swap brains with the neighbors as part of their invasion plot. The crime lord puts a hit out on the hero! Everything is rushing toward a big climax: We can see the two paths—success or failure—for the hero. We just don't know how things will go down or what the outcome will be. We're in the last levels of the game. All hell has broken lose and the player struggles to stay alive. Everything is faster, harder, and more intense.

6. **Finally, there is one last problem the hero must overcome, and it is the greatest risk of all.** The black knight transforms into a dragon! The alien overlord is going to swap brains with our hero! The crime boss tracks down the hero! This is the setup for the big confrontation. In games, this is a boss fight or the final puzzle.

7. **The hero must resolve the problem . . .** The hero slays the dragon. The hero tricks the alien overlord into swapping brains with a dog. The hero outwits the crime boss, who is caught by the police. Of course, you'll want to introduce the magic sword, the annoying dog, or the police detective earlier in the story so these story elements don't just show up when they need to be used. Try to wrap everything up with the characters, situations, and conflicts you've already created. The worst thing you can do is create a *deus ex machina* ending for your story, where an unrelated event or character swoops in and solves your hero's problems. That's lazy writing, and it is no fun for the player who has been waiting to learn how the hero solves the problem on his own.

8. **. . . in order to gain the object of his desire, and live happily ever after.** The hero rescues the princess. The hero goes back home . . . with a new pet dog. The hero buys the car from the police impound yard at a reduced price. Let the hero have her moment in the sun and give the player his reward. This is the big moment the player has been waiting for throughout the entire story—to come through all the trials and tribulations to see the hero get what he wants. It might be cliché, but everyone likes a happy ending.

See? Just follow these eight steps and you've got a pretty good story.

ANSWER 2: I absolutely, positively believe that story shouldn't be emphasized! Here's why:

○ **No one wants to wade through a story to reach gameplay.** Bad interface design, long-winded writers, poor pacing, and giving in to excess can all contribute to making a story unwatchable. But you can avoid these rookie mistakes with a little consideration for the player. Don't go overboard. Just because you have the budget for a 10-minute-long cinematic doesn't mean you need to make one[6]. The best game stories are simple and told simply. Don't dump a whole bunch of story points on the viewer at once; spool it out in interesting threads, loops, and kinks. Cut-scenes should be brief. Suck it up and cut that dialogue down, remove excessive scenes, get straight to the action. Some good screenwriting advice is "start your scenes 2 minutes into the action." Besides, no one wants to tap her way through a long-winded story to get to the game. She'll be tired of your game before even playing it!

○ **Tablet games are meant to be played in short bursts.** True, but that doesn't mean you can't tell a story in short bursts too. You just have to come up with a simple story: as long as it has . . . (wait for it) a beginning, middle, and end. Heck, even *Angry Birds* has a story, albeit a ridiculously short one (pigs steal eggs, birds strike back at pigs, pigs are defeated, and eggs are retrieved), but a story nonetheless. The trick is keeping it short; get in and get out, commando style. Let the world and the characters and the gameplay tell as much of the story as possible. Keep the jibber-jabber to a minimum or lose it all together. It's possible to tell an engaging story without any dialogue; just look at *Lego Pirates of the Caribbean* or *Bumpy Road*.

○ **Mobile players are not going to remember where they left off in the story.** Many games are starting to address this. The *Professor Layton* series of puzzle games has a recap page to bring the player back up to date. *Superbrothers: Sword & Sworcery EP* does the same thing, but in a more abbreviated manner and using a narrator character. These recaps don't have to be very long, they just need to provide the important plot points and remind the player why he cares and why he should keep playing.

---

[6]How about using that money to give the development team a bonus for all of their hard work?

○ **Game stories are predictable, contrived, and stupid.** The solution to this is to not write predictable, contrived, and stupid stories. Sounds simple, but the truth is, not everyone is a good writer. Here's where you have to be honest with yourself. If you don't think you are a good writer, then you should hire a professional (or at least find a friend with talent) to write your story for you. You can also avoid dumb dialogue by reading your text aloud. This even goes for help screens and instructional text. The written word and the spoken word sound very different. What looks great on the page often sounds really dumb when read out loud. If you don't want your game to be predictable or contrived, then make a practice of studying good writing. Watch movies, read books, play other games. Learn how to critically analyze them for what makes them work and what doesn't. Read books on screenwriting and play writing. Get a friend to read and edit your work, someone whom you know will give you constructive feedback and maybe even help you solve a few of your plot or dialogue problems. Most important of all, be honest with yourself when evaluating your own writing. If something doesn't make sense or fit together, don't try to make it work—change it! They're just words on paper.

○ **A game designer should make games!** Gameplay always comes first. Story should always be in service to gameplay. A great story, interesting characters, and an immersive world make the game better and keep the audience interested. But if your game isn't fun to play, then you've failed to create what makes a game a game. If you care more about the story than the game, you should write a novel (or a screenplay or a comic book or a play or whatever . . .) instead.

It's true that sometimes players don't want stories. They just want to play! You will have to make that decision for them as to how much story is in your game. However, you should allow them the opportunity to be as engaged or disinterested in your story as much as possible. *Bioshock Infinite* game designer Ken Levine says there are three kinds of players: those who "just want to shoot stuff," those who want to get a little deeper into the story, and hardcore players who want to know every detail of the fictional world they're playing in. You should cater to all three, but while it's easy to write for someone who is interested, how do you tell a story to someone who isn't? Here are a few ways to tell a story without getting in the player's way:

○ **Tell your story through collectables: videos, sound documents, computer documents, letters, and photographs.** Players can choose to look at these inventory items at their leisure. Of course, critical story points should be reinforced in the world and with gameplay. Don't create a situation where a player can miss something important. The intercepts in **EPOCH,** data tapes in **Dead Space** and biographies in **Batman: Arkham City Lockdown** all flesh out the game's world without slowing down the gameplay.

○ **Use the world to tell the story.** Give your places a backstory that tells a tale. Treat your levels and locations like a movie set. What's going on here? Posters in a hallway; hieroglyphics on a tomb wall; the aftermath of an invasion; posters; ticker tape displays; newspapers fluttering in the wind. Use details in the world to provide information that dialogue can't. Just being pretty doesn't cut it anymore.

○ **Eavesdrop.** Let players listen in on other characters' conversations. Let these other characters tell the story to each other rather than directly to the player; the latter type of conversation can get long-winded and stilted. The only response you will get from your player is them desperately tapping the screen in order to skip wordy dialogue. Plus, eavesdropping makes the player feel smarter.

○ **Don't forget the power of sound and music.** It's an effective way to communicate emotion to a player. Try playing a scary game with the sound off. It is just not the same experience. There's a lot I have to say on this, which is why I dig deeper into sound and music design later in the book.

Unreliable Narrators

I have one last thought on telling stories. Games don't necessarily need to have a story, but they still end up creating one for the player. It's something I call **narrative.** A story is crafted to tell a specific series of events, and the narrative is what players create in their heads after playing the game—kind of the post-game report. Depending on all the things a player can do in the game, the narrative can end up being different than the story. Your goal as a game designer is to create gameplay that influences the player's actions in such a way that the player ends up with the same (or at least similar) narrative to the story you are trying to tell.

But sometimes having the narrative and story match-up isn't a necessity. Some games are specifically designed to allow for wildly different player narratives—*The Sims* titles come to mind—but keep in mind that sharing stories is something that runs very deep in the psyche of humans. It brings us together as a species, and that's a powerful tool for game designers to keep in their bag of tricks.

Whew! That's pretty deep! Let's change the pace, lighten things up, and start looking at some games!

Game Design Spotlight 2

Helsing's Fire

Format: iOS (available in regular, lite, and HD versions)

Developer: Ratloop

Designer: Lucas Pope

When the implacable Professor Helsing and his assistant Raffton travel to The Shadow Blight, they need every weapon at their disposal to defeat Dracula's vampire horde. In this captivating, dark Gothic puzzle-adventure, use Dr. Helsing's powerful torch and tonics to save the world from the demonic uprising!

Helsing's Fire is a puzzler that uses an engaging mechanic, has lots of attitude to spare, and dishes out horror and humor in equal measures. The primary action is simple and unique. The player must cast torchlight into an environment to illuminate the monsters lurking in the shadows. Once the monsters have been exposed, our stalwart heroes can blast them with different-colored tonics.

The game sets the humorous horror tone right away. In the opening cutscene, a copy of the *London Times* is illuminated by flashing lightning. A headline reads: "Skies growing ever darker" and "5 more local women missing. Time to panic says top detective."

The game's selection screen represents city streets shrouded in London fog. The whole map screen is alive with motion. The map elements are animated, which is a nice touch, since it's unusual to see so much motion on a screen that didn't need to have it. The fog seethes, lightning flashes (temporarily illuminating the map), little red skulls that designate the enemies vibrate menacingly, and Helsing and Raffton jauntily bounce to the next fight when a puzzle is selected. The fog cleverly performs double-duty, not only providing some story context but also acts as a fog of war, exposing a block of the city at a time.

Helsing's Fire has a distinct visual style. It makes a stand thematically and doesn't give an inch. You can immediately recognize a screen grab from *Helsing's Fire*. The horror theming is laid on pretty thick. But then again, this is a game about blasting Dracula's minions with torchlight. The art reminds me of Mike Mignola's *Hellboy* comic book by way of 1960s artist Peter Max. Even the simple victory animations are hilarious. I have yet to meet someone who didn't laugh out loud at Helsing and Raffton's celebratory fist bump.

Helsing's Fire's controls are wonderfully simple. Players use their finger to move around a torch that sheds light in all directions with beams that shimmer and shine. Moving the torchlight around with your finger is quite satisfying, as you probe around with the light to illuminate the monsters. The effect is quite effective with its real-time shadow casting. The torch flame is huge, easily viewable from under a larger than normal digit. If an enemy touches the torch, it will extinguish.

While displayed very small on-screen, each puzzle starts by indicating the enemy's location. This gives the player a chance to strategize as well as see "cameo" images of the beasts. When monsters are caught in the light, they grow in size, throb, and are marked with an "activation" circle underneath them. It's more than enough visual information to let players know they've gotten a "lock" on the monster. Throw the tonic!

Puzzle complexity comes in many forms. The map layouts are well designed and it gets quite challenging to poke and prod around the corners of the maps in order to find the correct angle that will shine light on all the enemies. Colored circles surround the monsters to shield them from hits and must be broken using tonics of their corresponding color. Enemies struck by the wrong colored tonic will gain a shield. There is a wide variety of classic monsters: skeletons, rats, zombies, Cyclopes, mummies, and more. Some monsters move around after being hit by a tonic blast. Others require more than one hit to destroy. Ghosts disappear when lit by the torch. Others shoot back at the player's last position, requiring the player to move out of the way or get hit. Werewolves revert back into humans who can be destroyed by tonic blasts if the player isn't careful. Dracula himself turns into a bat and flutters around as the player tries to illuminate and blast him back to his tomb.

Time is tracked, but it never becomes a critical factor in winning or losing. It's used more for the game's leaderboard function than anything else. Although there is money to collect, the player almost never needs it. All puzzles can be solved with the tonics provided to the player.

The writing is spot on. Some of the sound effects for the monsters are so literal that they're hilarious. The hero's dialogue is drier than day-old scones, and Raffton provides a little color to the commentary during the puzzle. Dracula and his brood are a delightful mix of evil and bewilderment, almost as if the undead were as confused about the odd comments of the stoic vampire killers as we are.

The humorous sound effects are sparse but effective. The enemies pop, pop, pop as they appear on the map. The torch whooshes and crackles when ignited, and the tonics splort magnificently when activated.

The soundtrack, by Keiko Pope, begins as traditional Hammer horror organ music but radically shifts in the puzzle sequences to a cheesy Hammond organ beat, which surprisingly and deftly accentuates the action. It works particularly well during the victory sequence.

Helsing's Fire offers players a wide variety of additional features. It is supported by the gaming network Crystal, and has a journal where players can save their best times and favorite puzzles, a survival mode, and bounties where players can earn more gold by surviving several rounds. So why is *Helsing's Fire* so good? I chalk it up to the following:

- ○ A primary action that's easy to understand but still requires logic to use effectively
- ○ Style and attitude reflected in the art, music, and writing
- ○ A wide variety of puzzles based on a few well-designed elements and enemies

Helsing's Fire is available on iTunes.

chapter **5**

Puzzlings

PUZZLE GAMES. WHAT are they? Word scrambles? Math problems? Sudoku? *Angry Birds?* That game your mom likes where she tries to find rose hips hidden in the haunted attic? It's a riddle—hey wait, that's a puzzle too! And the answer is . . . *all of the above!*

Puzzle games comprise the broadest classification in the gaming universe. They've been played by humans (and a couple of very smart farm animals) for thousands of years. With each new form of technology that comes along, puzzle games have not been far behind. One of the first video games ever was *Noughts and Crosses,*[1] programmed by A.S. Douglas in 1952 on EDSAC. The EDSAC (Electronic Delay Storage Automatic Calculator) was a computer seven feet tall (the vacuum tubes

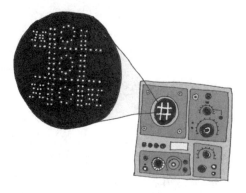

alone were 6 feet!) that filled up an entire room at the University of Cambridge's Mathematics Laboratory. Fortunately for our pants pockets, gaming systems have become a lot smaller!

Puzzle games and handheld gaming have always gone . . . well, hand in hand. Nintendo's Game Boy skyrocketed to success, partially thanks to the inclusion of *Tetris* with the system. Nintendo again acknowledged the power and importance of the puzzle game during the company's 2006 Game Developers Conference keynote speech when Nintendo Chairman Satoru Iwata gave attendees free copies of the math-and-word puzzle game *Brain Age,* requesting that audience members share the DS game with their non-gaming friends and parents. Nintendo knew that the popularity of puzzle games with casual gamers was instrumental to the success of the DS.

When the iPhone App Store launched in 2008, 30% of the titles offered were puzzle games. And at current count, there are over 1,000 titles under the classification "puzzle game". That's because puzzle games are perfectly suited for handheld gaming. They offer a quick burst of challenge with simple rules and controls. They're a good fit for game developers, too, because they require only a few simple gameplay mechanics. That means limited code and art requirements. Keep in mind that while this chapter is about puzzle games, the rules we'll be talking about can be applied to all types of games.

Regardless of the type of puzzle game you design, remember that simple is best. Your goal should be **elegance:** a clear, clean, easy-to-understand design that uses a handful of mechanics but offers a wide variety of ways for the player to reach the solution.

---

[1] Or as we Yanks call it, Tic-Tac-Toe.

I think one of the most elegant puzzles is the *Rubik's Cube* (Magmic, 2008). The objective of the *Rubik's Cube* is clear: Align all the sides' colors. How to manipulate it is clear: Twist the cube's sides to align all the colors. The only thing that isn't clear is how to get there: The cube can be rotated in 43,252,003,274,489,856,000 positions. And yet there is only one end point[2]. Simplicity, clarity, and complexity—all in one little cube.

Since puzzle games have been a part of humanity's leisure time for thousands of years, modern touchscreen users can easily understand their digital counterparts. Hand a newbie an iPad labyrinth puzzle and she'll get how to play it almost immediately (or even faster if she's played the "real world" game). This physicality of puzzle games is part of their appeal to players and developers. It's something that has to be considered seriously when designing even a brand-new-never-seen-before puzzle game. How will you interact with it? If it existed in the real world, what would it be like to hold it, to play it?

Which begs another question: How does one go about *creating* puzzles? Game developer Herman Tulleken knows. He says there are three different design methods: ***procedural, heterogeneous,*** and ***combinatorial.*** Take it away, Herman!

> At the one extreme we have procedural puzzle games. The designer designs the core mechanics and then allows the computer to put them together to create puzzles for the player—often randomly. Examples include Tetris and Minesweeper. The designer can control the difficulty by limiting the elements that the computer may use and by scaling the puzzle (making it bigger or faster). There is no level design in these games.

> At the other extreme, in heterogeneous puzzle games, the designer designs mechanics for each puzzle. Adventure games are typical examples of this type of puzzle game, and typical puzzles require a combination of common sense and lateral thinking to solve. The designer can increase the difficulty by making the solutions to the puzzles more obscure, or stringing them together into more complicated goal/subgoal systems.

---

[2]Solving a *Rubik's Cube* has been proven by computer to be achievable in just 20 moves (http://www.cube20.org/). Give it a try!

Between these extremes, there are combinatorial puzzle games, where the core mechanics are reused often, and in many combinations. Levels are carefully designed, and not created procedurally. Games like Portal *and* Braid *fall into this category. Difficulty increases when the designer introduces more mechanics, uses mechanics more cleverly, and combines more mechanics into each subsequent puzzle*[3].

Or, in other words, you can design a **code-driven** puzzle system that offers variation on a theme, **one-shot, stand-alone** puzzles that have no relationship to each other (and often require new art and code to create), or a **design-driven** puzzle that capitalize on a puzzle system but still offer unique content.

Another guy who really knows puzzles is designer Scott Kim, who gives the following advice on creating puzzles: "Determine the player's starting point and know the solution the player needs to reach. The designer must create choices for the player to make and dead ends that block the player from reaching the solution."

Along the way, the designer must create ways for the player to gain insight on how to avoid dead ends and make the correct choices that eventually lead to the solution. Mr. Kim warns that the insights must not obscure; otherwise, reaching the solution will feel unfair. He offers the following checklist for creating an appealing puzzle[4]:

○ The puzzle is visually appealing. The imagery is intriguing and yet somewhat familiar. *PuzzleJuice* (Colaboratory, 2012) bears a strong resemblance to both *Tetris* and *Boggle* and still has a unique and compelling visual style all its own.

○ The puzzle has simple rules. Even when creating puzzles with multiple steps, the steps are simple to understand within the process. In *Tetris*, rotating tetrominoes is the logical next step once the player learns how to manipulate, drop, and connect them together.

○ The puzzle is comprised of as few pieces as possible and those pieces work or fit together harmoniously. Start with a simple "tool box" of puzzle elements and use them to build increasingly complex puzzles. *Trainyard* (Matt Rix, 2011) uses very few elements overall and yet its puzzles can get quite complex just by the way they are repeated or orientated. By comparison, *Angry Birds* has more variation, but since the elements are kept to three classifications (birds, structure materials, pigs) the increasing complexity never gets overwhelming for the player.

---

[3]http://devmag.org.za/2011/04/16/how-are-puzzle-games-designed-introduction/

[4]Taken from his excellent website on puzzle design (http://www.scottkim.com/thinkinggames/index.html). Seriously, Scott Kim has probably forgotten more about making puzzles than most of us will ever know.

○ The puzzle is fun. It's pleasurable to manipulate the puzzle and players are rewarded with pleasing sound, music, and visual effects. The puzzle doesn't punish the player for missteps or wrong moves.

○ The puzzle offers a sense of progress. You can tell when you are getting close to solving the puzzle. The player gets that "Ah-ha!" moment where he knows he has solved the puzzle. He just has to do the work to reach the solution.

○ The puzzle has a clear goal. A puzzle can offer multiple solutions to reach that goal. The player should never be unsure when she has solved the problem or confused about the goal she is trying to reach.

Now that we've examined how to make puzzles, let's look at all the types of puzzles we can make. And there are a lot of puzzle "flavors" to choose from:

○ Logic puzzles

○ Math puzzles

○ Physics puzzles

○ Visual puzzles

○ Spatial puzzles

○ Word puzzles

Superior Logic

Logic puzzles can be found in adventure games like the *Monkey Island* series, *Machinarium,* or the *Puzzle Agent* series. Unlike traditional puzzle games where the puzzle is immediately presented to the player, logic puzzles often have to be found first, waiting to be discovered within the game's narrative or environment. They often rely on lateral thinking, deduction, wordplay, and object manipulation.

You can argue that (spoilers!) scaring Pegnose Pete out of his house with a duck is illogical, but the world of *Escape from Monkey Island* has its own silly logic that the player understands the more he plays. Maintaining the rules of your world and keeping a consistent tone are the keys to preventing your puzzles from becoming a frustrating exercise in "guess what the designer is thinking." Just as dramatic writing has a "three act structure", a puzzle breaks down into five moments:

○ Realization

○ Investigation

○ Understanding

○ Solving

○ Confirmation/Reward

First, the player *realizes* he has encountered a puzzle. This realization often comes when his progress is blocked. Solving the puzzle allows him to continue. This kind of puzzle is often prompted by a situation, location, or character[5]. Players explore the world as far as they can, making sure they haven't overlooked any alternative paths before they decide to confront the puzzle. They will switch into a slightly different mindset than the game normally requires. This is known in grade school as "putting your thinking cap on."

---

[5]Upon further thinking, pretty much any type of puzzle games is prompted by a situation, location, or character.

Next, the player searches for tools and clues to help her understand the rules for solving the puzzle *(investigation).* Here's where players engage in ***inventory manipulation.*** The player will hoover through an environment, grabbing anything that isn't nailed down (bottle, money, bone, flashlight, spoon, keycard, potted plant, broken sword, peanut butter, bowl of wax fruit, cat) and stashing it into her inventory. When designing a puzzle of this type, I recommend placing the necessary pieces within close proximity of the solution: only a few screens, rooms, or locations away. Players shouldn't have to backtrack through the entire game to find that sacred knob that fits into the temple door.

The player will return to the scene of the puzzle and in a worst-case scenario, try every logical (and then illogical) combination in order to come to a solution. Actually, an even-worse-case scenario is if the game has a "combine" function leading to many wasted hours combining and recombining objects in vain.

How can you prevent this from happening? Limiting options is one way. Creating clear puzzle elements is another. Avoid creating obscure or arcane object relationships. Peanut butter belongs on a spoon, but not on the back of a cat. If you feel like being a real jerk, you can plant deliberately false clues devised to throw the player off the track. Don't, however, include too many or else the player will get frustrated with the glut of false information. Personally, I think the puzzles in adventure games are complex enough without red herrings.

Also, keep the number of inventory items low. The player should be constantly cycling through objects. Once a puzzle item is used, it should leave the player's inventory. Avoid multiple use items if possible. If an object remains in the player's inventory too long, it's too easy to forget that it's there. Some games will gently remind players through messages or dialogue that they possess this item. If the puzzle needs to be solved by combining two items, the game will sometimes automatically combine them after they are placed into the player's inventory. It just boils down to how much effort you want the player to go through to solve the puzzle.

Once the player recognizes the patterns and logic, he will *understand* the solution. Be careful not to get so wrapped up in the complexity of a puzzle that the solution becomes arcane or unclear.

Now the player can **solve** the puzzle. He still has to do the legwork and heavy lifting, whether it is moving pieces into proper order or configurations, but he will approach the puzzle with a renewed energy and sense of determination because he is working toward an achievable goal.

There's one last step that is out of the player's hands: **Confirmation and reward.** I particularly like how *Professor Layton* "thinks" before announcing whether the player is correct or incorrect. If a correct guess is made, the player is rewarded in picarats (the game's currency) *and* the puzzle's solution is shown. Including the solution is particularly interesting because the player has already solved the puzzle, but the game still shows the "best possible solution." The player can profit from this knowledge later in the game.

Ultimately, the best rule to follow is to be logical with the logic in your logic puzzles. That way, you won't have players pulling out their hair.

The Problem with Math

Math puzzles challenge players with arithmetic, subtraction, multiplication, division, pattern matching, spatial geometry, or just plain ol' number ordering. Challenge players to solve problems quickly and accurately as in *Brain Age Express: Math* (Nintendo, 2009) or have them verify correctness of a displayed problem like in *Brain Tuner 2* (GreenGar Studios, 2011). Just because you are doing math doesn't mean you don't have room for creativity.

In the arithmetic game *Addicus* (Get Set Games, 2009), players must quickly select multicolored addends to reach a displayed sum. They gain points for being quick and accurate as well as matching colors into poker-like sets. In *Super 7* (No Monkeys, 2010), players "draw tiles together" to reach the number 7. Score multipliers are earned if combinations happen simultaneously while complication is added[6] when negative and multiplier tiles enter play. At first glance, *Math Gems* (Nerlaska Studios, 2011) looks like a classic gem breaker but with numbers and symbols (+, −) on the gems. Players create equations to reach a displayed sum. All three games have players use the touchscreen to choose numbers, turning the games into dexterity challenges as well as brain burners.

Ever since videogames first came out, parents have tried to make kids do more math and play fewer games. Math is the intellectual equivalent of broccoli, I guess. Never one to turn down a financial opportunity, many game developers have tried to "trick" kids into doing math. "Solve this math problem to blow up a spaceship!" These games say. "Find the sum of these integers to stop the ninjas from attacking!" "Divide the square root of the denominator to stop the skeleton invasion!" This never works. Kids are too smart and can smell these "edu-tainment" tiles a mile away. As a brilliant game designer, you have to at least be smarter than a fifth-grader:

○ **Hide it.** For goodness' sake, don't tell them they're learning. You can put learning into a game, but the minute you tell players they're learning, they won't want to play anymore. Make them concentrate on something else. For example, the goal of *Math Stickers* (Cloubble Adventure Team, 2011) is to solve math equations, but players get so caught up manipulating the match sticks to form numbers that the math stops being their primary focus.

○ **Use stand-ins for the learning.** If I have a 500 bullet capacity clip and I shoot 300 bullets into the Demon-Lord, how many bullets do I have left? You're going to need some quick math skills to reload!

○ **Distract with particles and effects.** Just because it's math doesn't mean it can't be exciting! In fact, you can never have enough particles, no matter the genre of game you're making. Particles make everything better.

○ **Be cool, but don't try too hard.** Nothing gives an edu-tainment game away faster than a hero with a punky haircut, sunglasses, or anything resembling a skate- or hover board. Grown-ups think they know what kids want, but more often than not, the "trying to be hip" developers fail . . . horribly.

---

[6]Pun intended.

A game that does none of the above and yet manages to be the most popular math puzzle game ever is **Sudoku**[7]. Created by Howard Garns in 1979, "Single number" puzzles are number placement games in which the player must fill a 9 × 9 grid with numbers 1 through 9 without repeating the same number in a line, row, or 3 × 3 sub-square. Single number puzzles were christened sudoku in Japan (su = number, doku = single) in 1984 but didn't really become popular until 2004, partially due to their success on mobile devices. On opening day of the Apple App Store, almost 10% of the games offered were sudoku.

Since most sudoku games play pretty similarly, make your sudoku game stand out by making it pretty. Cool or unique graphics go a long way to differentiate your game in an overcrowded market. Another way to stand out is to design interesting gameplay enhancements. The decreasing score multiplier in ▷Sudoku (Finger Arts, 2008) increased score multipliers for "runs" (uninterrupted completion of puzzles) as in Sudoku 2 Pro (Finger Arts, 2010) or the robust user-assist tools found in Sudoku HD (CrowdCafe, 2010). Want to make your own sudoku game? Keep the following tips in mind:

- ○ Keep your grids to the standard 9 × 9 cells. If you create fancy shapes and formations, players are going to spend more time trying to figure out where to place the numbers than what numbers to place.

- ○ Make sure your puzzle has only ONE solution. People like sudoku because it's simple.

- ○ Allow players to make notations (write in a temporary answer before committing to a final one).

---

[7]Sudoku is primarily a logic puzzle, but don't tell anyone; otherwise, other people won't be impressed that you are doing "math" . . . for fun.

○ Keep your graphics clear and easy to read, and your controls easy to use.

○ Add helpers (like the one found in *Sudoku vol. 1*) that highlight the answers if the player takes too long to solve a puzzle[8].

○ Allow for multiple levels of difficulty and challenge.

You know, looking at these tips I think that most of them work pretty well for most genres of games, not just sudoku.

I don't want to leave you with the impression that you should run out and create a sudoku game. Or that the sudoku market is a goldmine. It isn't. Not now. It's in fact an extremely overcrowded market, as there are hundreds of sudoku games for sale on the App store and you'll have to offer something extremely special and creative to even get the audience's attention. But what I do want you to do is **think.** Think how you could turn something as commonplace as sudoku into something extraordinary. This is where the gold lies.

Don't Be Difficult

That last bullet point reminds me of a topic that's important when designing puzzle games. Well, it's important when designing *all* types of game. Remember flow? Games need to challenge the players; otherwise, they won't stay in the flow. However, if a game is too difficult, they'll fall out of the flow. Wait a second! What's the difference between difficulty and challenge? I thought they were the same!

Difficulty strives to make things harder for the player. Game designers call the increase in a game's difficulty ***ramping.*** This is why the last level is harder than the first one. The player needs more skill and has less time to succeed. This margin becomes narrower until (a) the game is over or (b) the game becomes so "hard" that it is impossible for the player to win. (This is usually the end result of distance games, breaker games, and some puzzle and arcade games.) The following factors can be tweaked by the designer to increase or decrease difficulty:

○ **Aggression:** How often the game attacks or tries to thwart the player.

○ **Artificial Intelligence (AI):** How intelligently or accurately the game responds to the player's actions.

○ **Complexity:** How many steps the player has to complete in order to reach a successful solution.

---

[8]Player helpers are becoming increasingly more common in puzzle games; however, I'm torn about their inclusion. They're really helpful when I just can't see that three-combination move in *Bejeweled 2*. But other times, I just feel like a big dummy for being shown the location of that dog in *Little Things*. I guess I didn't really mind it in *Dragon's Lair* (Cinematronics, 1983), where it was first used.

○ **Frequency:** How often a new element is introduced into play or how often the player is forced to perform a particular action.

○ **Knowledge:** The depth of information (either in-game or real-world) that the player needs in order to reach a successful solution.

○ **Punishment:** What is the cost of making a mistake (or making multiple mistakes or making the same mistake over and over again) and how much punishment can be withstood as the player strives to reach the goal.

○ **Speed:** How quickly the elements in the game physically travel or how fast the player responds to events.

○ **Time:** The time a player has to solve a puzzle, travel a distance, reach a solution, or defeat an enemy.

All these factors can be tweaked so high that the players can't succeed; they just won't possess the dexterity, stamina, or knowledge necessary to win. As you work on your game, you may be tempted to "crush the player" and have him really work for victory. However, I believe that designing a game shouldn't be "designer vs. player." A game designer should do everything possible to **enable** players and lead them to victory. Be a gentle hand on the shoulder of the player, pushing him ever forward! You want players to succeed! If a player has a good time playing your game, then she will tell her friends what a good time she had. Some of those friends will in turn buy a copy of your game in order to experience it for themselves. You can claim that you want to make games because it's fun or you need an outlet for your creativity or because you want to make art, but the bottom line is, making games is a business. The only way you can stay in business is if someone (lots of someones, actually) buys your game. Making games that make gamers happy is a good recipe for making money . . . and making more games. And on it goes.

If this all feels a little too touchy-feely for you, you can always help players without them knowing by using **dynamic difficulty.** The player is given help or a clue when he most needs it, but because it's a "surprise," the player chalks it up to serendipity rather than the game monitoring the play. You can dynamically adjust the **difficulty level** from a higher to a lower one. Some games announce that the change is going to happen. I recommend giving the player the choice to stay at the current difficulty level. If you don't ask, you risk insulting the player, insinuating that he isn't "good enough" to succeed—whether or not it's true.

Challenge requires players to solve the puzzle or beat the boss using skills already earned. If they fail it's because they made a mistake, not because the game is out to get them. This encourages players to try again in order to improve their score or performance.

Those little stars in *Angry Birds* (and in just about every puzzle game since) are a great way to introduce challenge. A player can still succeed and progress to the next puzzle even if he doesn't get all three stars. But the stars motivate the player to try again.

It's win-win for the game designer and the player. The game designer has the player replaying levels, which means the player will be playing the game longer. The player will feel better about his performance by getting all three stars, or it will motivate the player to get a higher score so he can brag on leaderboards or to friends.

Or, you might just want to remove stress completely from the equation. Many puzzle games offer a 'free mode' or 'zen mode' where many of the losing conditions are removed so the player can get into a more casual mindset and focus on the challenge, enjoy the mechanics, or the pretty particle effects.

Physics: It's for the Birds

Physics puzzles simulate real-world interactions between objects and the environment to create challenges for the player. Objects can be pre-positioned to create a chain reaction, like in *Casey's Contraptions* (Snappy Touch, 2011), manipulated by the player's avatar, as in *Home Sheep Home HD* (Virtual Programming, 2011), or even set into motion by *No, Human's* omnipotent (and slightly malevolent) "hand of the universe" (vol-2, 2011). No matter the method, the goal of a physics puzzler is to use physics to produce the desired result.

Weight, density, momentum, motion, velocity, force, and kinetic energy are playthings in the hands of designers when creating physics puzzlers. All disciplines are fair game: balance and engineering as in *Sky Burger* (NimbleBit, 2008) and *World of Goo* (2D Boy, 2008), fluid dynamics like in *Sprinkle: Water Splashing Firefighting Fun!* (Mediocre AB, 2011) or *Enigmo* (Pangea Software, 2008), aerodynamics as in *Paper Toss* (Backflip Studios, 2010), and good ol' fashioned smashing stuff together like in *Trucks & Skulls Nitro HD* (Appy Ent., 2010) and that other game, I forget what it's called . . . something

about birds. Gaming is no stranger to physics. Some of the earliest arcade games, like *Lunar Lander* (Jack Burness, 1973), *Asteroids* (Atari, 1979), and *Marble Madness* (Atari, 1984), used real-world physics to challenge and confound players. Physics-centric games like the *Incredible Machine* (Sierra, 1993), *Ragdoll Kung Fu* (Mark Healy, 2005), *Crayon Physics* (Petri Purho, 2009), and *Crush the Castle* (Armor Games, 2009) were mainstays of PC and browser gaming. While touchscreen gaming had *Touch Physics* (Gamez 4 Touch, 2008) and the homebrew DS title *Pocket Physics* (Tobias Weyand, 2007), it wasn't until *Angry Birds* (Rovio, 2009) smashed sales charts and flew to the top of game-of-the-year lists that the genre took off in the touch-screen space.

So, in a sub-genre that is already becoming overcrowded, how do you make your game stand out? You allow physics to do what it does best . . . be physical. The slow slide of an object off a cliff. The lean of a tower before it settles or collapses. The roll of a stone or ball before it slows to a stop or crushes the pig that's mocking you. The problem is this kind of reaction cannot be designed. For this, you need a cracker-jack physics programmer or at least some kick-ass physics engine that you can put into your own game. However, physics can be a harsh mistress. Designing physics puzzles can prove more difficult and constraining than other kinds of puzzles. I recommend creating (or buying) your physics engine before design-ing your puzzles. Once you get the engine into your game, there will still be a lot of trial and error when designing puzzles. A designer can try to predict what the physics engine will do, but it is that unpredictability that is part of the fun of a physics game. It's like balancing a stack of cards. It's going to take a few tries to get things balanced just right. Since all the things in the game are connected by their physical properties, if you change one property (such as gravity) it will have huge ramifications on your game. You can try to design some-thing cool, but it may be physically impossible as the physics engine prevents it from happening.

Even fighting the forces of physics can be fun. ***Balance games*** like *Sky Burger* (NimbleBit, 2009) and *Monsters Ate My Condo* (adult swim Games, 2011) alternate between frantic movements and delicate balancing acts. When creating balance games, allow enough slowness in the physics to allow players to just barely recover from widely swaying stacks. It's the "whooooaahh!" factor that makes these games fun.

There is a joy to a good physics puzzle game as the player tries to find the "sweet spot" to knock stuff over. A good physics game will let you feel like you can make the right move and still get unpredictable results due to the reality of the physics. This is why physics games should be designed around cause and effect. It's kind of like when you play *Jenga*. You spend time analyzing the tower, looking for the right block to pull out. When you decide, you gently grab the block and pull. This is where the "teeth-sucking" moment occurs. In that moment, you are either going to be correct and get that block out safely or it will all come crashing down. However, in between those two options is a third . . . that moment when the whole thing wobbles and leans a little bit and you are praying that it doesn't fall over . . . that's when the teeth-sucking happens. And that's the feeling you want to create in your own physics game.

The forces of gravity make for good fun, but you need to consider all the variables used for gameplay:

- **Material density:** Wood, glass, metal, stone, rubber, foam, dirt, clay, gas, and water all have unique properties. Basing your materials on the real world is your best guide when creating physics and answering any "thrown rock vs. plate glass window" debate. Playing with these reactions can be as much fun as solving the puzzle. Twelve million copies of *Angry Birds* can't be wrong!

- **Ricochet** and **kinetic energy** create lots of questions. Does it bounce? Does it bounce far enough to bounce into something else? Does it keep bouncing and go faster as it bounces? Or does it eventually slow down and stop? Does it bounce off one surface and in another direction? How can all these decisions be used for gameplay? You've got some questions to answer.

- **Momentum:** This can be a double-edged sword for the player. Be careful when using momentum for the player character: It's too easy to overshoot a platform or slide right into a hazard. However, momentum is a blast when shooting, throwing, or tossing items, the player character included. The farther it flies, the more fun it is!

○ **Force:** *Home Sheep Home* has three sizes of sheep that can push with different amounts of force to solve puzzles. In *No, Human,* players must exert enough force to break through gravitational wells or ricochet long distances. One of the advantages of finger control is that it allows players to actually exert some effort to move an item.

○ **Velocity:** When thinking about how velocity works with gameplay, just remember the lessons of *Jetpack Joyride:* The faster it goes, the more awesome it is. The faster it goes, the harder it is to control. The faster it goes, the more spectacular the explosion is when the player finally smashes into a wall.

Another great way to make your physics games memorable is to create memorable characters. *Rolando* (ngmoco, 2008), *Angry Birds,* and *Where's My Water?* (Disney Mobile, 2011) all have charming and well-designed lead characters. As designer Sam Rosenthal once said, "Look at Papi Jump vs. Doodle Jump. A good character design can make all the difference." Indeed, Sam, indeed.

Let's Get Wet

Liquid physics make *Enigmo* (Pangea Software, 2008) and *Feed Me Oil* (HolyWaterGames, 2011) wet and wild fun. (I can't believe I just wrote that sentence!)

It's not like liquid physics games aren't exciting. After all, players are barely stemming the flow of rushing water, gushing oil, or toxic waste in a somewhat vain attempt to change the course of mighty rivers to activate bizarre water-powered devices. Here are some tips to make a splash with your liquid physics:

- ○ Remember that flowing water has **momentum.** Make your streams shoot across gaps, jump distances, and even loop-de-loop if you give them enough speed and pressure.

- ○ Adjust the **viscosity:** the thickness of liquids. Mountain spring water is going to flow differently than molten nacho cheese. The difference in the speed of flowing liquids can make the same puzzles feel different, especially when timing puzzle mechanics are involved. Using different viscosity will change the gameplay of these puzzles.

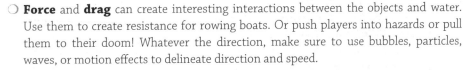

- ○ **Force** and **drag** can create interesting interactions between the objects and water. Use them to create resistance for rowing boats. Or push players into hazards or pull them to their doom! Whatever the direction, make sure to use bubbles, particles, waves, or motion effects to delineate direction and speed.

- ○ **Buoyancy** can be just as much fun as flowing water. The wild waves in *Plunderland* make bouncing ships as much fun as cannon blasting enemies. Why not base an entire game on flinging boats up and down on the waves and troughs of a stormy sea (or an agitated bathtub)?

○ Light objects in water are effectively weightless. Use water to change **gravity** and add a new twist on your dry puzzles. Why not base your entire game's physics on underwater dynamics? Instead of flinging birds, try floating penguins instead! Need a change of scenery? Remove the water and you've got outer space!

○ Don't forget **containers!** Water's got to flow so provide a place for it to go! *Enigmo* has players fill jars with water. Swampy (in *Where's My Water?*) just wants a full bathtub. The containers themselves can be part of the puzzle too. Use gravity to tip vessels over or create your own aqueduct system to get the water moving!

Do You See What I See?

Visual puzzles come in all shapes and sizes. And colors. And patterns. And negative spaces. They play with perspective, perception, and mental object transformation. (Is it a lady sitting at a table or a horrifying skull?!!)

○ **Spatial puzzles** like *Helsing's Fire* (Ratloop, 2010) and *Tomb Slider* (Alawar Ent., 2011) deal with the relative position and orientation of objects. They challenge players to manipulate objects to move them to a desired location or fill space with light or color. Spatial games often rely on move counters, which give the player a limited number of chances to correctly solve the puzzle. Make sure your game is smart enough to realize when it's impossible for the player to win and kindly reset the puzzle for him to try again.

○ **Falling block puzzles** like *Tetris* (EA, 2008) and *Jiggy* (Maverick Software, 2008) challenge players to align pieces before the stack of missed pieces gets too high. Make sure your puzzle pieces have distinct shapes and are colored differently to allow players to quickly identify them. Make it easy for players to rotate the pieces so they have a fighting chance to fit those pieces together.

○ Color and shape matching **"breaker"** games like the *Bejeweled 2 + Blitz* (PopCap, 2008) and *Puzzle Quest 2* (NamcoBandai, 2010) series. This last sub-genre is so popular and so large, we're going to talk about it in an entirely separate chapter.

○ Hieroglyphics, runes, icons. When words become pictures, it's time to break out the decoders and crack a **code.** There are plenty of real-world and fantasy languages and codes to choose from. Or why not take a stab at creating your own?

As the puzzle game genre evolves, exciting new **hybrid** puzzle games have emerged. At first glance, games like *Henry Hatsworth in the Puzzling Adventure*, *PuzzleJuice*, and the like resemble the same old puzzle games we're already bored with. Add some clever twists, engaging visuals, and innovative gameplay ideas though and you've created something exciting and new! Want to make your own hybrid? Here's how you start: it's (game #1) meets (game #2). What did you come up with? Here's mine!

Text Drive - The driving/word puzzle game!

Hmm. Maybe not all games should be hybrids.

Hiding in Plain Sight

Did you find the key in the junk pile outside Greywood Manor? How about a heart? The butcher knife? These kinds of **hidden object** games challenge players to identify several objects amidst a clutter of visual information. Titles like the *Nick Chase* series, the *CSI* series, and the *Laura Jones* series often rely heavily on genre such as mystery, adventure, and horror to invoke a sense of place or emotion. You'll even find romance, the most overlooked genre in gaming. This may be thanks to the popularity of hidden object games with female gamers.

But they're not the only ones playing these games. Casual gamers seem to be drawn to the hidden object genre too. As publishers like G5 and Big Fish release more and more titles[9], the hidden object sub-genre has begun to resemble traditional adventure games. Are *Mushroom Age* (Nevosoft, 2010) and *The Mystery of the Crystal Portal HD* (Artogon, 2009) any different than the classics like *Broken Sword* or the *Monkey Island* series? Complex stories, inventory systems, and mini-games help break up the action between static screens jammed with objects and images.

---

[9]Big Fish proudly boasts that they release "a game a day"!

One of the hallmarks of this genre is extremely detailed and often beautiful artwork that is used to disguise the hidden objects. There are exceptions: *Little Things* (KlickTock, 2009) relies on a lack of detail and a concentration on negative space to confuse the eye. Looking to test players' observational skills? Try these:

- Humans search for visual patterns: shapes, sizes, and colors. Change these often so players can't spot objects right away.

- Mess with player expectation and have players look for something they don't expect. Choose alternatives to stereotypical items. There are many kinds of leaves, keys, cards, and fruits, for instance.

- Hide in plain sight. The most overlooked image is often right in front of the player.

- Direction and rotation make a big difference in visually recognizing an object. A player doesn't expect a goblet to be upside down or a playing card to be face down.

- When all else fails, be sneaky. Hiding an object under some papers or in an armoire that must be opened will make the player really feel like he's rooting around the room for the items.

What not to do:

- Try to avoid using items that have no relation to the story or the genre. If you are making a horror game, then have the player look for rusty scissors, vials of poison, and shattered baby doll heads, not hairclips, lucky horseshoes, or sailing ships.

- Hidden object games will often use the jumble of objects as an excuse to reuse environments. Don't do this too often or the player will grow bored, or even worse, quickly spot all the items you have carefully hidden.

- Don't create a static screen. Add some animation. Granted, you don't want things moving all over the place, which can be too distracting to the player, but a little life is better than none at all.

- Avoid giving the player a time limit. It's one thing to focus concentration on finding objects; it's another to add the pressure of a ticking clock. Then again, if it's a *ticking bomb* . . .

Word Up

Word puzzles are games that focus on letters and words. Games that fall into this classification are guessing games like *Ultimate Hangman* (EnsenaSoft, 2011), knowledge games such as *Crosswords* (Stand Alone, 2008), word find games like *Word Detective* (Mighty Mighty Good Games, 2010), and even spelling games such as *Scrabble* (EA, 2008) and *Words with Friends* (NewToy, 2009).

When creating word puzzles, be careful about using slang, jargon, and colloquialisms when generating your words . . . unless you've alerted the player that these are valid options. Non-English words are often not allowed either. *Scrabble* doesn't even allow the use of proper nouns[10].

Word games should be visually uncomplicated. Design your interface with clarity and ease in mind. Lots of letters, word tiles, or slots to build words can make a screen look cluttered. You can combat this by giving the player the option to zoom in on a line of words or scale back on the game board to increase visibility. Use the touchscreen's natural pinch controls or a quick button tap; whatever method you choose, make sure the player can quickly get back into gameplay.

You'd be surprised at how many times developers forget little things like making their tiles a color so colorblind players can see them or making their fonts large enough to be legible on small iPhone screens or making game pieces large enough so they don't become obscured by a player's finger. I'm sure you would be embarrassed if a word in your word game was incorrectly spelled or your clue for your crossword was factually incorrect . . . yet these things happen. It never hurts to dot your 'i's and cross your 't's when creating a word game . . . so to speak.

---

[10]Yes, I know that in 2010, the board game's rules were amended to allow the player to use proper nouns, but publisher Electronic Arts informs me that this rule has not been included in any of its tablet versions.

Speaking of 'i's and 't's, **font** choice can make a big difference. A font is just a fancy way of saying letters or type. Choosing a font is important. Fonts carry just as much personality as characters and names do. You want to use the right font for your game, be it cartoony, horror, sci-fi, or something completely different. You can find a wide variety of fonts at sites like `http://www.fonts101.com`, `http://www.fonts4free.net`, or `http://www.dafont.com`. Even though these sites offer a wide variety of really cool fonts, be careful when using super-stylized fonts or very narrow fonts that can cause aliasing when displayed on-screen. You can avoid this by either using simple fonts, or making your font size large. Fonts that are sans serif (serifs are the little flourishes found on the tips and ends of some fonts) can make text harder to read on smaller devices so I suggest avoiding them unless used for large images like title screens. Programs such as *GameMaker* contain built-in tools for creating screen-ready fonts. For retina display devices, a font size of at least 16 points is recommended.

SERIFS   SAN SERIFS

Word games often have **_player assists._** *Scrabble*'s "Best Word" function automatically finds the best word on your rack of tiles and places it on the board. There's another term for this . . . cheating. I'm kidding, but it is a design decision that has to be made. It's a fine line to walk: Some players just want to get onto the next puzzle and don't mind skipping past a stumper. It's your responsibility as a game designer to keep the player playing, so it doesn't hurt to provide a way out. However, if you feel strongly about giving the player such a powerful advantage, then make it cost something (score points, "coins," or tries, for example) to skip. And always allow the player the option to turn the functionality off.

When creating a visual for a player assist, make the hint stand out by using a glow, highlight, twinkle, or some other visual effect. Normally, subtlety has no place in games. This is one of the few times when I feel that subtlety is appropriate, however. You don't need to tip the player off by using a huge glowing, pointing arrow to do it. If you can make the player subconsciously think he solved the puzzle himself, then more power to ya!

Word games are social games. Create "single system/multiple player" functionality like *Words with Friends*' "Pass and Play," which allows players to physically pass the tablet to other players in the room.

Word games can sometimes be a little bland in their presentation. Think about what you can do to "theme them up" to make them more appealing to the "I don't normally play word games" audience. What would a World War II code-cracking word game look like? What would a pirate treasure map–deciphering word game be played on? What about a word game that exclusively uses a made-up alien language? Remember, creativity is what makes any game stand out. Explode those brain cells and come up with something good!

Speaking of explosions, real-world puzzle game counterparts have distinctive sound effects associated with them: Don't disregard the scratch of a pencil on paper, the rattle of wooden tiles in a bag, or the rasp of a piece sliding into place to add atmosphere.

Themes can extend to the puzzles themselves, too. Crosswords and word finds do this all the time ("How many Christmas words can YOU find!"), but you never see a *Scrabble*-style game do this. Maybe there's a reason for it. Or then again, maybe I just invented a new game . . .

And the Solution Is . . .

Whew. That's a lot of puzzles to choose from! Which one's the best? Who knows?! Just pick a type and go for it! Remember that many of the rules and strategies listed here apply not only to puzzle games, but to most game types in general. Just remember to play fair, keep the objectives simple, the pieces few, and the logic sound.

DEVELOPER INTERVIEW 3

Erin Reynolds

Developer profile: Erin Reynolds has worked with Disney interactive and mobile studios designing Nintendo DS titles. She is currently working with USC's prestigious interactive media department on an unannounced project.

Current project: *Nevermind* (TBD)

Company website: http://www.nevermindgame.com/

Previous titles: *Ultimate Band DS* (Nintendo DS)

Erin, thanks for taking the time to talk with *Swipe This!* What excites you about designing games for touchscreens and tablets?

What excited me both then and to this day is the fact that touchscreen games offer developers a whole new array of tools in creating novel and engaging experiences for their players. The "traditional" video game has been fine-tuned to find effective and entertaining ways to leverage the controller-and-screen interface that has been the de facto standard up until recently. However, with this constraint now removed, we can break those rules and, in many ways, have the freedom to redefine what user interaction can be within virtual environments.

What are some of your favorite touchscreen/tablet games?

Having played so many touchscreen-centric games that I loved, it's a bit of a difficult task to narrow it down to just a few. However, one that I think leveraged the touchscreen especially well (and in a way that couldn't be replicated by any "standard" interface) was the 5th Cell/ THQ game *Drawn to Life*. In particular, I really enjoyed being able to participate in the game experience not just as a player, but as a creator as well[1]. In *Drawn to Life*, the player was able to "draw" his own character, enemies, environment assets, and other elements, which he could then interact with throughout the game. To me, that particular use of the tablet inter-action felt like bringing my sketch book to life . . . and then going on an adventure within it! To my inner 5-year-old, it was truly a magical moment.

What advice can you give to someone who wants to get into designing games for touchscreen/tablet space?

My advice when it comes to designing games for touchscreen/tablet interaction is to simply think outside the box—as hackneyed as that may sound. Given all of the new tools and tech-nology that have recently become available to us developers, it seems like it is now up to our imaginations to catch up with the technology. My feeling is that all of us—both experienced and brand new developers alike—need to approach this tech with a fresh perspective that isn't dulled by the habit of designing non-touchscreen games.

What gameplay and control challenges did you face when designing your touchscreen game?

I found that striking a balance between "literal" gestural actions and more elegant abstract gestures (for example, ones that don't interfere with screen space, are fun to perform repeat-edly, are technologically feasible, and so forth) to be a reoccurring challenge. As a designer, you want to provide the player with what he wants and expects . . . but not at the cost of the usability of the experience.

Ultimately, I came to learn that the trick lies in guiding the player into wanting and expecting the gestures that are most fun and effective for the game. One game that does this well is *Trauma Center* for the Nintendo DS. Players initially may be wont to apply sutures through gestural interactions that mimic sewing. However, that ultimately ends up being slow, bor-ing, and eventually repetitive. By presenting the quick "zig-zag-across-the-wound" as an abstraction of skilled doctor technique, the player is primed to readjust his expectations and adjust his actions to reflect how gestures are performed in-game.

---

[1]Full disclosure: I worked as THQ's creative manager on *Drawn to Life*. Despite this fact, Erin still really likes the game.

What game design opportunities and player interface considerations do AR game designers face?

Ultimately, the challenges that touchscreen technology initially presented—learning to think outside the box and not relying on antiquated design techniques—will be key to tapping into the potential of AR games. AR interactions are not merely an upgrade from "controller-and-screen" or even touchscreen interaction schemes. Augmented reality is its own beast, and we, as game designers, are responsible for learning what works, what doesn't work, and what players want/need in order to know how best to "tame" it.

Any predictions for the future of the touchscreen game space?

My hope is that people will continue to innovate and push the possibilities of touchscreen interaction to its limits. However, I fear that players and developers will start jumping on the next interface technology before the touchscreen can reach its full potential. Nonetheless, these devices are so ubiquitous now that there will always be a host of developers looking to squeeze the most out of what the platform has to offer.

chapter 6

Arcade Crazy

WHEN I WAS a kid, I was crazy for arcade games. Absolutely crazy. I was hooked and I would do anything to play them. I had played pinball and I had played electro-mechanical games, but nothing matched the intense visual bliss and the sweet, sweet beep, boop, wakka that only an arcade game could give. I'm not proud to tell you that I stole quarters from Dad's huge bowl of coins to play games at Scotty's Arcade. I embarrassingly confess that during the 1981 Boy Scouts jamboree, I caused Troop 649 to mobilize a search for me because I hadn't told anyone that I had dashed across the highway to a nearby mall to look for an arcade. I freely admit that I attended birthday parties of kids I didn't like because they were having their parties at Golf Land, which had the gnarliest arcade in all of Northern San Diego County.

Because my parents wouldn't let me spend all of my time in an arcade and I couldn't afford to own arcade cabinets[1], I lusted after two surrogates during my whole childhood. The first was a **Vectrex:** the first home system with graphics **exactly** like the arcade. The eye-searingly bright vector line graphics were **identical** to those found in *Asteroids* and *Star Castle*. Even cooler was the fact that the Vectrex was a self-contained gaming system, a rarity in 1982. The screen, processor, and even the controller were built right into the Vectrex! It was a modern miracle as far as I was concerned[2]. The Vectrex had a side slot for cartridges (the total catalog was around 30 games) and, even cooler, most of those games came with screen-printed plastic overlays that magically transformed black-and-white graphics into **color!** Add in the miniature joystick and buttons and you had your very own home arcade. Bliss! As Christmas approached, I explained to my parents that the Vectrex was my ticket to escaping the obligation of lame birthday parties. Sadly, I didn't receive a Vectrex that year (or the next), and by 1984 the Vectrex was no more.

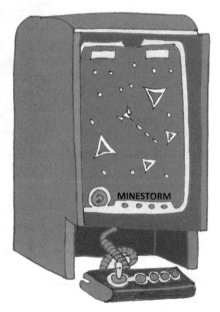

---

[1]Buy an arcade game for my HOUSE? Who am I, Rockefeller?
[2]And quite possibly the reason why I later got a Macintosh Plus back in 1986.

My other childhood desire was for Coleco's line of mini-arcade games: *Pac-Man, Ms. Pac-Man, Frogger, Galaxian, Donkey Kong Jr.,* and my favorite, *Donkey Kong.* The tiny cabinets looked like they were imported straight from a Lilliputian arcade. These little guys were things of beauty, complete with original graphics on the sides of the cabinets and a teeny-weeny little joystick that you could push around with one finger. Okay, so maybe the game's VFD graphics resembled *Mattel Pocket Football* more than the games they were based on, but I didn't care. Next to the Vectrex, they were the closest thing you could have to an official looking arcade cabinet at home. And you guessed it: I never got that for Christmas, either.

This brings us to the present and the reason why an Icon's **iCADE** is sitting on my kitchen table. The iCADE is a desktop sized arcade cabinet peripheral for the iPad that **"will provide hours of action and nostalgic fun for years to come."** I haven't made up my mind about the iCADE—it seems indulgent to strap a foot-tall fiberboard cabinet onto the sleek and elegant touchscreen iPad, and it does seem a little silly to give up finger control for clunky analog controls. While it might be a step backward on the gaming evolutionary chart, I have to admit it is fun to play games with an honest-to-god joystick and buttons that make those very distinctive clicking sounds when pressed. The iCADE does make games like *Velocispider* (Retro Dreamer, 2011) and *Arcade Jumper* (BlackHiveMedia, 2011) more fun to play. What I realized is that I didn't buy the iCADE for any logical reason: Instead, I bought it as a misplaced desire for some of those never-had-as-a-child toys. Which brings me (finally) to the connection between the arcade games of my youth and games on touchscreen devices and what I love about them: **nostalgia** and **simplicity.**

The "Good Ol' Days"

Even the word "arcade" conjures nostalgic visions for guys like me—players wistful for the golden age of gaming. If you've ever visited an arcade, then you already know that these dimly lit shrines to gaming were designed to do one thing . . . suck all your money right out of your pockets. And those arcade game developers knew plenty of ways to do it: They used mysterious cabinets that grabbed your attention with gorgeous and exciting panel art and beautiful imagery that compensated for the games' primitive graphics[3]. Lit marquees dared you spend money for a glimpse into the fantastic gaming world. And when they really wanted to pull you in, they would let you sit in the seat of an X-wing fighter, a race car, or Captain Kirk's command chair.

Those early arcade games screamed fun. They tugged at the sleeves of your eyeballs with flashing attract modes, beckoning beeps and boops, and they even begged for your quarters with synthesized voices. Once a coin dropped into the slot, an arcade game just had to be simple enough for the player to get through a wave or two, just enough to entice you to spend another quarter for "just one more try" when the difficulty ramped up and the game killed you. The insidious thing was, it wasn't the game that killed me; it was just that I needed to be more skilled at playing it[4]! Skill that could only be gained by playing more. They were simple, but effective. And the lessons about game design that can be learned from those early games are still applicable when designing mobile arcade games. What lessons, you ask? Here they are:

○ **Simple controls:** With a few exceptions[5], most arcade game controls are comprised of a single joystick, a couple of buttons, or maybe a trackball. Follow this example when designing your own games. In the words of *Pong* creator Nolan Bushnell, an arcade game should be "Simple. Simple enough for a drunk to play[6]."

---

[3]Note to my 1980 self: The centipede on the side of the cabinet is waaay scarier than the one in the game.

[4]I am convinced my entire generation was transformed into obsessive/compulsives thanks to video games.

[5]*Robotron 2084* had twin joysticks and *Defender* had what seemed to be a half-dozen buttons.

[6]*"All Your Base Are Belong to Us: How Fifty Years of Videogames Conquered Pop Culture"* by Harold Goldberg (Crown Publishing Group, 2011).

○ **Fast-paced gameplay:** Players should constantly be moving their avatars around the playfield. Change direction. Switch modes. Alternate between a finger move and a button press. Standing still equals death. Dodge that invader's missile, jink around that ghost, and roll out of the way of that spider. This is the key to heart-pounding, adrenaline-pumping gameplay that keeps players coming back for more.

○ **Increasing difficulty:** As gameplay gets faster, the hazards should get deadlier, the enemies smarter. Ramping difficulty toward the unplayable has recently made a comeback in the otherwise casual gaming space. This return to hardcore gaming is a nostalgia-fueled reaction to years of player cuddling and coddling on challenge-less console games. It's time to earn those high scores! Games like *Tobor* (Atomic Games, 2011), *Canabalt* (Semi Secret Software, 2009), and *Robot Unicorn Attack* (adult swim, 2010) are unabashedly proud of their insane difficulty levels where players measure their victories in inches. Luke Muscat of Halfbrick shares an observation about increasing difficulty: there's only so fast that a human can react to high speeds and obstacles. In *Jetpack Joyride* (Halfbrick, 2011) the player's speed increases until the player can barely react to the oncoming hazards. But rather than increasing the speed even further to cause the player to fail, instead the intervals between hazards is decreased and randomized to create challenge and variety. In the end "(you) want the game to be a little unfair."[7]

○ **No endings:** Play until death, that's how we rolled in the old days. Even if you were good at playing a game, you still died in the end. If you were really good, you reached the game's kill screen but you still lost your quarter. Today's audiences like a little story and every story has an ending, preferably a happy one. But we all know that true retro arcade games are like the Energizer bunny; they just keep going and going and going . . .

○ **Scoring:** Once upon a time, scoring in video games was *this close* to being passé. Many game designers considered score to be too old school, a remnant of an older time when games couldn't display more than a few digits to prove to the neighborhood who was the game master. As casual gaming took off, people remembered how much they liked bragging to their friends about their high scores. High scores flourished. Modern gaming lets you display your *entire* name to the whole world—which makes the bragging all that much sweeter. Social gaming networks like Open Feint, Plus +, and Gameloft Live provide applications to make it easy for developers to plug links to **leaderboards** and other score-related features into their games.

When allowing for high scores, consider the following: How long should the high score be displayed to the world? What happens to the score when it is beaten? What does the player get for attaining a high score? How many characters does the player get to write her name (classic games = 3 characters, modern games = 16 characters)? How high can the score go? To 999,999[8]? Higher? What happens when the score "flips"? So many things to consider!

---

[7]"Depth in Simplicity: The Making of Jetpack Joyride" by Luke Muscat (Game Developers Conference Lecture, 2012)

[8]When visually designing your score bar, make sure you use 8s, 9s, or 0s as placeholder numbers. Narrow numbers like 1s and 4s do not provide an accurate gauge for required spacing.

○ **One more try:** Fast-paced action. Simple controls. Catchy music. Crazy animations. Big explosions. Creepy (and funny) enemies. Stunning background art. Achievements. Purchasable virtual goods. Tradable items. Multi-play. Money. High score. Sex. Extra lives. Free games. Cheat the game in favor of the player. Err on the side of drama. Deliver on the promise of New! Exciting! Novel! Bizarre! Random! Fun! It doesn't matter how you do it—as long as you can get the player to play one more time. Give him a hundred reasons to keep playing . . . and then give him one more.

○ **Bite-sized gameplay:** Arcade games broke play sequences into waves. Levels. Mazes. Chapters. Break your own game into ***bite-sized chunks*** to promote stop-and-go play. Touchscreen gamers usually don't have the time for long, involved games[9]. This is why repeatability is stressed over length. In the world of console games, the average game length is 8 to 10 hours. In touchscreen gaming, the average[10] target game length is 2 to 3 hours, but those 2 to 3 hours are repeatable . . . which could turn into more hours, days, weeks, or even months of play. Of course this number depends on the game you are making.

Bite-sized gameplay sounds delicious, but how can you prevent biting off more than you can chew? Let's take it one bite at a time. Start by having a good idea of your entire gameplay experience. How long does it take to play your game[11]? Next, determine a complete sequence of play. Is it wiping out a single wave of alien enemies? Is it clearing a maze of pickups? You can prototype this single sequence or just imagine yourself playing it. It will be easier to break up your gameplay if it is built around a single play-through. Static screens, solitary objectives, single solutions. To keep things from feeling too thin, you might want to add a secondary objective such as targeting a randomly appearing enemy, collecting a limited number (like three) of pickups, or uncovering a hidden object. You can give the player a time limit or a mission/objective to complete during the sequence.

Here's a way to help promote bite-sized gameplay: Visually segregate your chunks on your level selection screen. The more levels you can display on one screen, the better. It makes a player feel like he's getting a good deal for his money. Look at all those levels! There are so many of them! This game is a great deal for the price I paid!

---

[9]Even "longer" made-for-mobile games like *Superbrothers: Sword & Sworcery* break their stories into pieces to allow for short-burst play sessions.

[10]This, of course depends on the game's genre. One can expect (hope) that players will play more sessions of a puzzle game like *Hanging with Friends* or *Draw Something* than a story-based game.

[11]Remember? 2 to 3 hours!

Letting players know that they are playing a bite-size level has three benefits: First, as the number of completed levels increase, players gain a sense of progression and accomplishment. The faster they rise up the ladder, the more they will feel like they are getting somewhere. Secondly, visually breaking up the experience, no matter how long it is, gives the players permission to take breaks and lets them catch their breath, rub their aching hands, and mop the flop sweat from their brows before plunging back into the action. Thirdly, the players feel that because the experience is so short, it isn't a big deal to give it one more try. The more they play your game, the more compelled they are to complete it. And if they complete your games, they'll want to play (and buy) the next one.

Okay, designers, now that you know some tricks, let's figure out what genre of arcade game to make! Smash open those piggybanks, grab your dad's quarters, and let's go to the arcade!

Games? I'll Give You Games!

Before arcades were reduced to grim dens of *Skee-Ball* alleys and redemption machines, they had variety. The *Mario Bros.* lived happily next to *Sinistar*. Dirk the Daring braved dungeons while Major Havoc explored space stations one cabinet down. Thank the maker that this variety lives on in touchscreen gaming. Every genre of arcade game is represented on touchscreens[12] and there's plenty to choose from.

Some of the earliest arcade games were **shooters.** While *Space Invaders, Asteroids, Galaxian*, and *Tempest* live on in spiritual successors like *Super Crossfire, Alien Space Retro, Warblade HD*, and *Orbit1*, you can still play the original games on touchscreens: *Space Invaders Infinity Gene*, *Atari's Greatest Hits*, and *Galaga REMIX*. It's kind of amazing that these games are still popular to this day; retro is the new cool.

---

[12]A sampling from one row on my personal iPad: *Gesundheit, Paper Wars, Rage, Jelly Car*, and *Zombie Gunship*.

If you want to design your own shooter, first determine what kind of shooter you want to make. The shooter style will determine your character, your controls, your camera, your background, and how your enemies attack. In a **single-screen shooter** like *Blasteroids*, the players can move around the entire screen as enemies and hazards come in from all directions but they cannot move beyond a single "fixed camera" screen. However, players sometimes can travel off-screen in one direction and "wrap around" to emerge from the other side of the screen. In other single-screen shooters like *Earth vs. Moon* (*Low Five Games*, 2009), the player is locked to the bottom of the screen as enemies advance toward him. This screen format is similar to a **scrolling shooter** like *Boss Battles* (Backflip Studios, 2011), where the player is only allowed to move left and right or up and down for a limited distance. The word scrolling in these types of games refers to the background—which scrolls down behind the player's avatar, giving the illusion of flight to the player. Enemies and hazards mostly attack from the top and work their way down toward the player. If the enemies or hazards reach the bottom of the screen, it often means death for the player.

A **cursor shooter** like *Zombie Gunship* (Limbic Software, 2011) allows the player access to the entire playfield, but the player isn't represented on-screen with a ship or a character. If the player fails to stop enemies or achieve an objective, the game is lost, rather than getting "killed" from a collision. The cursor shooter's counterpart is the **twin-stick shooter,** and includes games like *Cowboy Guns* (Chillingo, 2011), where the player moves a character or ship that shoots. The name of the sub-genre comes from the two control sticks the player uses. One (usually virtual) joystick guides the player around, and the other enables him to shoot in any direction. A **rail shooter** like *Rage* (id software, 2011) or *Star Fox Command* (Nintendo, 2006) shows the player from either a first- or third-person camera view. The player does not control the character's movement, which in turn allows the player to concentrate on enemies and hazards that pop up. Imagine this kind of gameplay but remove the movement and you have a **shooting gallery** shooter like *Snow Ballistic* (Big Blue Bubble, 2010) or *Bang Bang BOOM!* (Circle Star Software, 2011).

Did you pick a style? Good. Now you want to think about how the player is going to shoot! There are many factors to consider: shooting method and direction; projectile type, size and speed; what happens when the projectile hits and misses . . . . There are so many, I'm going to have to make a chart!

Basic Shooting Pattern Chart

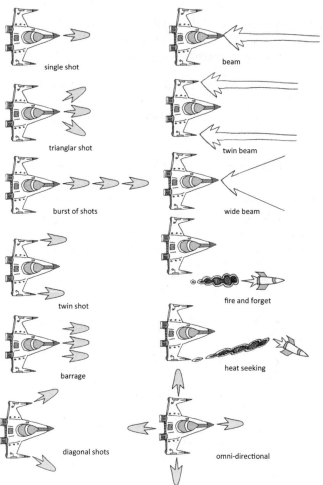

Every great shooter needs awesome weapons. Machine guns, laser beams, heat-seeking rockets, shotgun blasts, drones that shoot when you shoot, whirling blades, flamethrowers, ice cannons, cluster bombs, tiger-launchers, laser beams that shoot laser beams: They all add variety and excitement to your game. The more spectacular, ridiculous, particle-filled they are, the better!

If players can shoot, then they should have something to shoot at. You need waves and waves of enemies. When one wave is cleared, the next one isn't far behind. Make waves unpredictable and challenging just by adjusting their movement patterns. Get some randomness into their movement . . . but not so much that the player feels like enemies are zipping out of the way right as the player has them dead to rights. Players like getting into the rhythm of a game and the enemies are a big part of creating that rhythm. There are so many ways to configure enemies; I feel another chart coming on!

Start with these basics and then go ahead and layer in additional mechanics—dangerous hazards, moving elements, ground-based weapon emplacements, pickups, imperiled non-player characters . . . you get the idea. Just don't overcomplicate the environment; otherwise, the player will be too distracted to remember to shoot!

Don't overlook the importance of sound in your shooter, either. Distinctive firing sounds, robust explosions, happy pickup collection sounds—create pleasing sounds that the player won't mind hearing over and over and over again. Some shooters like *Radio Flare REDUX* and *Child of Eden* incorporate the rhythm right into the gameplay. Music can add excitement and tension to any game—remember the ominous march of advancing space invaders? This is true for just about any genre of game. See how many genres you can combine with rhythm action!

Shooter Enemy Movement Chart

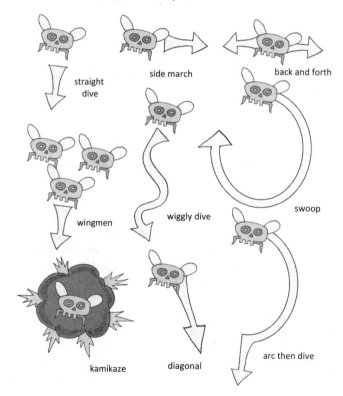

A-mazing Games

Another tension-filled arcade genre is the **maze game.** The grandfather and undefeated champion of maze games is *Pac-Man,* who is also the star of several touchscreen games, including *Pac-Attack, Pac-Chain, Pac-Mania,* and *Pac-Man Remix.* The original *Pac-Man* invented most maze play mechanics, including **constant motion.** The player can control the direction of the character but cannot adjust the speed at which that character travels[13]. Even tilt maze games like *Labyrinth* (Codify AB, 2009) make it extremely difficult to come to a complete stop. The constantly moving character forces the player to pay attention; missing one opportunity to make a turn or grab a power-up could result in game over. Not giving the player an opportunity to stop and catch her breath[14] adds tension. Maintaining tension is important for any game, not just maze games. To achieve tension, the player must be (a) powerless, (b) outnumbered by hazards or enemies, and (c) extremely fragile—killable in one hit.

Another way to build tension is timing. *Sr. Mistu* (We Choose Fun, 2011) relies on timing to create tension as players avoid environmental hazards such as moving cars and walking pedestrians.

Another control variant is the **drawn-line maze game.** Games like *SPY Mouse* (Firemint, 2011) and *Sr. Mistu* have players first draw the character's path through the maze and then watch to see if those characters succeed or get flattened by a moving car.

No matter if it takes place on an open city street or a tight maze, remember that collecting is the primary action of maze games. Make sure players know what they are collecting and that it is easy to find. Make your collectables count. The brilliance of *Pac-Man* is the energizer: the power-up that allows the hunted to become the hunter and gives the enemies their comeuppance. It provides a break in the tension and gives the player a moment of invulnerability or a way to strike back. It is not only extremely rewarding, but it also reminds players of their vulnerability once everything has returned to normal.

---

[13]This differentiates the maze game from its cousin, the stealth game, with which the maze game shares many gameplay features.

[14]Whether or not Namco intended it, there's a spot on the *Pac-Man* maze where a player can hide from pursuing ghosts. This location is where the record-breaking *Pac-Man* players hide in order to take food or bathroom breaks.

Pac-Man is a good starting point for inspiration, but you don't need to limit your level layouts to traditional labyrinths. As long as you have a complex path, enemies to avoid, and items to collect, then you can have similar gameplay. *Mappy* (Namco, 2011), *Crime Spree* (Skyworks, 2010), and *Rally-X Rumble* (Namco, 2011) all follow this formula.

Cuteness Counts

Speaking of *Rally-X*, did you know that Namco thought that the car maze game *Rally-X* was going to be the big hit of 1980? Boy, were they wrong! Both games had similar gameplay, but I maintain that *Pac-Man* became a hit because he's a cute character[15]. Look at many of the popular early videogame stars—*Pac-Man, Dig-Dug, Mario, Donkey Kong, Q*Bert*. The cuter the character, the more the player will want to keep it safe from harm. Here are a few pointers on creating cute characters:

○ Big heads: particularly with a large forehead like a baby

○ Large eyes

○ Simplify features like nose and ears

○ Give your character a small body with short arms and legs

○ Use primary colors

Awww, even a disgusting zombie can be made adorable! Another genre that knows the importance of cute characters is the **platform game.** Plucky heroes like Mario, Kirby, Cordy, Pizza Boy, and whatever the heck that thing in *Mos Speedrun* is brave all manner of bizarre environments that are chock-full of deadly traps, adorably vicious enemies, and more collectables than your local comic book store to save a princess or the world . . . or a slice of pizza pie.

---

[15]Let's just say that nobody ever wrote a song about how much he loved *Rally-X*.

Another super-important thing to do when designing a platform game is to establish your **metrics**—the player character's relationship to the game world. Character metrics should be one of the first things you develop when you design your game. To design metrics, you need to know your character's **dimensions.** The easiest way to design dimensions is to get out a piece of graph paper and draw your character like so:

Notice how the character is three squares tall on the grid and two squares wide? This means that your platforms cannot be smaller than two wide. Entries cannot be shorter than three high. If we want the player to jump twice his height, the height of the jump would be six and the height of the platform he is jumping onto cannot be higher than six. If you want an enemy to look small compared to your hero, then the enemy has to be shorter than three squares. You get the idea. Now that you know the character's dimensions, you can determine:

- ○ Distance the player can walk, jump, run, or slide
- ○ Height the player can jump, reach, or hang
- ○ Distances the player can attack, shoot, and interact
- ○ Height of world objects like doorways and crates
- ○ Size (height and width) of enemies
- ○ Distance of camera to player

See how important metrics are to the game? Besides metrics and memorable characters, the best platform games all have the **Three S's:** Story, Skill, and Surprise:

○ **Story:** You should already know how to write this; after all, you just read Chapter 4, didn't you[16]? In addition to cutscenes (which no one watches anyway), you should strive to tell your story *within* the level by using backgrounds, enemies, environments, and mechanics. For instance, your hero could start out on a ship and have to jump over smokestacks, fight angry merchant marines, and collect something nautical like . . . I don't know . . . conch shells or those donut-shaped life preservers. Then the ship could strike an iceberg and the player would have to fight the forces of gravity to hop to safety while dodging sliding chunks of ice, deck chairs, and confused musicians. Lastly, your level could end with the ship sunk and the hero hopping from ice floe to ice floe to keep from falling into freezing cold waters. The hero would then reach the cause of the disaster—the dreaded Iceborg, the cold-hearted, cybernetic iceberg of death! See? You've just told a story about a ship that is whacked by an iceberg and the hero's fight for survival. If this story can win James Cameron an Oscar[17], then it should make for a good level story.

The dreaded
ICEBORG

---

[16]Unless you time-travelled straight to this page.

[17]I think I just wrote the sequel to *Titanic*.

○ **Skill:** Players need skill to survive a platform game because so many things are trying to kill them! Accurate and intuitive-feeling controls are essential to platform gaming because much of the play is based on quick reactions and last-minute escapes. If controls feel too sluggish or jumps feel too floaty, examine the physics, the metrics, and the animation cycles of your characters to get to the root of the problem.

The **mechanics** (things that the player interacts with), **hazards** (things that the player interacts with and that try to kill said player), and **enemies** (things that the player interacts with, that try to kill the player, and that possess artificial intelligence) all challenge the player's ability to stay alive.

○ **Surprise:** To keep players interested in your game, you must provide variety. And surprise is variety that the player doesn't expect. Surprise can come in the form of an enemy leaping out from an unexpected place, a treasure chest that turns out to be a horrible enemy disguised as a treasure chest, a jewel that splits into two when selected, a slow-motion effect when a ball is about to hit the final peg, or a burst of energy when the player is least expecting it. Use surprises to delight, reward, scare, and amuse your players. If you are going to have unpleasant surprises, then give the players a warning first, such as an animation, sound effect, or particle effect.

There's so much more to learn about platform games for touchscreens that I'm going to devote an entire chapter to them. In the meantime, let's talk about another character-centric genre—fighting games.

The First Rule of Fighting Games . . .

Fighting games are not commonly found on touchscreen systems[18]. Sure, the old standbys like *Street Fighter* and *Mortal Kombat* are represented on the Nintendo 3DS, but most of the fighters found on iOS platforms feel closer to *Super Punch Out* than to *King of Fighters*. This is probably because fighting games traditionally use complex joystick and button combinations to pull off combat moves, and touchscreen just can't approximate an eight-button combo very well. It's also why you find fighters on gaming systems with pad controllers—where the touchscreen is used to execute a super move but not act as the primary controller. There are several sub-genres of fighters to be found:

---

[18]Game developers take note!

One-on-one fighters are where two fighters enter, one fighter leaves! Whether it's boxing, wrestling, or duking it out for the fate of the universe, one-on-one fighters feature realistic (like *Super KO Boxing 2*) and bizarre (like *Beast Boxing 3D*) characters—each with unique stats, powers, and attack moves. Players often rely on combination attacks to beat their opponent down to be finished off with a super blow or technical move. On touchscreens, directional swipes often stand in for stick controls with varying results.

Consider how realistic your fighting game will be. Do you want to make a straight-up realistic wrestling game like the *UFC Undisputed* series (THQ, 2010), or mix magic and brawling like in *Mortal Kombat?* You don't have to limit your fights to bare knuckle variety, either. *Infinity Blade* is a one-on-one fighter stripped down to the bare essentials: a sword, shield, dodges, and some swipe attacks. Players of *Batman: Gotham City Lockdown* rely only on their fists, dodges, and an occasional batarang!

After you determine the level of realism, start figuring out who your characters are. When designing a one-on-one fighter, make sure each character brings something unique to the fight. *Street Fighter*'s characters each represent a different style of fighting. This gives players a reason for playing all the characters and helps flesh out their personalities. Personality goes a long way in fighting games.

Beat 'em ups like *Knight's Rush* (Chillingo, 2010) or *Tap-Fu* (Neptune Interactive, 2009) combine platform gaming with fighting in a satisfying blend of punching and brutality. When designing a beat 'em up, remember it's all about over-the-top action, a variety of attacks, and hordes of cool-looking enemies. We'll get more into how to design fighting and creating enemies in the next chapter.

Thanks to the wonders of Wi-Fi and Bluetooth, multiple players can bash on each other simultaneously in **group brawlers**—a combination of a platformer, a one-on-one fighter, and a party game. But instead of beating the health out of each other, players gain damage until they are knocked off a platform or out of the battle arena. Player controls are often very simple compared to other fighting games. Players can move, jump, attack, grab, and throw.

Group brawlers are often populated with unique characters, and giving each of these characters distinctive moves and attacks is par for the course. Like many one-on-one fighters, characters will have over-the-top finishing moves that can deal lots of knockback and damage to players at once. These moves should be the "signatures" of your player characters. If you have a ninja char-acter, then he could execute a "hundred throwing star" finishing attack or dive in with a blinding flurry of katana strikes.

When creating a group brawler, arena design is very important. Arenas occupy a single screen with a fixed camera. Arenas are often extremely simple, designed with only a layer or two of platforms. Sometimes, they can have moving or rotating platforms, electrified floors, and spike pits. Gaining higher ground is another common strategy, so make it interesting and challenging for players to reach the top levels.

Conversely, the **boxing ring** game has almost no level design. These one-on-one fighters rely less on complex combos and more on the player's timing of delivering blows. Opponents will strike at the player who blocks or dodges attacks while waiting for an opening in the opponent's patterns, hoping to land a mighty blow. The camera in a boxing ring fighter is usually positioned directly behind the player or from an over-the-shoulder perspective to give the player a clear view of the opponent (and makes the player feel right in the middle of the action).

Make sure your characters are distinct from each other. Creating realistic characters is one thing, but at least give them each one memorable feature—whether it's a unique face, a crazy hairstyle, or a different body type. I once played a boxing game where the player characters were identical models except for the color of their jerseys. I had no idea which character was mine until he was on the floor and I had lost.

When designing a boxing game, work with your programmer to really nail collision. Nothing looks worse than when someone's boxing glove passes into or through another person like Patrick Swayze in *Ghost*. Hit reactions are another important thing to nail in a boxing game. If the boxer throws a punch and it doesn't feel powerful enough, the player isn't going to realize they connected. The payoff for players is landing a good, solid blow, so make sure players really feel like they've connected! Effects like speed blur, bursts, flying teeth, and sweat really sell the impact of the fight. Don't be afraid to get a little cheesy with some good-old fashioned slow-motion camera work. If it's good enough for *Super Punch Out,* then it's good enough for you!

Get on the Ball

Another gaming system I'd love to own is an old-school Pinball machine. The lights, the artwork, the sounds, the digital readout, and the physicality of a pinball machine all remind me of my youth. Once again, there's that arcade nostalgia at work. Speaking of you young whippersnappers, many of you younger readers might not be familiar with pinball jargon, so here's a short glossary:

- **Backbox (**or **backboard):** The vertical back of a pinball machine where graphics, score, and display can be found.
- **Board:** The horizontal gameplay area of a pinball machine.
- **Bumper:** An upright, often lit target that pushes the ball horizontally when hit.
- **Dot matrix display:** A distinctive monochromatic pixel display screen used on most pinball games from the 1990s.
- **Drain:** The spot between the flippers—if the ball goes down the drain, then it is lost.
- **Flippers:** A player-controlled bat that is used to hit the ball, usually found in pairs at the bottom of the board (but frequently in other locations as well).
- **Lane:** The path for the ball to travel around the board; in-lanes lead to the flippers while out-lanes lead to the drain.
- **Multi-ball:** A mode that releases more than one ball onto the board: Multi-ball increases difficulty but gives the player a chance to earn a higher score.
- **Plunger:** A player-controlled spring-loaded shaft that launches the ball into play.

○ **Popper:** A target that launches the ball upward, often to another level.

○ **Rail (or Habitrail[19]):** A wire-enclosed tube that allows the ball to travel through without falling off the track.

○ **Tilt:** An anti-cheating system that activates if the player violently pushes the pinball machine in an attempt to influence the ball's movement. If the game tilts, the player loses the ball.

There were some really awesome pinball machines back in the day, like *The Creature of the Black Lagoon, Indiana Jones: The Pinball Adventure, Funhouse,* and *Scared Stiff*[20], that merged traditional pinball play with story and mission-based gameplay. They would have the player shoot the ball toward particular locations or targets. When the player "collected" enough of these targets, the objective was achieved . . . usually with great fanfare and a short video on the dot matrix display. Mobile games *Pinball HD* (Gameprom, 2011) and *Retro Pinball* (Fuse Powered Inc., 2011) do an admirable job of capturing the classic pinball experience, but aside from pulling back the plunger and tilting the board you just don't get that feeling of physicality. This may be my bias toward real-world pinball, but I feel that touchscreen pinball loses something in the translation to digital.

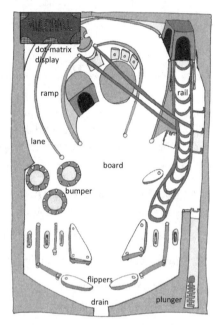

Game designers have taken this as a challenge rather than a disadvantage. Many touchscreen games have merged pinball with other genres: Tower defense in *Undead Attack Pinball* (Lucas Mendes Menge, 2009), RPG as in *Pinball Massacre* (Nuclear Nova Software, 2011), action with *Pinball Ride Unlimited* (Massive Finger, 2009), and sports with *ESPN Pinball* (ESPN, 2010). There are even pinball games that let you design pinball games like *Pinball Wizard* (Zidware, 2011). Whether your design is traditional or hybrid, here are some factors to consider:

○ **Physics:** Well, duh. Without good physics, you just don't have a pinball game. But remember that physics extend beyond the ball. Realistic reacting flippers, poppers, and bumpers (you want to avoid "dead bumper syndrome," where the ball hits a bumper and immediately loses all its inertia) help make the game feel solid and realistic.

---

[19]Named after the famous clear plastic tube for pet hamsters to crawl through.

[20]This chapter is beginning to resemble my Christmas wish list.

Camera: Personally, I don't like it when a camera moves around on a pinball board. I like being able to see the position of the ball in relationship to the rest of the board. However, in a virtual landscape, one of the freedoms you have is that you aren't limited by a static board. For example, when the ball drops in *Monster Pinball* (Matmi, 2009) it goes to a completely different screen. You could have the ball drop down into a sublevel, climb up floors, or perhaps shoot into outer space.

place your camera here*↘

*and treat the player as invisible

You're limited only by your imagination! But if you go that route, keep in mind that it's very easy for a player to get lost if the camera doesn't make things super-clear. No matter if you go static or active with your camera, pull it back a bit to keep the ball in view. Avoid whipping the camera around so the player doesn't lose sight of the ball. (Or get nauseous!)

Feedback: The proverbial bells and whistles. Sound and lights are some of pinball's most exciting features. I suggest placing several score bumpers and intractable objects in your game. Arrange three bumpers in a triangular shape to get that cool bouncing-between-them-several-times sound effect that players love hearing. If you think traditional bumpers and lights look a little old-fashioned, try disguising them like *Pinball HD*'s *The Deep*, where the bumpers and lights look like the skylights of underwater buildings and the smokestacks of a ruined ship.

Theme: Most pinball games have a theme: unless you are trying to emulate a vintage pinball game like *Wooden Pinball* (devforfun, 2010)[21]. There have been pinball games about river rafting, rollercoasters, magic shows, and many popular comic book and movie characters. Any story genre is fair play; you are limited only by your imagination. Use the theme to inspire the elements found on your board. Start by listing all the elements found on a pinball game (Hint: there's a list of them a few pages back) and assigning themes to them. For example, in *Pinball HD*'s *Jungle Style*, you can find Tiki-shaped bumpers, a blue lagoon, a wrecked helicopter, a Mayan temple, and a ball-eating ape!

I believe the pinball genre, like puzzle games, still has plenty of room to expand in new directions. Digital pinball designers are not restricted by real-world concerns like wear-and-tear or even reality! What great pinball hybrids are out there for game designers to discover?

---

[21]Which in retrospect has the theme of "vintage pinball game," so I stand by my previous sentence.

Baby, You Can Drive My iPhone

Racing games were some of mobile gaming's most popular games, thanks in part to their novel tilt-controls. Within the racing genre, there are three sub-genres: Realistic racers like *Real Racing 2* (Firemint, 2010) and *GT Racing: Motor Academy* (Gameloft, 2010), arcade racers like *Reckless Racing* (EA, 2010) and *VS. Racing* (Maciek Drejak Labs, 2011), and kart racers like *Mario Kart DS* (Nintendo, 2005), *Cro-Mag Rally* (Pangea Software, 2008), and *Sonic & SEGA All-Stars Racing* (SEGA, 2008).

Realistic racers concentrate on precision handling, accurate controls, realistic physics, and vehicle customization. Some realistic games allow players to obsess over their cars—from the engines and tires to the paint jobs—and let them have the car they couldn't own in real life. Realistic racers are mostly displayed from a third-person perspective, giving the player a chance to switch into a first-person point of view.

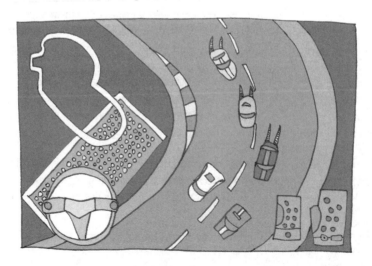

Arcade racers concentrate on speed and thrills. The track designs are more fantastical than their realistic cousins, with an emphasis on in-race events and hazards designed to create epic moments, such as colossal jumps or even loop-de-loops. Cameras in arcade racers vary the most, from a third-person point of view to an isometric to a top-down perspective. Smash-up racers like *Smash Cops* (Hutch, 2012) and *Reckless Getaway* (Polarbit, 2011), where crashing is just as important as racing, have become a popular sub-genre in the arcade racing classification.

Kart racers feature cartoon characters racing in crazy themed vehicles on fantasy tracks. Kart racers focus the battle for the finish line by using weapons and power-ups. Cameras are almost exclusively third person to see the driver and any incoming projectiles!

Now that you've picked a genre (you have picked a genre, right?), ask yourself how the player is going to drive. How about tilt controls? Players can grip either side of the mobile device to "steer" their vehicle, making for a (somewhat) realistic driving experience. It's better to have the player make extreme gestures rather than subtle ones; otherwise, the car will slam its way left and right as it drives down the track. You can even combine tilt controls with touch-screen gas and brake for extra realism. How about a virtual steering wheel? Be careful that the wheel snaps back to center if the player's finger slips off the wheel. Some games have the player draw a line for the car to follow rather than directly controlling it. Other games simulate the player "pushing" the car, which allows the player to see the car in front of their finger as they steer. What I am trying to say is, you have plenty of options when designing a racer.

Game design lecturer Luke McMillian offers the following sound advice on track design no matter if you are designing a realistic, arcade, or kart racer[22] (or even a chariot, horse, or sailboat race):

○ Never have the player stop accelerating. Players want to consistently race, not constantly brake!

○ Build in straights at regular intervals on the track to allow players to get an exciting boost of speed.

○ Design your track with occasional tight spaces. "Threading the needle" will give your players a burst of excitement.

○ Scale the tracks to be larger than life (about 33% larger) to allow for more appealing camera angles as well as cleaner passing opportunities.

○ Have the track slant (or camber) toward the *inside* of the track to allow for smoother cornering on curves.

○ Put down lots of "paint"—markings on the road—to help increase the player's feeling of speed.

○ Reduce the height of the vehicle (or raise the camera) to allow for a greater line of sight. The more of the road the players can see, the less anxious they will be about oncoming turns and hazards.

○ Use "rubber banding"—opponent cars speed up or slow down to match players' pace so they have someone to race against. No one likes to be "blown away" by AI-controlled cars. It just feels like cheating.

Or you could throw all that advice out the window and design a driving game like *Enviro-Bear 2010* (Blinkbat Games, 2009), which can be described only as "... as realistic of an experience as I can imagine if I were a bear driving a car.[23]" You see, the most important thing about making a racing game is that the player feels awesome—no matter if it's blasting through a tight spot between two opposing drivers or roaring through a stream while collecting salmon. Make it fun. Make it awesome.

Beat It, Kid

Starting on consoles with games like *Parappa the Rapper*[24], the **rhythm game** genre took over arcades in the late 1990s with Konami's *Dance Dance Revolution* (or *DDR*). Rhythm games came to touchscreen gaming in three flavors: **rhythm action** games like *Elite Beat Agents* (iNiS, 2006), **repeat rhythm** games like *Rhythm Nation* (Nintendo, 2008), and **matching rhythm** games like *Guitar Hero: On Tour* (Vicarious Visions, 2008).

Rhythm action has players react to the beats as they appear. To increase a rhythm action game's difficulty, speed up the appearance of beats and decrease the time between the beat's appearances. This style of rhythm game is as much about quick reactions as it is about keeping a beat. Sometimes it has almost nothing to do with keeping a beat.

Repeat rhythm plays like that classic game, *Simon*. A beat (or song) is played once and the player must repeat the pattern as well as match the timing of the tune. Difficulty ensues when the tune's speed is increased or made more complex by increasing the number of notes that have to be memorized and repeated back. The tune doesn't have to even be musical, just distinct enough for the player to repeat it.

---

[23]http://toucharcade.com/2009/07/10/enviro-bear-2010-the-best-bear-driving-simulator-in-the-app-store/

[24]Okay, this isn't entirely true. *Quest for Fame* (Virtual Music, 1995) was a PC (and later arcade) game that not only featured a plastic guitar controller 10 years before *Guitar Hero*, but also starred those rock band pioneers of music-themed video gaming, Aerosmith.

Matching rhythm is where the player can see the beats coming down a track and use dexterity to hit the beats as they cross a marker or enter a specific zone. Difficulty is created by making the pattern of beats into complex patterns, creating beats that require different fingering positions such as holding a note or by increasing the speed that the beats travel down the track. Of the three styles, matching rhythm games feel the most like playing musical notes. Speaking of which, here are a few "notes" on creating music games:

- The average length of a rhythm game song is 2 minutes. Many licensed tunes have parts cut out of them to make them friendlier to the player.

- Rhythm games should be as fun to watch as they are to play. Even if your game is about matching dots, give the player something interesting to look at on-screen. *Elite Beat Agents* shows dancing comic characters, while *Guitar Hero* spotlights a band performing on stage.

- The longer the music goes on, the harder the game gets; and by harder, I mean that the beats appear faster and in more complex patterns. The player has to perform "moves" more often and with more variety—requiring the player to dance her fingers all over the screen.

- Audio and visual feedback is extremely important in rhythm games. *Guitar Hero* doesn't just show when the player has missed a beat; an off-chord note plays to indicate the player has screwed up. Play poorly enough and the crowd will boo the player! The "guitar strings" on the track will vibrate when a flub is made or glow with "star power" when the player is doing really well.

When picking music for your rhythm games, consider creating original music for your rhythm game. Although it is nice to have the most popular songs or the latest and greatest top hits, original music allows you to cater the music to the design of your gameplay. Much better than having to fit your gameplay to a song that just doesn't work. Original music is also cheaper[25] for a novice team to license! Avoid these headaches and choose your songs carefully!

Everything New Is Old Again

As you can see, just as arcade games come in a variety of gameplay genres, they also come in a variety of art styles: drawn sprites, pre-rendered art, true 3D characters and environments, vector graphics . . . but nothing says nostalgia like 8-bit graphics. Big, chunky pixels were all the rage back in 1979 (but then again, that's all we had).

---

[25]In some cases, ridiculously cheaper; EA paid over $40 million in royalties to use the songs in *Beatles: Rock Band*.

Once the Atari 2600 and Nintendo Entertainment System were surpassed by 16-bit systems, 8-bit graphics were quickly abandoned by deeper pixel depths, larger color palettes, and alpha layers. But 8-bit graphics never really went away[26] and the blocky pixel art never left Nintendo's handheld systems, from the Game Boy to the Nintendo DS.

It was the resurgence in **retro games,** titles like *Canabalt* (Semi Secret Software, 2009) and *Bit-Trip Beat* (Namco Networks, 2010) that refired the imagination of developers who wanted to capture the simplicity and feel of the late 1970s arcade and home system games. As appealing as this vintage art style is, Eli Hodapp of the *Touch Arcade Podcast* has an opinion that I generally agree with: When it comes to retro style graphics, the art style only really works when the gameplay is simple[27]. Having created pixel art for console games back in the day, here are a few pointers I picked up to help you make some blocky, chunky 8- and 16-bit art of your own:

- ○ Use graph paper to create a template of what you want to draw.

- ○ Create a box that will contain what you want to draw.

- ○ It might be tedious, but draw one pixel at a time. Use the pencil tool; other brushes tend to blur.

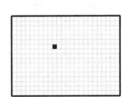

- ○ Draw an outline of your image first, and then use the fill tool to block out large areas of color.

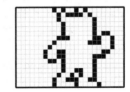

---

[26]Atari 2600 home brewers have been making 8-bit games since 1995, only 3 years after the system was discontinued. If you are curious about the Atari 2600 home brewing community or want to create your own Atari 2600 title, then I suggest starting with http://reviews.cnet.com/4520-11261_7-6298931-1.htmltag=tnav and http://www.alienbill.com/2600/.

[27]That didn't stop Ed Fries from relatively de-making the complicated console game *Halo* into *Halo 2600.*

○ Edge images with darker colors to give depth and light colors to make edges pop up.

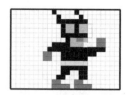

○ To create texture, use dithering—alternating colors in a checkerboard pattern, usually a light color with dark.

○ To create rounded edges, remove one of the pixels from the corner of a squared-off edge.

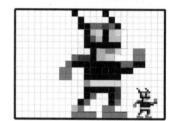

○ Reduce down your drawing to make sure it is readable at a smaller scale.

○ Zoom out and check your work from time to time. It's easy to get lost in the pixels as you draw. Otherwise, you'll end dazed like Cameron staring at *A Sunday Afternoon on the Island of La Grande Jatte*[28].

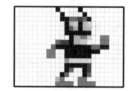

Speaking of paintings, you will need to consider the orientation of how your game will be displayed on-screen. There are two screen formats to choose from: **portrait** and **landscape.**

Portrait or vertical format displays the screen so the play space is shown as taller than it is wide. This was the most common configuration during the earliest days of gaming, as seen in arcade titles *Space Invaders* and *Centipede*.

Portrait games are best for descending visuals and mechanics—be it the scrolling icons in *Tap Tap Revenge* (Tapulous, 2009), descending jewels in *Bejeweled Blitz*, or dropping candy in *Cut the Rope*. Of course, what goes down must go up; so when I say descending, I also mean ascending gameplay, like in *NinJump* (Backflip Studios, 2010) and *Tiny Tower* (Nimblebit, 2011).

---

[28]Yes, I did just make a *Ferris Bueller's Day Off* reference.

Landscape format is used to emphasize horizontal environments: scrolling levels, like in *Canabalt* and *Jetpack Joyride* (Halfbrick, 2011), and platformers, like *Cordy* (Silver Tree Media, 2011) or *Nicky Boom* (Chillingo, 2009). Landscape format is perfect for showing off real estate and works well for single-screen puzzle and adventure games, like *The Secret of Monkey Island (Lucasarts, 2009)* or *Spider: The Secret of Bryce Manor* (Tiger Style, 2010).

Consider how the player is going to interact with the screen no matter which orientation you choose. Matching the wrong control layout with your game can cause all types of problems, from a reduction in reaction time to hand fatigue.

When designing any sort of game, I like to get an idea of the screen layout first. This means mocking up all the elements you think will need to be displayed on the screen at once. I've included a template for you to use in Appendix 2. Use it to determine the placement of:

- Player character and player-controlled pieces
- Gameplay framing device or level geometry
- Background art
- Enemies or other AI characters
- Power-ups and pickups
- Particle-based effects like projectiles and explosions
- HUD elements like Score, Health Indicator, and Timer

○ Scrollbar and directional indicators

○ Virtual controllers

○ Instruction and dialogue boxes or text

You will want to create several of these mock-ups during the course of designing your game to help you solve spatial problems and see if you are displaying too many elements on-screen at once—which can cause your frame rate to slow down as well as clutter up the screen.

Another great nostalgia trigger is electronic or 8-bit **"chiptune"** music and sound effects. Sound is a powerful memory trigger, and many people associate old-school arcades with the bleeps and bloops of this bygone era[29]. Play *Retro Gaming Challenge* or *Forget Me Not* with the sound off. It just isn't the same. Don't ignore sound effects and music, and don't leave your sound design until the last minute. Creating the right sound effects for your game takes time and much iteration, especially if you are creating sounds from scratch. Making distinctive sounds and music for your games is always worth it in the long run. If you create the right sounds, you can create something so distinct that players will associate it with your game.

Remember that sound and music are often hard to hear on mobile devices without earplugs. Competing noise in the world and tiny speakers don't make them the most ideal listening devices. Keep your tones low and non-intrusive to the gameplay. Support voice with text whenever possible. The players might not always read it, but they'll appreciate it. Just like with retro gameplay, keep your retro sounds simple.

So, what have we learned from the arcade games of the past? That these games offer lessons in simplicity and can act as springboards for innovation. Be inspired by the past, create something original, and one day the games you create might be the ones future generations of gamers look fondly back upon.

---

[29]If you missed out on the arcade era and your time-travelling DeLorean is in the shop, you can still relive the experience online at http://arcade.hofle.com/ and http://www.coinopvideogames.com/sounds.php.

GAME DESIGN SPOTLIGHT 3

Where's My Water?

Format: iOS (available in regular, lite, and HD versions)

Developer: Disney Mobile

Designer: Timothy FitzRandolph

Swampy the Alligator lives under the city and yearns for a more humanlike existence. He is especially fond of cleanliness. Cranky and the other gators do not take kindly to Swampy's eccentricities and have conspired to sabotage Swampy's water supply. Help Swampy by guiding water to his shower!

Where's My Water? is a water-based physics puzzler[1], and although that isn't anything new, it does have something that feels in short supply in tablet gaming: a character with a charming personality. I'm not saying that there aren't some great characters already on touchscreen games. Mario, Professor Layton, and Barry Steakfries (to name a few) are all memorable characters. To be fair, though, these characters have had several years and/or games to build up their personalities. *WMW?*'s main character Swampy is charming right out of the gate. And this has everything to do with character design and animation.

---

[1]What can I say? I like physics puzzlers!

It isn't surprising that Swampy is well ani-mated. *WMW?* is from Disney, after all. They know a thing or two about character design. Swampy's animations have personality. He doesn't just stand around idly while he waits for the player to fill up his tub. Swampy gazes hopefully at the shower head and cud-dles with his rubber ducky. He impatiently bangs and chews on the pipes. He loofahs himself and dances with joy when the tub is finally filled. You don't need to be a Disney animator to make your main characters lik-able. Just give them a motivation and a few idle animations.

The story goes further to make Swampy relatable. Swampy is slightly pathetic, which also makes him charming. He's a fish . . . er, reptile . . . out of water who wears water wings and prefers his cozy apartment to the sewer. Then again, can you blame him?

But charming character alone does not a great game make. *WMW?* features some cleverly designed puzzles with just enough hooks for the player to try "one more time." The game play is a mix of *Dig Dug* and *Sprinkle*. The primary action is to dig in order to divert water to a pipe that leads to Swampy's bathtub. Gravity must always be considered as the water sloshes around. Players have to cause waves or create drips to solve puzzles.

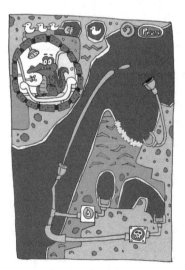

Complications arise with the introduction of mechan-ics such as squirting pipes, switches that need a drop of water to activate, and platforms that divert the water flow. Hazards include green moss that absorbs the player's precious water, hydro-activated bombs, purple toxic ooze that absorbs water, and green slime that eats through dirt. If one drop of ooze or slime gets into Swampy's bath, then it's game over.

Gameplay is extended through the now-becoming-traditional three-star systems; in this case, three rub-ber ducks need to be "filled" with water to be earned. This is a lot harder than it seems; water often needs to be measured out by the drop to fill Swampy's tub. A drop in a duck is a drop away from level completion. It provides a nice risk/reward system that gets the player to think "do I really need to get all three ducks?" Secondary rewards can be uncovered within special levels. Dig to find hidden items such as a loofah, a moldy toothbrush, and Mickey Mouse ears.

Collect all six items from the game's five chapters to earn two completely new gameplay levels that use tilt control mechanics (not used in the main game) to collect three duckies before time runs out. The radically different play scheme is a nice change of pace for the player. Finding all these items adds to the player's score. Other scoring conditions include puzzle completion time and an "overflow bonus" for filling Swampy's tub to beyond capacity. In addition, there is a system for earning 25 different achievements, such as cutting away dirt with two fingers at once, playing a level more than seven times, and filling a bathtub with exactly 20 drops of water. The achievements are buried a little deep in the interface for my taste, and it wasn't until I actually earned one that I realized they were in the game.

You would expect a game by Disney to have great visuals, and *WMW?* doesn't disappoint. The start and selection screens look fantastic, the level art is great, and the character designs are top notch. The puzzle select screens are well animated, with Swampy snoozing in a bubble-filled tub. *WMW?* chapter cutscenes are charming, though not animated; rather, they are images that the camera pans over to reveal the whole image/story. The style doesn't impede the storytelling and sure beats sitting through over-produced animated cutscenes. The only visuals that aren't fantastic are a couple of in-game mechanics that look out of place from the rest of the game considering how much care went into its theming. And the water, although up-to-par with other water physics games, moves a little more like Jello than water. And finally, there's the awkward scrolling bar that is used for some of the larger puzzle screens. Given that the game's digging mechanic would get in the way of any finger-based scrolling system, it's easy to understand why the design team made it the way they did: They wanted to make some of the puzzles more than a single screen. It's a solution, just not perhaps the best solution.

WMW?'s theme music is catchy, but it can get a little repetitive. The in-level sound design is more pleasing, especially the sounds of Swampy grousing for his bath and the sizzling of toxic waste burning away green moss.

Where's My Water? is an excellent puzzle game with great visuals and a fun story. It's interesting to see story creeping back into casual gaming, and I'm curious to see where it goes. So why is *Where's My Water?* so good? I chalk it up to the following:

○ A charming character that the player cares about and a story where the player wants to see what happens

○ Challenging puzzle gameplay with several compulsion systems to drive replay ability

○ Overall great visuals and presentation

Where's My Water? is available on iTunes.

chapter 7

Action Guy

IF ARCADE GAMES are about nostalgia, then action/platform games are all about character. Some of the most memorable characters in gaming are from the action/platform genre: Mario, Sonic, Rayman, Master Chief, Kratos, Nathan Drake. However, as I write this, some touchscreen game characters are becoming as recognizable as their console game cousins: Angry Birds, Om Nom, Barry Steakfries and Swampy. These game characters come in all shapes and sizes but share one thing in common: They are all built the same way, with these three shapes:

These basic shapes are the building blocks used to draw anything, be it a person, a monster, a tree, a car, or a house. But they're not just boring, inanimate shapes. Oh, no. Shapes can be used to convey **_personality._** Hey, look: Here comes a posse of cowboys:

While all these cowpokes wear a 10-gallon hat, sport a mustache, have squinty eyes (probably from staring into the desert sun for too long), and have a handkerchief around their neck, they all have different personalities. They look stupid, heroic, wicked, or stoic, all depending on their shapes. Early animators (we're talking 1930s here[1]) discovered this trick and used shape language to help distinguish their characters' personalities. Mickey Mouse's design started off gangly and rubbery but eventually evolved into the rounder character he is today, thanks to the animators realizing that a circle made a character look friendlier. Bugs Bunny was more of a smart aleck and his personality was conveyed by drawing with longer ovals. Humorous characters are often drawn with bigger, fatter circles, while a villain can be constructed from triangles. Pointy shapes create dangerous and sinister silhouettes. Rounder shapes convey feminine, softer images. Harder angles are more masculine, implying both strength and danger.

Think Like an Artist

A character's silhouette is extremely important. It allows the player to quickly differentiate between heroes and villains or to even tell the difference between different player characters. By using shapes and distinctive features, you can make your characters instantly recognizable even if you cannot see any of the details. Can you identify these characters by their silhouettes?

---

[1]The animator who really perfected this technique was Fred Moore, who redesigned Mickey Mouse for *The Pointer* in 1939.

Of course you can! That's because these characters all have distinctive silhouettes. If you have teams of heroes, give them all distinct shapes to set them apart from each other. Look at the distinctive silhouettes of these characters. Each of them is based on a unique shape: square, triangle, and circle (and lines).

Square   Triangle   Circle

If you have opposing characters (for example, heroes and enemies), then make their silhouettes opposite shapes from each other. By that, I mean if you are using a circle, then a triangle or a line is the opposite shape. If your hero is long, then make his enemies squat. If your hero is round, then make the bad guy spikey.

In fact, I recommend using stereotypical imagery so the player can tell that the bad guys are bad. Stereotypes are stereotypes for a reason! You should be able to tell that an enemy is dangerous just by looking at him, her, or it. Bad guys often can be seen wearing the following:

- Skulls and bones
- Horns and spikes
- Helmets or fancy hats
- Capes or cloaks
- Weaponry
- The color black

Speaking of black, color is extremely important when creating heroes and enemies. Color theory has been a field of study for many years. Do yourself a favor and learn some color theory to maximize the impact your colors will have on your characters. For example, primary colors red, blue, and yellow are great for heroes' costumes, while secondary colors purple, green, and orange work better for bad guys. Creators used to do this all the time in comic books from the 1940s: Superman, Batman, and Captain America all wore costumes with primary color elements, while their enemies, Lex Luthor, the Joker, and Baron Zemo all wore secondary colors[2]. The guys who created *Angry Birds* must have known this trick. The birds are red, blue, and yellow, and the pigs are green! In fact, *Angry Birds* uses colors, shapes, and silhouettes to help players distinguish their characters even while they are in flight.

Shapes, colors, and silhouettes become doubly important when creating mobile games. Mobile screens are so small that players need to quickly be able to tell the difference between game elements like characters, puzzle elements, enemies, and power-ups. Size also matters. The larger your game elements, the easier they will be to make out on the screen. But there's another reason why size matters: Knowing the size of your character will help you determine the player's metrics.

The Metrics System

Metrics are the yardstick for building everything in your game. You start with the following measurements:

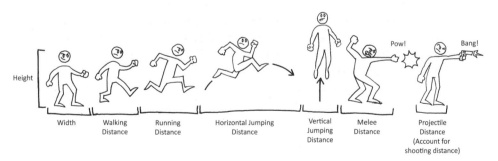

I call the proportions that are determined by the height and width a metric unit. You can call it whatever you want, as long as you keep the measurement consistent during the design and production of your game. You should **NEVER** change your metric unit after you have determined it. The metric unit will be used to determine the proportions of **EVERYTHING** in the game, be it the height of a doorway, a floating platform, or an enemy or the width of a vehicle, the player's shield, or a deadly pit. The metric unit is used to determine:

- **Height of everything:** Always consider the height of the player character and his/her relationship to things in the world. This comes in useful to determine the height of a doorway. A bad guy isn't going to seem very impressive if the door is shorter than the hero, and you can't design a tabletop that the player can reach if he or she is too short! If you need your puzzle pieces to fit together nicely, you must make sure they are uniform in height.

- **Width of passage:** This value must be wider than the character; otherwise the character won't be able to pass through! As a starting point, I design walkways and roads three metric units wide. This goes for vehicles as well. What good is a *Tower Defense* unit if it's too wide to get out of the tower or down the path?

- **Player's walking speed:** This relates to how far the player travels per second or within a particular length of time. If you want to determine the overall length of your level or play space, walk the character through the environment. This will be the bare minimum amount of time it takes a player to get through the level[3]. Note that this metric won't apply to "endless runner" games like *Canabalt* and *Temple Run* where procedurally generated level geometry creates limitless level length and play time.

- **Player's running/flying/swimming speed:** This value should be gauged against the slower walking speed. If you don't know how far or fast your character's walk is, how are you going to increase it when running? You should always make your enemy's running speed slightly slower than your character's running speed; otherwise, the player will never be able to escape! If you are dealing with multiple flying objects (like, say the rockets in *Flight Control Space*) you want to make sure they are consistent per type so the player gets a sense of how long it will take the ship to reach its destination. The player gets used to the movement speed of a character or vehicle or game piece and any increase or decrease is going to throw your player off. If you are going to have your game pieces adjust their speed, make sure you are doing it for a good gameplay reason.

---

[3]That said, remember that walking is never ever gameplay.

○ **Player's jump distance:** The width of the character should help determine this distance. For example, if the character's width is a metric unit of one and he can jump a distance five times his width, then a deadly spike-filled pit should not be wider than three metric units. (Unit one is for the player's starting position, units two through four are the width of the pit, and unit five is the spot where the player will land after making the jump.) These rules don't just apply to a jump, they can be used for any player movement that covers distance, like *Bike Baron's* jump or the gas blast in *Ow my Balls*.

○ **Player's jump height:** In a realistic game, most characters can barely jump higher than half their own height, if at all. In an unrealistic game, players can jump as high as the designer wants them to! Use the metric unit of height to determine how high the player has to jump to reach cliff ledges and floating platforms. If your player character cannot hoist (hang or grab onto a ledge and pull themselves up), then the height should be two units lower than the overall height; otherwise, the player will not be able to land on it!

○ **Melee attack distances:** Barring characters with stretchy arms, most characters can reach their own width. Starting with this metric unit, the designer can determine how far a character can reach with a punch, a sword strike, a slide attack, or any number of combat moves. The inverse of this is also true: You need to know how far players can strike if you want an enemy that dodges or blocks their attacks.

○ **Projectile attack distances:** Knowing the width of your character and how far he or she can move is the starting point for determining the projectile attack distance. Generally, this distance is farther than the player can walk or run (or reach). A gun isn't that useful if it can shoot a character only a few feet away. Take into account the effect of the attack as well. *Battle Nation's* (Z2Live, Inc., 2012) flame throwing tank has a short distance but a wide range, while the penetrating bullets fired by *Gem Keeper's* (NCSoft, 2011) turrets will shoot in a straight line all the way down the playfield.

○ **Camera distance:** You can't tell the difference between a long shot and a close shot if you don't know the size of your character. What if your character is HUGE? How high or far do you need to place the camera to see him? What if he's tiny? You need to know where and how to position the camera so he doesn't get lost. All of this starts with a metric unit.

Movement, combat, world building, camera distance. Who would have thought that something so small as a metric unit would help you decide so many things about your character? But one thing it doesn't answer is "who is my character?"

Didn't We Already Talk about Character?

Not really. We learned how to start your game idea with a cool character, but what makes a really cool character? A cool design? A great name? An awesome weapon? Sunglasses and a leather jacket? These all help, but remember the first rule of video game design:

Form follows function

You must know your character's primary action first. Then it's time to come up with a name. The simplest naming method is to have the character's primary action inform his or her name. In the original *Donkey Kong* arcade game, Mario's original name was "Jumpman" because all he could do was jump[4]. *Paku-paku taberu* is Japanese slang for opening and closing one's mouth, which inspired the name of Pakkuma (or Pac-Man for you Westerners). Pizza Boy delivers pizzas. The Hero rescues people. These names might be a bit too **literal** or generic, but players will immediately understand what these characters are about.

Naming characters ***descriptively*** is a good method. Solomon Dark is an appropriate name for an evil wizard-in-training. King Cashing is a great name for a character in a fantasy themed slot-machine game.

You can do some ***research*** when naming your hero. *Hero of Sparta*'s Argos translates to "shining brightly" in Greek and is a perfectly good name for a Grecian hero. *Dead Space*'s Isaac Clarke is named after two famous sci-fi writers: Isaac Asimov and Arthur C. Clarke. Audiences appreciate researched names. It means that you spent time thinking about the name of the character and wanted it to have some significance to the player and the game.

If research isn't your thing, then give your hero a ***silly name.*** Guybrush Threepwood is a good name: It's memorable, and the least pirate-y name you could imagine for the hero of the *Monkey Island* titles. I also like Barry Steakfries, the hero of *Age of Zombies, Monster Dash,* and *Jetpack Joyride* and not just because I like steak fries[5]. It's a funny name that makes me smile. And there's nothing wrong with that, especially if your game is lighthearted.

What's the best name? Stereotype or go against type. There's no hard and fast rule when it comes to names other than they should fit the characters. Oh, and do some research and check to see if the name already exists in some other medium, like a movie, comic book, or novel. There's nothing worse than coming up with the BEST NAME EVER only to find out "Batman" is already taken. Who would have thought?!

---

[4]Do I really have to recount the story for the billionth time, the story how Mario was named after Nintendo of America's warehouse landlord? He was.

[5]Mmm. Steak fries.

Or you could just let the player **customize** their character's name. There's a far greater emphasis on customizable characters in the tablet market. Give your player the freedom of choice to give their character a silly name, a literal name, a descriptive name or their own name if they want[6].

World Building for Fun and Profit

You have a character. You know what he looks like. You know what he does. You even have a name. But where does he live and fight and explore? Let's channel our inner creation myth and let's make a world. Of course, just like with everything else, you start with the hero's primary action. The world must support your gameplay[7]. The world of a platform game is going to be different than that of an action game. The layout of a puzzle game is going to be different than that of an object search game. Gameplay is first and foremost, but once you know that, you must choose the story genre[8].

Knowing the story genre will help you develop what the player finds in the game. I like to brainstorm all the major components you would find in the world: locations, mechanics, hazards, enemies, and rewards. Just what are these components?

Locations are the places players go on their adventures. Locations also can be the place where the gameplay takes place. They can be a helpful location like a store that sells the player weapons and magic healing potions. They can be a deadly location like a trap-filled tomb of horrors. They can be a maze filled with dots, or a location that simulates a table-top gameboard. Locations are where you will find **levels,** where the gameplay occurs. Levels are filled with sequences of **encounters** involving mechanics, hazards, puzzles, enemies, and rewards.

Good locations: An amusement park funhouse. A sewer. Dracula's castle.

Boring locations: A warehouse full of crates. A fabric softener factory. A living room.

When all else fails, put it in space. Why not? It worked for *Angry Birds*, *Flight Control*, and *Cut the Rope*.

---

[6]Scott's as good a name for a hero as any other, right?

[7]Form follows function, remember?

[8]Remember this from Chapter 4?

Mechanics are gameplay objects that the player interacts with. They can operate independently, operating like factory machinery left on for eternity. They can be player initiated, activating when the player is nearby or completes a set of conditions. They are doors that open and close, blocks that can be pushed, switches and levers, conveyor belts, moving platforms, or sticky or icy floor surfaces. They can even be natural forces like a blowing gust of wind or a strong current of water. Mechanics don't kill the player. At best, mechanics challenge the player, and at worse, complicate the player's progress.

Good mechanics: An opening and closing hatch that the player has to slide under to get through. A moving platform that the player has to hoist to reach. A magnetic wall that the player can walk on.

Bad mechanics: A door that opens halfway. A switch that activates another switch that causes a third switch to rise up. An invisible wall.

Hazards are deadly mechanics. A player that touches or is touched by a hazard will take damage or immediately lose a life. Hazards include electrical fields, swinging blades, spikey pit traps, pools of acid, machine gun turrets, smashing blocks, and exploding barrels. Hazards have limited movement and little to no intelligence. If they move, they travel in a predetermined pattern. If they have **artificial intelligence** (or *AI*), it is to track the player's movement or to respond to a certain action (like spring when the player steps on a floor trigger). Hazards may or may not harm enemies when they activate. That's a design decision you have to make for yourself, but it is more fun for the player to be able to turn the tables on the bad guys. Something I don't recommend is killing players without letting them know they're in danger. Don't drop a big rock on a player's head. She should always know why she died and what she can do to avoid it. Learning by dying is not as much fun as learning by succeeding.

Good hazards: Smashing chandeliers you can trick enemies to stand under. Rocket cannons you can man after avoiding. Electrical floors that you can knock enemies onto.

Bad hazards: Floors that damage you no matter where you walk. Objects that explode without warning. The hand of God randomly smooshing a player.

Enemies are characters who move, think, and live to annoy, harass, and kill the player. Enemies move, fly, swim, teleport, crawl on walls—in short, they really get around! And they attack! Most enemies will follow a **path** that can be created on the fly by the game code or predetermined by the game designer. To follow a path and decide what to do, your enemies need to think. To make them think, they need AI. As a designer, you need to take into account everything your enemy needs to do:

○ **Movement:** How does your enemy move? What speed does it move? Is it quick or slow? Does it move in a unique manner? Does it teleport, jump, or fly?

○ **Attack:** How does your enemy attack? With a hand-to-hand melee attack or does it shoot a projectile? What happens when an attack hits the player? Does the player lose health or get stunned or get knocked back? How much health does the player lose? How far back does the player get knocked? Does the attack have any special effect on the player?

○ **Health:** How many hit points does your enemy have? What happens when it has low health? Does it fight harder? Will it fight to the death? Does it run away and hide? What happens when the enemy dies? Does it drop on the floor? Explode in a harmless cloud of dust or an explosion that hurts the player?

○ **Rewards:** When the enemy is defeated, what does the player get for his or her victory? Treasure? Experience? A key that opens a nearby door? Does a gate to a new area magically open?

If I'm making a fantasy game, my initial brainstorm list might look something like this:

Castle, tower, princess, treasure chest, armored knight, living armor, crossbow, arbalest, castle gate, molten lead, opening and closing portcullis, raising and lowering drawbridge, battering ram, goblins, barbarians, angry mob, peasants, peasant farm, farm animals, haystack with treasure inside, smashable fence, cattle, wolf, werewolf, forest, oak trees, pit trap, thorns you can cut back, man-eating plants . . .

What I want to do first is separate out the components. My list of locations includes castle, tower, castle gate, peasant farm, and forest. These can be places the player visits in the course of the adventure or a background environment for a static screen if I were doing a puzzle-style game.

The hazards on my list are crossbow, living armor, arbalest, molten lead, angry mob, pit trap, and thorns. These could be mechanics that the player has to avoid during the action. Notice that some of the items on this list are repeated. These elements sometimes can serve double duty and sometimes should just do one thing to avoid confusion.

Enemies in the game from my list are armored knight, living armor, goblins, barbarians, angry mob, wolf, werewolf, and man-eating plants. I will determine the function of the enemy's behavior and then assign a visual for said enemy.

The rewards for the player include the princess, the treasure chest, and the crossbow. These are things that the player wants to possess and can be of use during the course of the game.

Looking at the elements I've listed, we can start to fashion an order of events and craft a story. Let's say our hero starts in the forest where he encounters wolves on their way to attacking Grandma's house. When the hero gets there, it's really a tower that is under siege by an army of werewolves. The hero has to fight his way through a pitched battle between the humans and the wolf-men to reach the tower where Granny and Little Red Riding Hood are holed up. The exciting climax occurs when the hero dashes from one defense to another, pouring hot lead and firing arbalest bolts at the werewolf horde scaling the tower. I'd play that game!

So as you can see, it's really easy to use the story genre as a starting place for building a world. But some story genres are used over and over so often that they can end up feeling stale. But I believe that even the most worn-out cliché can be made awesome. It's all in the presentation. This is where my **_Theory of Mexican Pizza_** comes into play. I can hear you now: "I like Mexican food as much as the next guy, but what in the wide world of sports does pizza have to do with making an exciting video game world?"

Well, it's safe to say that pizza is a pretty common food item. Maybe even a little boring if you just stick to the basics. You know you can find pizza pretty much everywhere, and if you are like me and attended college, you might actually be sick of eating it. The same can be said for Mexican food[9]. While considered exotic in some locations of the country and world, it is starting to become a pretty common selection. Both of these foods on their own can be boring and predictable. No surprises. But if you combine them together . . . then voilà, you've created something new and exciting! You've created something that sounds intriguing. Once you've heard about it, you just have to try it. _That's_ the point of the Mexican pizza.

---

[9]I grew up in San Diego county, where you can't go 5 miles without tripping over a taco shop.

When I was designing video games, I would use the Mexican pizza technique to make my clichéd levels unique. A dull graveyard became a swampy graveyard. A predictable ocean became interesting when it was drained of water: a dry ocean. A stereotypical factory became a circus factory[10]. Just by adding an adjective to my noun, I created some interesting and memorable locations[11].

So what if your game doesn't have traditional levels? What if they are single boards like in pinball or simulated table spaces like in word games? I recommend you still "theme it up." Theming makes everything better. Really. I have scientific proof (in the form of a list):

Top Five Reasons Why Theming Makes Everything Better

1. **Theming attracts players to a genre of game they wouldn't normally play.** *"Pirate Mahjong"?* Why not!

2. **Themes come with their own characters, enemies, music styles, story tropes, and even lighting!** (Film Noir! Disco!) It makes creative choices that much easier.

3. **Theming saves time.** It gives the player backstory that you don't have to supply. The zombie apocalypse doesn't need to be explained; players already understand what it's all about.

4. **Theming gives you keywords.** This can be very important when trying to get the attention of a consumer. There are lots and lots and lots of games out there. If you keyword your game to a popular theme, your game will be included, which gives it a higher likelihood of being bought.

5. **Theming can be applied to any game genre.** Take *zombies,* for example. On touchscreen devices, you can find zombie action games, zombie shooters, zombie puzzlers, zombie physics games, zombie RTS games, zombie tower defense games, zombie typing games. There are angry zombies, burning zombies, fat zombies, burping zombies, zombie BBQ . . . . No matter what your favorite gameplay genre is, you'll find a game with a zombie in it.

---

[10]Those miniature clown cars have to be made somewhere!

[11]If I do say so myself!

I guess game developers love zombies. Zombies are fun to design and animate and do the voices for. I've been known to throw a zombie or two into my own game designs. I have found that theming helps teams "get into" making their game. This enthusiasm is apparent to the player. You can tell when a team isn't into the game they are making. But even a mediocre game can be a blast with the right theming.

What's with All the Zombies?

Your game enemies don't have to be zombies. They just have to be something you think is cool, whether it's ninjas or pirates or cowboys or furious cockatoos. But more importantly, it's ninjas, pirates, cowboys, and furious cockatoos as obstacles that will challenge your players. Now I know it is great fun to design monsters and bad guys. They are awesome to draw. I design at least six of them a day. See?

But before you start drawing awesome monsters for your game, you should remember that *form follows function*. That means that you must first know what your enemy does and then figure out what it looks like. And nowhere in a game design is *form follows function* truer than when you are designing your enemies.

How to Design an Enemy in Six Easy Steps

1. Determine the enemy's **function.** An enemy exists to create complications for the player. A complication can be blocking the player, stealing her treasure, or just trying to kill the player.

2. Determine the enemy's **movement.** How does the enemy move around? Does it walk or run? Does it hop or fly? Does it drive around or not move at all? Is it intelligent enough to move around objects and find the player? Is it so dumb it can only march back and forth?

3. Determine how the enemy **attacks** the player. Does it attack at close range or from a distance? Is it a melee attack or a projectile attack? Does the attack affect a radius, or does it target a specific part on the player? Is it a fast attack requiring quick reactions, or is it slow, giving the player time to strategize?

4. Determine how the enemy's attack **harms** the player. Does the enemy do damage to the player? How much health does it deduct from the player's overall health? Does it kill in one hit? Rather than taking health, does it harm the player in another way? Does the attack do knockback, entangle the player, or stun the player? Does the attack cause the player to lose all of his coins? Does the attack turn the player into a hopping toad?

5. How does the enemy **defend** itself? Shields? Armor? Camouflage? These defenses are definitely going to impact appearance since the player should be able to tell at a glance what they are going to need to do to overcome them.

6. Determine the enemy's **appearance.** NOW is when you can go ahead and draw that awesome monster. I'm giving you permission. Here, I've even left a little room for you to draw it in. Draw six if you want!

DRAW YOUR OWN BAD GUYS HERE

A **boss** is a special class of enemy that is usually bigger, nastier, healthier, and harder to defeat than a plain ol' enemy. Bosses have very long health bars, which makes them very scary when you realize how tough it will be to defeat them. Bosses are also often HUGE, which makes them seem even scarier. And even worse, bosses generally come in three varieties: table top, ambulatory, and doppelganger.

Table-top bosses are so big that you only see their torso and above peeking out from a ledge or a building. They will smash or blast at the player who runs around on a "table top" (aka the floor or rooftop) trying to hide or at least keep from getting pulped by the boss. While this style of boss shows off scale really well, they often are not that dynamic. Boss movement is limited and the player has to endure invulnerable states before getting a chance to attack.

Ambulatory bosses are also really big, but they move around a lot more than their table-bound brothers. These are the "big stompy bosses" that try to squish the player underfoot. They don't have to stomp around; these bosses can float or fly around or be a spaceship or a dragon. Like table-top bosses, they have several attack and defensive states during the fight. Sometimes they are invulnerable. Sometimes they need health and time to rest. This is when you kill them! Strike, darn you, strike true!!

A **doppelganger**, besides being a German word for "twin," is a boss that is the player's size and sometimes has the same abilities. Bosses in fighting games are often of this variety. Players can defeat their doppelgangers with creativity, cleverness, and exploiting systems.

But before you start designing your boss, you need to decide how the player is going to fight the boss. By my count, there are three ways to approach the boss fight:

○ **Learn as you go:** The boss fight is built around the player learning how to use a new weapon or ability. The learning curve is built into the time it takes to play the boss fight. The upside is that the player always gets something new. The downside is that the player has a steep learning curve when starting the fight.

○ **Culmination of knowledge:** The boss fight is built around using everything you've learned how to do up until that point in the game. The upside is that you are using moves, weapons, and abilities you already know how to use. The downside is that you have to take all these abilities into account as you get deeper into the game. Of course, you can always focus on only having the player use one or two of his abilities to defeat the boss.

○ **Drama:** This boss fight focuses more on an intimate battle between the characters rather than an epic, stompy fight. Sometimes this style of boss fight comes down to one moment where a decision has to be made. This often comes in the form of an exceedingly simple move or a quick timer event.

Of course, you can combine any of these three into one fight, but changing the rules of the fight midway might get a bit confusing to the player. Why? Because boss fights are often built around **patterns.** Like enemies, they move in patterns, attack in patterns, and do special moves in patterns. It's up to the players to decipher when to attack and prepare themselves by counterattacking or defending. Some classic boss fight patterns include the following:

○ Boss attacks from a static position and then runs around while invulnerable.

○ Boss makes a huge attack that taxes him, and player can attack while boss is "recovering."

○ Boss fires projectiles at a steady rate and then fires at a furious rate for a short period of time.

○ Boss has a shield component that must be "beaten open" by the player, revealing a vulnerable spot (eye, glowing heart, brain, and so forth) where damage can be inflicted.

○ Boss has a sequence of attacks and heals all or a portion of his health at the end of the sequence. Player must do significant damage or kill the boss before he gets a chance to rejuvenate himself.

Also significant to a boss fight is the environment. In many cases, the location where the battle takes place is just as important to the gameplay as the actual battle. Hazards like fall-away floors, fire-spewing vents, or shifting or moving platforms. Mechanisms that the player can use against the boss, like a cannon or crushing blocks, can put the boss into a state (stunned, wounded, trapped) that gives the player a chance to land an attack.

I believe that it's important for a boss to have a "boss bar" or a health bar so players see their progress during the fight. Without it, boss fights tend to feel really long. If players know they are close to victory, they usually redouble their efforts to win. Always let the player land the killing blow. After all, why would you want to have the player go through the entire process of fighting a boss without the satisfaction of destroying it?

So, all this knowledge about boss fights is great, but many touchscreen developers have asked, "Do boss fights really have a place in touchscreen games?" I think it's a valid query. Boss fights are often very time-consuming in contrast to the short nature of a normal level. Poorly designed boss fights often rely on the player learning by dying rather than learning by learning. Don't torture the player by killing them repeatedly. That's the best way to get a player to stop playing your game. Besides, boss fights require lots of extra production effort (art, animation, effects, sound, and gameplay design) and unique code to make fun. Do some genres like puzzlers, distance games, or breakers even need a boss? That said, there are still touchscreen games with epic boss fights, including *The Legend of Zelda: Spirit Tracks* (Nintendo, 2009) and *Boss Battles* (Backflip Studios, 2011), that are *nothing but* boss fights. Whether boss fights will still have a place in touchscreen games is really up to you, the game designer.

Fighting for Cash and Glory!

The primary function of an enemy is to fight (or complicate life for) the player. And since you will be doing a lot of it, fighting should be fun! But in addition to being fun, touchscreen game controls should be simple.

Touchscreen games are simpler than arcade, console, and computer games since the method of input is limited. This challenge has birthed some very clever solutions as in *The Legend of Zelda: The Phantom Hourglass* (Nintendo, 2007), which introduced some novel combat systems to touchscreen audiences. The player would tap enemies once to have Link swing his sword. Moving enemies were dispatched by a forward swipe that would propel the hero forward—sword first. The most interesting attack move was with Link's boomerang weapon, which the player controlled by drawing the flight path. Once the path was drawn, the boomerang was released, bonking the bad guys along the path.

Since there is little room for buttons on most touchscreen devices (the Nintendo DS and PlayStation Vita being the exceptions with their luxurious multiple buttons and finger triggers), most games have one button do all the killing. This means that combat is ***contextual.*** When a player attacks, no matter what weapon he has, be it a fist or a sword or an atomic bomb, the character has unique animation during the attack. Players will be able to choose or pick up a new weapon, but the control scheme is always the same: Press the button, strike the enemy.

When striking the enemy, make sure the animation plays quickly. Nothing is more frustrating to the player than when a delay occurs between pressing the attack and seeing the character act. This delay can create moments for the enemy to attack as the strike is being carried out. In these cases, I recommend the "tie going to the player" approach, meaning that the player's action should always take precedence over that of an enemy (or hazard).

Another source of player frustration can come from long attack animation cycles. While it may look great, an excessively long attack animation can cause the same delay between when the button is pressed and the attack lands. Games like *Out of the World* or *Lost Mars* pride themselves on their lush animations, but remember that those games are not combat-based (although they do have some shooting in them) and the delay in the command and the animation is part of the "style." Just be sure players know the rules of your game's metrics, and they will adjust their pace for these longer animations.

The downside of a one-button attack is that things get very repetitive quickly, especially if that attack is all the player does. Strangely, I've found players mind the repetition less if the game is shooting-based rather than melee. I think it has something to do with the nature of shooting. The animation cycles are shorter, repeat shooting is often encouraged, and firing a "real-world" gun is a simple action: Just pull the trigger. Pressing a button or tapping a screen is a short hop of logic away. Some games make shooting a by-product of movement, like in *Jetpack Joyride*, or "automatic" while operating a virtual joystick in the twin-stick shooter *Age of Zombies*.

In a twin-stick shooter, the weapon fires as long as the joystick is pushed in the desired direction. The basic weapon of a twin-stick shooter (usually a plain vanilla pistol) often has unlimited ammunition so the player has a weapon to shoot at all times. I suppose you could have a twin-stick non-shooter, but it just doesn't have the same catchy ring to it.

In a twin-stick shooter, the timing of firing the weapon becomes the variable that the player learns to manage during the game. Variation is introduced when the player finds new power-ups like double firing rate and other kinds of weapons like machine guns, flamethrowers, and grenade and rocket launchers. New weapons improve the player's basic attack in ways that obviously (mostly) start with the letter "r":

- Rate of fire

- Reload time

- Range

- Radius (explosions and 45 degree shotgun blasts)

- Effect (fire, freezing, stunning, and so forth)

Despite having only one button or control stick to operate the attack, changing these variables will keep fighting fresh and fun for the player.

If you want them to fight with more skill, however, then try the **high/medium/low system.** The player's combat range is divided into three distinct attack zones, like so:

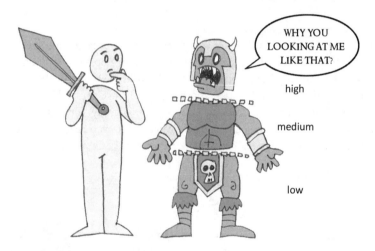

The enemy is divided up into three zones: head, body, and legs. *Infinity Blade* and *Sid Meir's Pirates* use this method, where it requires a modicum of strategy to win a sword fight. However, even on a larger screen, it's still easy to get confused in the heat of battle and make the wrong swipe. The player's hand gets in the way, resulting in the player making unintended moves.

This problem is pretty easily solved by telegraphing to the player. What does a 19th century wired communication device have to do with touchscreen gaming[12]? Nothing! You're thinking of a telegraph. We're talking about something else!

Telegraphing is when you let the player know an attack is coming, sometimes way ahead of time, sometimes only seconds before it happens. In the previous example, (A) the Mighty Bedbug is fighting his arch-enemy, the Grave Robber. In this example, the Grave Robber is in his "ready position," a pose from which all other animations begin. (B) The Grave Robber jabs out with his shovel and hits Bedbug in the head. This attack happens very quickly. The strike feels sudden and a bit cheap, like it came out of nowhere. The player might not even have enough time to block the attack. *A player can learn by failing, but I prefer a player learn by succeeding.*

Now let's look at the same move *with* telegraphing.

(A) Bedbug once again squares off against Grave Robber. (B) This time, Grave Robber telegraphs his attack by "winding up" with his shovel. This animation not only lets the player see the attack coming, but it also gives a chance to block or counter-attack. (C) Another benefit to telegraphing an attack is that it shows the player that the enemy has exposed a vulnerable spot that the player can exploit. There's nothing wrong with giving players a chance to succeed, especially if they are observant or quick enough!

---

[12] -.-. --- -. --. .-. .- - ..- .-.. .- - .. --- -. ... . / -. ---- ..- ! / .-.. --- ..- / .... .- ...- . / -. .-. --- .-.- . -. / -.-- --- ..- / -.- -. --- .-- / -- --- .-. ... . / -.-. --- -.. . / .-. .. --. .... - / -. --- .-- .-.-.-

The high/medium/low system's roots lie in the kid's game *rock, paper, scissors*. Depending on the elevation/attack the player selects, one of three results can occur: failure, block/parry, and success.

Failure occurs when the combatant makes the worst strategic decision. A failure can result in a miss, causing humiliation and prolonging the combat. It can be fatal, causing the character to stumble or overshoot the target, exposing the character to attack from the back or flank. In rare cases, a combatant can drop a weapon, requiring the combatant to scramble to retrieve it to continue the fight.

A **block** stops the combatant's attack cold. A block can be done with a shield, a magic spell, or even crossed arms, as seen in fighting games. Often, a block move is maintained to stop several attacks. Games that use this benefit from block-breaker moves allow the player to shock an enemy out of his defensive pose opening up an opportunity to follow up with an attack. Some games with swordplay allow combatants to lock blades, requiring a quick-time event or button-mashing to break free. The victor of these encounters usually gains a temporary advantage over the opponent. A **parry** is another move that originates from fencing[13], one that allows the combatant to deflect an attack giving her a chance to counterattack.

---

[13]No, not building fences, but sword fighting.

A player can score a ***successful hit*** in several ways:

○ Strike an enemy as it is telegraphing an attack.

○ Strike at an unprotected part of the enemy.

○ Expose a weakness by hitting one part of the enemy, and then striking the spot that is exposed as a result.

○ Knocking armor or shielding away to expose "softer parts" underneath.

○ Stun, daze, or juggle an enemy into the air, allowing the player an opportunity to attack while the enemy is still recovering.

○ Perform an unblockable attack (often referred to as a **super-move**) for which the enemy has no defense.

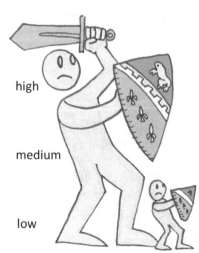

The high/medium/low system can also serve as a defensive system.

Just reverse the directions and remap attack moves to defensive blocks and voilà! You've doubled the depth of your controls!

high

medium

low

Pain, Pain, Go Away, Come Again Some Other Day

Of course, you can't have all this fighting without someone getting hurt. And when players get hurt, they take damage. Here's where you have to do a little math. Don't worry; it won't hurt you as much as it will hurt the player. First, determine how much health the player has. How do you do this? Metrics, of course! But the magic formula for calculating health is a different yardstick than the player's height and width[14]:

Enemy Health </ Player's Health < Death

Start by determining your toughest enemy's strongest attack, BUT set it **without** thinking of a number value. For example, your giant Cyclops does the most damage to the player. But how much damage does the Cyclops do? Will it kill the player with one blow? Totally doable, but it makes for a very short fight. What if the Cyclops's attack takes off half of the player's health instead? This means the player will die in two hits. Perhaps the fight should go on a little longer. Let's say the player can withstand three hits from the Cyclops.

Okay, keep that ratio in your head for a second. Now think about the weakest enemy in your game. Let's say it's an animated skeleton. How many hits can the player withstand from this bag of bones? About 10 sounds like a good number for one off the top of my head. But wait a second: If the skeleton kills the player in 10 hits and the Cyclops kills the player in 3, then something is off. Three doesn't go evenly into 10. Maybe we should adjust the Cyclops's damage to kill the player in four hits instead. Or maybe we should adjust the animated skeleton to kill the player in eight hits. From this, we know that the player can take eight hits overall and can die if the Cyclops hits him four times. Eight is the starting health before any increases from experience or power-ups. This value doesn't need to stay the same throughout the entire game. Or maybe it does. It's your choice.

---

[14]I warned you that game designers sometimes use the same term for different things!

To determine the enemy's health, you do the same exercise but this time from the player's perspective. The animated skeleton might explode into bones with just 1 hit from the player while the Cyclops might need to be hit 20 times to die. You can determine the damage a weapon does by thinking about what effect you want it to have on the enemy. A standard weapon will require the maximum amount of hits to slay the enemy, while a really powerful weapon can kill an enemy with a single blow.

Putting the "Ack" in "Feedback[15]"

When players or enemies take damage from an attack, the first rule is to make sure they know it:

○ Start with an animation of the character getting hurt, such as recoiling in pain, limbs extended out, and a pained look on the face.

○ Next, play a vocal cue to let the player know he either has been hit or has scored a hit: A yelp! Or an Ow! Or that old favorite since the days of Cain and Abel: "That hurt!"

○ Finally, spray out some particles. It doesn't have to be blood; it can be sparks or stars or Pow! marks that come out of the player. Just make sure the particles are noticeable.

○ If the player or enemy has a health bar, then make it flash or turn red or both as its health bar graphic or number decreases. Or better yet, make the enemy flash or turn red to indicate vulnerable bits that should be attacked!

I don't recommend making the entire screen turn red or dim out (as if the player were seeing through a haze of blood or darkness). Don't punish the player twice. It's bad enough that the player is losing health, but adding loss of vision is just a low blow. Speaking of blows, did you know there are other ways to hurt a player besides losing health? It's true!

○ **Knock back:** The player or enemy is displaced in space. If the knocked-back character is standing next to a ledge or hazard, the results can be extra painful.

○ **Stunned:** The player or character cannot move or act and is thereby vulnerable to attack. I recommend not making the stunned state last too long because it can be very frustrating.

○ **Loss of control:** This happens when the player is mesmerized, entangled, or otherwise incapacitated by an enemy or opponent. Like with the stun, I don't recommend making this state last too long. There's nothing less exciting for players than not being able to play the game (other than not getting to play the game and taking damage while not getting to defend themselves, that is).

---

[15]It's a better title than "Putting the "Ow" in "I Know I've Been Hurt.""

○ **Loss of treasure/pick-up item:** Instead of spraying blood, why not spray coins? What's fun about this is that it immediately changes players' behavior from fighting an enemy to scrambling to reclaim all their lost treasure.

○ **Dropped/broken weapon:** Much like with the loss of treasure, players lose their current weapons and must reclaim them. Or even worse, players' weapons are destroyed and they must find a new one/replacement if they want to keep fighting. This is a pretty cruel way to punish the player. I recommend that the player have some sort of hand-to-hand attack to balance out the fact that you have just broken her only way to hurt the enemy.

Of course, if you hurt players too much, then they will **_die._**

The Only Good Player Is a Dead One

There are two schools of thought when it comes to killing the player character: quickly and as horribly as possible. Killing the player **_quickly_** means that the player doesn't have to spend too much time watching the character die, which is fine since all the player wants is to get back into the action. Although too graphic and possibly offensive or inappropriate for younger audiences, killing the character as **_horribly as possible_** can provide a shock or gallows humor.

How you kill off your character really depends on the tone and genre of your game. Players of platform games, puzzlers, and shooters prefer to get back into the game as quickly as they can; therefore, the quick method is preferred. In a horror, fighting, or adventure game, seeing the character die slowly and graphically can shock the player into caring about the character's well-being and might make the player try harder to stave off the inevitable *game over* screen. Now that I mention it, the concept of game over, which had been mostly abandoned in most console games, has returned with touchscreen games, with high scores and leaderboards. Providing a cut-off point for players makes sense when the goal is to see how long players can last or how high a score they can achieve.

Whether to have a game over screen or let the player keep playing upon death is just one more decision that designers have to make. Making the player restart a level or puzzle works well for the abbreviated gameplay of most touchscreen games. "Game over" is perfectly acceptable in genres where the player can fail or die: puzzlers, distance games, retro arcade games, platformers, horror, and RPG titles.

However, if you'd prefer the player to keep playing, then I recommend creating a "keep going" screen. When the player dies or leaves gameplay, show a preview of the next level, treasure, weapon, vehicle, or plot point. Give players a sneak peek to get them excited enough that they won't want to stop playing!

Another end-of-gameplay system that keeps players playing is the three-star achievement system popularized by *Angry Birds*. This system has the players shoot for a three-star ranking. One star is earned by successfully completing the level or puzzle. The second star is earned by completing the puzzle or finishing the level within a specified time. The third star often requires players to go out of their way to earn or attain the goal without losing a life or some other criteria of "perfection." *Cut the Rope, Casey's Contraptions, Jelly Car 3, Tomb Slider,* and *Where's My Water?* are just a few of the games that have used the three-star system. Where the three-star system shines is clearly rewarding players for their accomplishments, motivating players to become better at playing and driving players to play completed gameplay all over again. And isn't a game designer's ultimate goal to keep the player playing[16]?

---

[16]If you said no, then you haven't been paying attention! Go back and read the book from the beginning again!

DEVELOPER INTERVIEW 4

Blade Olsen

Developer profile: Blade Olsen recently graduated from USC's prestigious interactive media department. His senior project, *Dance Pad,* was the star of demo day: a showcase where industry professionals scout new talent. As a result, Blade landed a job as an assistant producer with EA games.

Last completed/published project: *Dance Pad* (iOS)

Company website: http://gamepipe.usc.edu/usc_gamepipe_laboratory/R&D/ Entries/2010/12/14_Dance_Pad.html

Blade, thanks for taking the time to talk with *Swipe This!* What excites you about designing games for touchscreens and tablets?

I originally wanted to make a game involving funk music and have it be really energetic. However, I conceded early on that I'm a lazy video-game player and wanted to make sure the "energy" of the game didn't translate into an overly active experience. I don't have anything against active gaming *a la* the Kinect, Wii, and Move; I just personally have the patience of a toddler, the energy level of a sloth, and muscles that have atrophied from years of gameplaying. When I want to play video games, it's because I need to relax.

In the end, my college buddies and I thought the idea of physically using your fingers as tiny legs was hilarious and immediately recognizable to anyone who owns a pair of hands. Consequently, we decided "dancing with your fingers," for example, the moonwalk, the Stanky-leg, or the C-walk, would make a wonderful senior project—think Tech Deck for dancing. Tablets were just hitting the stores when we came up with the idea, and the wide touch space was a perfect fit for what we wanted to do with the game.

Mobile devices offer great accessibility and convenience for the player, awesome distribution channels for the developer, and new, exciting interactions for everyone involved. As these devices get more powerful, it's going to be really fun to watch mechanics evolve or be discovered.

What are some of your favorite touchscreen/tablet games?

I've always been a sucker for puzzle games, especially ones that involve simple interactions with a vast number of outcomes. *Cut the Rope,* a puzzler, has consistently been the game I show off to people who don't consider themselves a mobile gamer. It's a tight, well-crafted experience, and it follows a golden three-pronged design philosophy: very simple interactions, deep gameplay, and a finely tuned learning curve. Even better, *Cut the Rope* is a game that is best played (and I think could only be played) on a touchscreen device. If you're reading this and haven't played it, you should go find an iPhone and download it.

What advice can you give to someone who wants to get into designing games for touchscreen/tablet space?

First, I'll give a few design philosophies I've learned from creating a touchscreen game from the ground up and from interviewing a lot of experts in big companies about this stuff: Scope small, make every second of the user's time be incredible, and get the user to the "fun" part of your game as fast as possible. Every second counts. I actually used to think this applied only to mobile/touchscreen games, but it's now a philosophy I'm trying to carry over to every game I create. The market is absolutely flooded with different experiences for the user to choose from, and the only way your game will survive is if you make your game incredible and have it be something your players want to actively tell other people about and show off. By the way, that's an actual issue that you should **playtest** when designing your game: "Do they actively tell other people about the game after the play it?" Word of mouth will carry your game.

Second, for those who are unsure about whether developing for mobile is fun: The development time on mobile is much quicker than a console or PC game, so you typically don't experience the exhaustion that most game developers face. It's also cheaper, so your hair isn't falling out from stress as you try to manage bloated teams and inescapable budget problems. Most importantly, the current mobile landscape of games is but a precursor of what is to come. If you like 2D games, you'll be right at home on the iPhone or Android. However, if 3D games with large budgets are where your heart is, you'll also be right at home on the iPhone or Android. *Infinity Blade* is a great glimpse into the future of what kind of mobile games are in the pipeline.

What gameplay and control challenges did you face when designing your touchscreen game?

Our game relies heavily on coordination and finger dexterity. We had to playtest almost weekly for a year to determine which "dance moves" were realistic and which moves would be unfair for someone over the age of 40. This might be specific to our game, but finger length really became an issue. The things I now know about the index and middle fingers . . .

"Direct finger" vs. "virtual joystick": Which do you prefer and why?

Direct finger is by far my preferred control scheme. We need to embrace what makes touchscreen gaming cool: the lack of any confusing buttons or joysticks that would normally make your parents spike the controller into the ground with frustration. The more of the interface we can remove, the better. Ironically, I think the best interface designer will try to have the very least of his work noticeable on-screen.

Removing the controller is more of a design opportunity than a challenge. Now that we have this new method of interaction with the touchscreen, we should do something interesting with it. I will echo what I've heard many times: We are only just beginning to see some of the interesting mechanics that will come out of a mobile, touchscreen device. Let's not take a step backward.

Any predictions for the future of the touchscreen game space?

You can hold me to this prediction: Mobile will consume console in time.

chapter **8**

DoodleCat

Learn the rules in drawing and perspective. It is an absolute must, even for the abstract artist, to learn the rules before perfecting a personal style

—*William Band*

There are no rules, only tools

—*Glenn Vilppu*

An artist is only as good as his tools

—*Someone*

CRUD. I GUESS artists can't agree on anything . . . except that you need to have good tools if you are going to make good art. Heck, you need good tools even if you are going to make bad art—especially if you are going to design a game for a player to make bad art (or good art) while playing a touchscreen **drawing game.** Before touchscreens, drawing in video games was mostly pretty crummy[1]. You either drew using a game controller, which was about as easy to use as those little knobs on an Etch-A-Sketch, or with a mouse, which was like drawing by remote control with a bar of soap. Even if you owned a thousands-of-dollars CAD tool, drawing in games was no fun[2]. Without simple and intuitive drawing tools, you risk creating not only bad art but also creating a bad game. Let's create some good drawing tools instead!

Get to the Point

The Nintendo DS took the stylus from the CAD artists and put it into the hands of the players. It was an inspired idea, but this stylus/controller combination still had a few disadvantages: Players had to juggle between using the stylus and the D-pad and button controls. Balancing them between fingers, clinching them between teeth, or repeatedly sheathing and redrawing the stylus from the DS became most players' ways to deal with the combo. As a result, many DS game developers adopted a strict "one or the other" design approach. When making your own stylus-controlled games, do the following:

- ○ Create longer stylus-only or controller-only gameplay experiences so the player doesn't have to switch as often.

- ○ Give the player an opportunity to set down or put away the stylus when shifting to non-stylus play sequences.

---

[1]Arguably, a sole exception was *Mario Paint* (Nintendo, 1992), which came with a mouselike controller and pad. Granted, the images you could create looked about as good as ones made with *Windows' Paint 1.0,* but it was pretty cool to draw on a SNES back in the day. What can I say? We were easily impressed back then.

[2]As CAD tools were used for making games and not playing games, there really wasn't anything to play.

◯ Develop a "control theme" where the stylus has a specific use (for example, the stylus is only used for magiclike casting spells or throwing fireballs, while the D-pad is used for movement or physical attacks).

◯ Keep the stylus motions simple. Tap, swipe, circle, line. Anything else on the small screen might be too complex.

◯ Avoid repetitive motions. Vary the variety often, too: Alternate between tapping, swiping, scrubbing, and so forth.

◯ Substitute button presses for stylus taps. Use the stylus to clear away dialogue balloons, select options, and save game files.

◯ Emulate real-world motions. *Trauma Center: Under the Knife* (Altus, 2006) does a great job making players feel like they are cutting, sewing, and using tweezers, all with the stylus.

The stylus can be used in several ways, simulating many things. The stylus is a pencil in *Brain Age: Train Your Brain in Minutes a Day!* (Nintendo, 2005). It guides dancing agents in *Elite Beat Agents* (iNis, 2006). It's used to draw magic runes in *LostMagic* (Taito, 2006), and for a variety of things in *WarioWare Touched!* (Nintendo 2004), including a knife to cut steak, a chisel to carve statues, and a finger to pick a nose!

When it comes to drawing gameplay, there are two ways to approach the act of drawing. Fast vs. slow. Creation vs. reaction. Art vs. action. **Artistic drawing games** enable players to create the most beautiful art they can, while **action drawing games** have players drawing as fast as they can. If you want players to create beautiful art, you must give them a ***drawing tool.*** Think of it as the player's painting set. And as I said earlier, you must start with the right tools.

Finger Pointers

Fingers! The original drawing tool! Touchscreens are perfect for quick and easy drawing and image manipulation using digits. *Sketchbook Pro* (Autodesk, 2011) provides a very robust set of drawing tools that can be manipulated just with the user's fingers. The developers of *Katana Jack* (Ivanovich Games, 2011) used their fingers and the App tool *Brushes* (Steve Sprang, 2010) to create all of its in-game artwork. But touchscreen drawing isn't just for work. Finger painting is one of the great joys usually left behind in childhood. A touchscreen allows adults to get back in touch with their inner child without any of the mess! When letting players finger-paint, follow these facts to facilitate fun:

○ Use clear moves. Don't misinterpret a flick meant for scrolling as a swipe that draws unwanted lines.

○ Allow toolboxes to open wherever the player's fingers are. Don't make the player hunt for where to resume drawing.

○ Let the player use more than one finger for non-drawing moves, such as a pinch-and-expand to zoom and enlarge images or swipe with three fingers to bring up a palette.

○ Develop a "finger language" for summoning tools: A tap could change from a brush to an eraser, while a tap-and-hold could bring up the palette.

○ A finger isn't meant to draw straight lines. Creating in-game auto-correction can straighten lines and round out shapes like circles. Always give players the option to turn off this function if they so desire.

Of course, sometimes fingers aren't enough. This is when you break out your ***toolbox.*** Having the right tools in your box is very important. At the very least, include the following:

○ A pencil tool to draw with.

○ A variety of pencil-tip sizes, from a large circle or square to a single pixel.

○ An eraser (you have to be able to correct mistakes!).

○ A line tool that creates straight lines.

○ A palette of selectable colors, starting with ROY G. BIV[3], plus black, white, and at least two shades of grey. If you have room in your palette, then you should also have a tint and a shade of each primary color (in other words, one lighter version and one darker version, such as pink and scarlet options to complement the primary color red).

Those are just the basics. Depending on how complex you want your drawing tool to be, you also could include other features, such as . . .

○ A zoom tool for scaling images up or down, great for pixel-by-pixel drawing.

○ Shape tools (usually brushes) for quickly creating squares, circles, and other shapes.

○ A paint bucket for quickly filling in large areas.

○ A drawing brush for creating lines with anti-aliasing to avoid that pixelated jaggy look.

○ An eyedropper tool for "pulling up" a color without having to go to the palette.

○ A stamp tool for creating premade images like facial features, body parts, and patterns.

○ Templates for tracing or modifying players' own designs.

○ An Undo function, preferably one for undoing several steps.

○ A lock color function to prevent players from erasing something they don't want to.

○ A grid overlay enabling artists to draw pixel-by-pixel and create proportions easily.

○ A scroll function for moving around when zoomed in close to their art.

○ A preview window displaying players' art as they draw it. (This is important because if players are drawing something that moves, like a character, they need to make sure the character animates properly, which includes seeing how all the parts move in relation to each other.)

You don't need your tool set to be as complex as *Photoshop,* but the more features you add, the more beautiful the art the player will be able to create. As your feature set grows, where you place your tools on-screen becomes just as important as the tools you give the player.

---

[3]ROY G. BIV is a mnemonic way to remember the basic color palette: red, orange, yellow, green, blue, indigo, and violet.

Artistic tool sets aren't just for drawing! You'll need a tool set if your driving game lets players design custom decals or paint jobs. Your action game where your Street Artist hero creates art to "stick it to the man" will need some sort of art tool. You might want to use an art tool if you have Space Marines whose armor needs spiffing up. Whatever the game, keep your art tools simple—you don't need to invest too much energy creating something complex. Just have your tool be robust enough to do what you need it to do, nothing more.

What's wrong with this layout? Everything! The brush tool is one of the most used functions, so put it within easy reach of the stylus[4]. Don't make players have to repeatedly go back and forth between tools. Since players use one tool at a time, hide additional brush widths with roll-over windows. Place the eraser on the main screen, preferably within reach of the brush tool. Get rid of unnecessary framing devices and "fancy artwork." Dedicate as much room as possible for drawing space. Don't make the player have to open another page to reach additional functions like the color palette. When you avoid basic layout mistakes like these, players will be on their way to creating great art!

The Artist's Way

Artistic drawing games emphasize player creativity and personal expression. In an artistic drawing game, the players draw their character, backgrounds, and even mechanics and hazards. Most of these games start with the players drawing these elements. It's a perfectly fine way to begin the game, but remember that players need time to draw their creations. If you want to get the player into the gameplay quickly, spread this creative process out over the course of the first level, if not the entire game.

---

[4]Or if you want to cater to left-handed players too, put the erase function on a button control.

Many artistic drawing games make the mistake of only letting the player draw at the start of the game. Don't limit the drawing! Artistic players LOVE to draw! Artists want to personalize their game. There's nothing cooler than having two players create artwork and then compare to see how different they are[5]. Give the player plenty of opportunities to draw. My motto when helping create the *Drawn to Life* games was "Draw, draw, draw." The design goal: If the player wasn't jumping, fighting, or erasing, he should be drawing. The creative team solved this issue by letting players draw mechanics and power-ups in order to progress through the levels. Once an item was drawn, the player not only could marvel at his creation for the rest of the level, but also could use the item to achieve something during gameplay. When prompting players to draw something, rather than providing a specific boundary box like this . . .

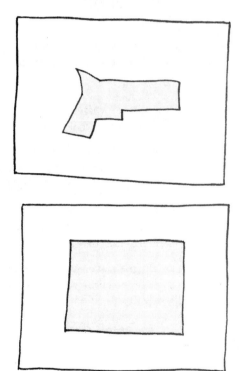

. . . we created a simple box that showed how much room they had. We didn't, however, make them draw a specific object.

We wanted the players to know what their drawings were to be used for, so we gave players a text prompt. Players were asked to draw a gun (or a car, or a pretty flower), but they could make a fish (or the Batmobile, or a hand) if they wanted to instead. The team also provided pre-made templates for artists who wanted inspiration, a place to start, or just lacked the confidence to create something on their own. We didn't want the drawing to get in the way of the fun for less artistically inclined players. *Doodla!* (Applied objects, 2011) uses a trick similar to *Drawn to Life*'s templates. The drawing game provides a small starting shape that players use as the basis of their own drawings. A blank page can be an intimidating thing. Even the best artists can benefit from a little push from time to time.

---

[5]Ask five friends or family members to draw the same character or object. You will never get the same image twice! Even if someone has drawn something before, he or she hasn't drawn it the way YOU would draw it. That's the beauty of art!

Don't forget that *erasing* is gameplay too! Players enjoy scrubbing away inky blots, scribbly monsters, and other messes. When creating a game with erasing as a mechanic, keep in mind the following:

- ○ The inky blots (or whatever the player is cleaning up) should look hazardous or threatening. The ickier they look, the more the player will know they need to be erased.

- ○ Give your inky blots some life. It will clue the players into what they have to remove, and add some pizzazz to the screen. Consider making your inky blots move threateningly or like the jittery artwork in A-Ha's famous *Take on me* video[6].

- ○ Let the players see the result of their cleaning! Reveal interesting images, sparkling clean landscapes, hidden treasure, or power-ups! No one scratches a lotto ticket only for fun; make sure there's some sort of reward underneath.

- ○ Don't make the player erase *too much*. All that scrubbing can get a bit repetitive over the course of the entire game. Like I always say, if something feels too long or too boring, then it is!

---

[6]http://www.youtube.com/watch?v=oHg5SJYRHA0

Of course, no section on drawing games can be complete without mentioning *Draw Something* (OMGPOP, 2012); the Boggle-meets-Pictionary multiplayer sensation. The game has been a genuine phenomenon, going from nowhere to over 35 million play sessions in a matter of weeks and leading to the acquisition of developer OMGPOP by Zynga for over $200 million. The genius of *Draw Something* isn't the simplicity of the concept (you draw something and I'll guess what it is using a limited number of letters) or the simple drawing tools (a pencil and eraser with four brush sizes and a limited palette of colors) or even the appeal of drawing (after all, who doesn't like to draw?), but watching your partner (*opponent* isn't really the right word since both players get points when a guess is correctly made) vainly guess the solution to your lame drawing as it is recreated in real time. It is knowing that on the other end of your connection there is a thinking, creative human that gives the game its heart and makes it so appealing.

A Line on Fun

If you find artistic drawing too long and boring, then design an **action drawing game** instead. In an action drawing game, players just need to draw a line to get the job done: no artistic talent required. *Draw Jump* and *Drawn to Life: The Next Chapter* (5th Cell, 2009) require players to quickly draw lines and shapes to bounce characters to greater heights. Connect objects with lines, like in *Super 7;* draw circles around specific shapes or characters as in *Zoo Lasso* (Launching Pad games, 2009); draw shapes to create formations of angry purple dots in *Dark Dot* (GAMBIT Game Labs, 2011) or use lines to quickly defeat enemies and capture treasure like in *Dungeon Raid* (Fireflame Games, 2010).

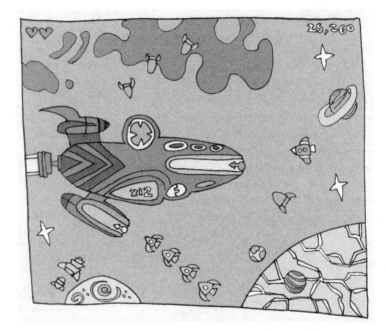

The most popular style of action drawing is **line drawing games.** In line drawing games, players . . . well, draw a line . . . often to guide their avatar (or several avatars) to a specific location. The first touchscreen line drawing game to gain popularity was *Flight Control* (Firemint, 2009). Since *Flight Control*'s debut, players have been creating paths to perform a potpourri of primary actions. Use a single line to guide vehicles into safe landing zones, like in *RocketCop* (Headlight Software, 2010) and *Harbor Master* (Imangi, 2009). Sneak players past peril, as in *SPY Mouse* (Firemint, 2011) and *Sneak Out!* (42games Limited, 2011). Guide your blind master to safety, as in *Sr. Mitsu*. Sail ships into battle, as in *Crimson: Steam Pirates* (Bungie Aerospace Corporation, 2011) and *Sid Meier's Pirates* (2K Games, 2011). Create a slide to career down, as in *Line Rider iRide* (inXile Entertainment, 2008). When all else fails, you can always set your game in space like Firemint did with *Flight Control Rocket*.

As you can see, a line can be a powerful way to guide players' fun. Just don't stray too far by making these mistakes:

○ Leaving the previous line behind when a new one is drawn. Clearing the palette lets the players know they have a chance to draw a new line.

○ Not giving players enough time to draw the next line. You may have to fudge the physics to make this work. Err in favor of the player.

○ Not giving the line a clear ending point. Players will use the metrics of the line to help them gauge how far they can draw. Coming up short or failing to making a connection will result in player frustration.

A line is just a rope. A rope is for swinging. And with that brilliant transition, we come to the last of the action drawing games: ***swinging games.*** In swinging games, the player's primary action is . . . you guessed it. Swinging. On a rope. Or a vine. Or a string. Or a grappling hook. Or a rope. Look, there aren't really many options here. The player characters, for some reason, launch into the void without realizing that there isn't any safe ground underneath to land on. Or if there is some sort of ground, it will horribly kill them and end the game.

The only way to save the player characters and prevent them from smacking into the ground is to throw or draw a line that connects to some sort of hanging element, like a roof, a stalactite, or a floating, very viscous cloud. The player then uses gravity to swing to the farthest extension of the line, let go of it for some insane reason, and draw a new one in the hopes that there is something to actually connect to. This keeps going until player fatigue sets in or the player misses making a connection. Along the way, players can collect treasure, dodge obstacles, and avoid enemies . . . essentially all the stuff you can do in a distance game. *Swing the Bat* (Chillingo, 2011), *Jungle Swing* (Category 5 games, 2009), *Hook Champ* (Rocketcat, 2009), and *Super Quickhook* (Rocketcat, 2010) are all fine examples of this "swinging" genre.

Meow Meow Meow

You know who else loves string? Cats. There's scientific proof that adding a cat makes any game better[7]. Let me tell you a little secret: Cats are the new ninjas. Cats are the new pirates. Cats are the new . . . dare I say it . . . zombies.

I have a great idea! You should totally put a cat in your game! The great thing is cats work in any genre!

- ○ Platform games: *Bulba the Cat* (C4M, 2010)! *Burger Cat* (Ravenous Games, 2012)!

- ○ Puzzle games: *CatDoku* (elogicpuzzles.com, 2009)! *Cat Burglar* (Cygnis Labs, 2011)!

- ○ Distance games: *The Last Ace of Space* (Astro Crow, 2011)! *Cannon Cat* (Loqheart, 2011)! *Nyan Cat* (Mark Ellis, 2011)!

- ○ Physics games: *Catshot* (DAN-BALL, 2010)! *Bike Baron* (Mountain Sheep, 2011)!

- ○ Arcade games: *MAPPY* (Namco, 2009)! *Box Cat* (Rusty Moyher, 2011)!

- ○ First-person shooters: *MeWow* (Wowsystems Informatica Lda., 2009)!

- ○ Line drawing games: *Cat and Mouse* (ivMob, 2009)! *SPY mouse* (Firemint, 2011)!

- ○ Tilt games: *Rocats* (DAN-BALL, 2010)! *Copy Cat* (Zealogic, Inc., 2010)!

- ○ Racing games: *CatRun HD* (Demonual, 2010)!

- ○ Reaction games: *Touch the Cat's Numbers* (SuiNekoKan, 2011)!

---

[7]According to *Touch Arcade's* Brad Nicholson, "You put cats in your game, your sales go up 1,000%. Truth. Cats are hot, son!"

[8]Yes, *Bike Baron,* I'm looking at you.

Cats can be the heroes. They can be the villains. They can even be there for no reason at all[8]. Cats are everywhere! Why beat them when you can join them? Besides, cat games practically design themselves:

- ○ Cats jump far and high. Can anyone say platformer, distance game, or vertical jumper?

- ○ Cats eat mice and birds. This means they make great enemies and/or health-ups.

- ○ Cats love yarn and cheezburgers. Both make great pick-ups and collectables. Besides, they both come in a variety of flavors and/or colors.

- ○ Cats cannot swim. Unless they are driving a submarine.

- ○ Cats like to be scratched behind the ears. And scratching is very similar to tapping on a touch screen; which must be why *Tap Pet Hotel* (Pocket Gems, Inc., 2011) is so popular[9].

- ○ Cats have claws. That means they can climb. Like a ninja. Do pirates have claws? I don't think so[10].

- ○ Cats can play the keyboard[11]. 'Nuff said.

- ○ Cats are adorable. The cuter the cat, the more your game will sell.

Cats. It's the next big thing. You read it here first.

---

[9]Even if it has a dog for an icon.

[10]A hook doesn't count.

[11]http://www.youtube.com/watch?v=J---aiyznGQ

GAME DESIGN SPOTLIGHT 4

Jetpack Joyride

Format: iOS (Universal)

Developer: Halfbrick Games

Designer: Luke Muscat

Suit up with a selection of the coolest jetpacks ever made and take to the skies as Barry Steakfries, the lovable hero on a one-way trip to adventure! From the creators of the worldwide phenomenon Fruit Ninja *comes the action-packed* Jetpack Joyride.

Tell me, who can resist stealing an experimental jetpack? Not hero Barry Steakfries. And not me! *Jetpack Joyride* delivers exactly what the title promises . . . a thrilling joyride for as far as possible without getting fried by electrical fields, blasted by rockets, or ... well, that's about it!

Jetpack Joyride's controls are as simple as you can get. You use just ***one finger*** to control this game. One finger! Touch anywhere on the screen to make the jetpack lift Barry up, and release it to make him drop back down to the ground. Even though the controls are limited to staccato bursts that move Barry up and down, believe me, it's more than enough to keep you challenged. The player's path is complicated by electrical zappers, some short, some long. Some that rotate, some that are slanty. In addition, deadly fields of flying laser beams zoom about. If you don't jet up and maintain your elevation, you get fried.

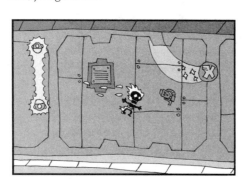

Jetpack Joyride's simplicity extends to the story: Barry steals a jetpack from an underground/underwater/outer space base populated by scientists who create experimental jetpacks. That's it. No further information is offered or required. If *Jetpack Joyride* is about anything, it's greed. The temptation to grab coins while risking getting fried by zappers is everywhere. Floating coins are arranged in patterns like arrows and smiley faces and text that reads BARRY and COINS!!! Collecting coins is very satisfying, thanks in part to the sound effects that feel ripped straight from *Sonic the Hedgehog*. The simplest stretches become dangerous when the player passes a tempting grouping of coins. Capture floating spin tokens to play The Final Spin, *Jetpack Joyride's* in-game one-armed bandit. Prizes include second chances, speed boosts, double coin values, and small to huge explosions that throw Barry down the endless corridor.

Coins are used to buy a variety of things in "the Stash," the game's store. Loot comes in a variety of flavors: Bullet-blasting jetpacks to steam-punk jetpacks to rainbow-powered jetpacks. Costumes are available, as are utilities like Head Starts that blast you forward 750m to Quick Revive that gives you a little more of a chance to go the distance. You can also buy coins using real money ranging from 99 cents to $12.99 for one million coins (which could probably buy everything in the Stash at least once). Or you can get the counterfeiting device to turn every coin you earn into two! There are just enough items and utilities in *Jetpack Joyride* that are worthwhile and fun to own to make a little coin grinding worth it. And some of the game's achievements and missions are item dependent, which is guaranteed to keep you from hording those coins.

Jetpack Joyride's tool kit of game mechanics is extremely limited, but the game is much better for it. As *Jetpack Joyride* is a distance game, the camera never changes, the background is constantly scrolling, and the gameplay is wholly dependent on the player's reaction time to narrowly avoid electrocution. Screen orientation plays a large role in the design. The player is kept to the left of the screen, giving her enough time to react to hazards or plan for collecting coins. Spin tokens leave a trail giving the player enough time to consider the risk or reward of capturing them.

This is twitch gameplay at its finest. But as simple a control scheme as it is, moving Barry takes skill. Want to collect every coin floating in a line? Then you'd better be good enough to fly straight for the entire length of the line. Want to pick up that helix of coins? I hope you know how to dip up and down. Need to avoid that incoming rocket? Controlled dropping becomes a valued skill. Last-minute blasts up and over a zapper

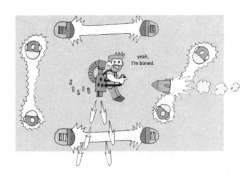

take split-second timing. And to make things more difficult, the farther Barry goes, the faster he flies. Levels become a blur as Barry blasts through the world. And since the hazards and treasure are procedurally generated, no two joyrides are the same.

Jetpack Joyride offers control variety in other ways. The player can occasionally ride vehicles, each with its own movement mechanics. The Gravity Suit allows Barry to run on ceilings and even "bounce" between the ceiling and floor by repeatedly tapping. Barry tears up the road on the Bad As Hog, shotgunning scientists out of his way. The Crazy Freaking Teleporter lets Barry blip around the screen and narrowly avoid hazards. Mr. Stompy the mecha tromps through the level while the Profit Bird leaks dollar bills with each player-controlled flap of its wings. And Mr. Cuddles is a robotic fire-breathing dragon with reverse controls. They are all great fun to pilot and even better when you purchase the magnetic coin-collecting add-on.

Jetpack Joyride excels in the details from the get-go, including the "do not steal" sign at the beginning of the game. The player's farthest distance is displayed on another sign at the start of the game. The graphics and animations are charming, with nods to 16-bit classics like *Gunstar Heroes* and *Metal Slug*. Barry's slightly oversized head provides enough expression to make us wince when he wipes out and slides 50 feet on his face. However, to *Jetpack Joyride*'s credit, a tie often goes to the player: Coins and spin tokens can still be collected in death. That doesn't mean that the game doesn't have fun messing with the player. During the final spin, fake outs are just as common as spins in the player's favor. There's nothing worse than the third heart icon clicking "one past" and an off-screen crowd "oohing" their disappointment. Talk about twisting the knife!

The most compelling feature is *Jetpack Joyride*'s achievements and mission system. Players are automatically assigned three missions they can choose to complete . . . or not. The missions are pretty fun, whether it's high-fiving scientists, having close calls with missiles, or ending your run at a particular distance. Sometimes you "just earn" a mission by playing; others require conscious efforts to achieve.

The achievements system works the same way, though some of the objectives are more esoteric, such as flying 2 km without touching any coins, scientists, or tokens, lose the final spin 100 times, or fly over 1 km in a top hat, classy suit, and traditional jetpack[1]. It's this "play how you want" attitude that makes the missions and achievements so appealing and definitely brings you back for more. If earning achievements and completing missions isn't enough, just about every significant player stat is tracked—from distance covered to coins collected to how many times you died by what to how far you slid on your face[2].

I would be remiss if I didn't mention the great sound effects. From the blast of the machine gun jetpack to the clank of the vehicles assembling, every sound effect (sfx) is chunky, fun, and effective. And a shout-out to *Jetpack Joyride*'s music composer. Even though there are only two tunes in the entire game, neither of them gets old after playing the game for several hours. That's the sign of a great composer.

So why is *Jetpack Joyride* so good? I chalk it up to the following:

- Super-simple controls
- Attitude and humor in equal measures
- A compelling prize/achievements/mission system that encourages the player to give it "one more try"

Jetpack Joyride is available on iTunes.

---

[1] All available for purchase at the Stash.

[2] 4,643m at my last count.

chapter **9**

Casual Fryday

OH DEAR, INTERNET, what is it now?

Red alert! The interwebs are on fire[1]! What could have sparked the flame wars that rage across gaming forums and blog sites? What could have caused such ire and outrage in the hearts of gamers? **Casual games,** of course. Furious bloggers ask, "Is casual gaming ruining gaming?" and "Casual games . . . Are they destroying the industry?" Industry insiders proclaim that "Casual gamers are ruining the industry!" and they're sick and tired of "casual gamers ruining games for us hardcore players!"

The irony is casual gaming existed waaaay before hardcore games—like thousands of years before hardcore games. Originally, games were simple. Light. Fun. Casual. For example, there was no such thing as a hardcore game of chess, unless you were Garry Kasparov or playing on one of those three-level Vulcan boards. Sure, there were poor winners and sore losers and my dad usually cheated when we played *Monopoly,* but mostly games were about having fun. Everything was chill.

The truth is, if anything made gaming hardcore, it was video games.

The first commercial arcade games, like *Pong* and *Space Wars,* were created to make money. These games' creators quickly learned that the best way to separate money from players was to get them to want to play the game more than once. The best way to challenge players was to make the game easy enough to play, but not easy enough to win. If players won, they would stop spending money. The trick was to keep them coming back. As time went on, it became more difficult to challenge the player. Players kept getting better. As players got better, the games got harder. The term **gamer** came to mean someone who not only played video games, but who also enjoyed difficult games. A **core gamer,** as defined by NPD, is anyone who spends 18 hours a week or more playing console videogames. **Hardcore gamers** thrived on the hardest games—games that deliberately ignored the casual audience, featured longer playtimes, possessed a higher degree of difficulty, and demanded game completion as the mark of ultimate mastery.

---

[1]Again.

But something happened. As the games got more difficult, the gaming audience contracted. Arcade and home gaming, which once had offered a variety of gameplay genres to players, now catered exclusively to the hardcore audience. The general audience, who once flocked to arcades, felt marginalized.

The Nintendo Game Boy had already struck a chord with the casual audience by including *Tetris* with the handheld gaming system, but Game Boy was an exception to the game consoles that catered to the hardcore audience. *Minesweeper* and *Solitaire* were bundled with Windows operating systems on personal computers; these games were played by millions of people, but the gaming community never took the "free" games seriously. Classic arcade games migrated over to these systems[2], but the real change happened in the late 1990s when the Internet exploded and developers started creating original games for websites using Macromedia's *Flash*—a platform for adding animation and interactivity to web pages. The casual gaming market found a brand-new audience online. These web-based games made their way from computers and Game Boys to mobile phones. When touchscreens were introduced to mobile phones, games were not far behind, and the casual gaming audience finally had the gaming platform they deserved. This casual audience had been disenfranchised by the ultra-niche subject matter of hardcore games, high time commitment required for completion and high dexterity required to operate game controllers. Mobile gaming's simple touch controls and arcade-like titles brought these 20- and 30-somethings back in droves; offering them short gameplay sessions that fit nicely inbetween the moments of their busy lives.

It is a pretty common practice to translate or convert games from one platform to another. But some games work better on touchscreen devices than others. Knowing how to convert your game and what to look out for is pivotal to your game's success. For example, lack of Flash support has slowed conversion of this generation of games to Apple's iOS platform. There are many genres to cover, so hold onto your hats and let's ride!

Board Games

Whether it's an age-old favorite like *Chess*, the latest from Dr. Reiner Knizia, or an original effort, board games have successfully made the jump from reality to the virtual tabletop. I think it has something to do with the shared **tactility** of the board game and the touchscreen.

---

[2]Over the years, many of the most popular arcade games like *Pac-Man, Galaxian, Dragon's Lair,* and *Breakout* have been adapted (or "ported") onto the latest and greatest gaming hardware. I'm sure that in the year 3000, we will be jacking into our Thought-Blaster Neuro-Plug gaming system and still be playing *Pac-Man*.

Part of the appeal of board games is how they feel. A virtual game will feel real if the player can move a game piece or flip a card. Technology provides advantages for boardgamers such as cards that expand to provide greater space for text displays and dice that can't roll off the table or knock over game pieces. Let the player replicate real actions with your controls. A flick move simulates pulling a *Uno* card from the deck. Shake the accelerometer to roll dice. Give a *Monopoly* player token inertia as the player slides it down the game board. Make easing a *Jenga* block out from the stack the same precarious motion as it is in real life. Why reinvent these motions if you can model them on reality? Of course, all of this novelty eventually wears off: players get sick of shaking their phones to roll dice. The key is to strike the right balance between gimmick and functionality.

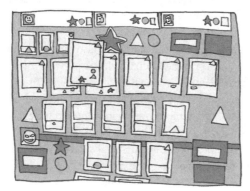

Cluttered play surface

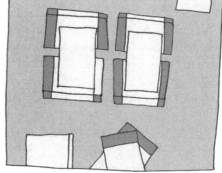

Clean play surface

Another thing touchscreen games do well is to **consolidate** elements that are normally cumbersome in real games. Managing a hand of cards, drawing a tile from a pile, calculating how much money a player gets—these are all functions that can be simplified by the game. If it causes the gameplay to slow down, then it is best if it's automated. Another rule to follow when translating board games is to stick to the core rules. Keep things **simple.** These board games are games that players have been enjoying for many years before you came along with your newfangled technology and your fancy touchscreens. There's no need to complicate matters. If your adaptation doesn't resemble the game you are adapting, then why bother adapting it? Of course, you can just create something new instead and save everyone the disappointment of screwing up the adaptation.

When you are adapting an existing board game, you probably want to stick with the graphics from the original game. However, if you are creating an original board game, don't skimp on the artwork. Make it as beautiful as you can afford. Your players are going to be looking at the game board and cards for quite a while. Many times, an old classic can be given a thematic twist to make things more interesting to modern gamers. Look at all the existing variations of *Clue, Risk,* and *Battleship.* Need some ideas on where to start? Try these themes on for size:

- **Fantasy:** Players' tokens can represent knights, elves, and dwarfs. Players can earn gems instead of dollars and explore a dungeon instead of a candyland or boardwalk.

- **Pirate:** Tokens become ships, money becomes doubloons, and the game board becomes an ocean full of dangers!

- **Horror:** A game board becomes a deserted city or shopping mall. Instead of money, collect and spend bullets instead to eliminate zombies that bar the player's path.

- **Sci-Fi:** Astro-Rangers vs. hideous aliens. Armies become fleets of space cruisers and instead of capturing countries, they conquer planets instead!

- **Steampunk:** Gears and woodwork can adorn cards and game boards. Players' tokens can be fantastic contraptions such as clanking automatons, zeppelins, and steam-powered auto cars that can transport the players around the world, through time or just around the block[3].

- **Something foreign[4]:** According to Boardgamegeek.com[5] there are two types of gamers: **Eurogamers** and **Ameritrash** players. Ameritrash players like to play games with lots of dice, blind luck and space marines fighting zombies. Eurogamers like games about agriculture, 14th-century economic principles, and sheep. Most Eurogames are named after a foreign country or body of water, like *Carcassonne* (TheCodingMonkeys, 2011), *Catan* (USM, 2009), and *Tigris & Euphrates* (Codito Development, 2011). If you want to design a Eurogame, I suggest you hurry, as there aren't too many foreign names left to take.

Some games don't immediately appear to have a theme. *Scrabble* and *Words with Friends* come to mind. But don't be fooled, these games have theming just as much as any other game. Scrabble's uses the "academic" theming used in the original board game. The wooden tiles, scrollwork logo, and vivid red coloring remind me of the cover of a dictionary. On the other hand, *Words with Friends* ditches the history (read "baggage") of its inspiration with a clean, friendly, and icon-centric theming that appeals to modern audiences.

---

[3]Take my word on this; steampunk is about to pop in a cultural sense. It just needs one good movie to get things going. Come on, Hollywood, I need a reason to wear my pith helmet and welding goggles in public!

[4]Again, I apologize to my foreign readers for my American-ness.

[5]If you want to lose a week of your life, I highly recommend logging into `http://boardgamegeek.com/`—the best board gaming database on the interwebs.

While it's fun to add theming to your game designs, don't get carried away. Keep your graphics **clear;** otherwise, they'll be distracting to the player. Art should be in service to the information on the card, not the other way around. Use the following trick to check if your card design is too cluttered: Turn the card upside down. If you can still make out the image and read the information, then it's just right. This is true for gameplay. Keep things simple. Don't give the player too many cards, pieces, dice, and rules to keep track of. The screen will get overcrowded, and players may accidentally grab the wrong things. Don't make manipulating pieces the hard part of the game: The hard part should be beating your opponent!

For many players, the most appealing part of playing board games is the **social** aspect. Games like *Scrabble* and *Words with Friends* feature asynchronous play, allowing many matches to be played simultaneously. Other games, like *Ticket to Ride* (Days of Wonder, 2011) and *Bang!* (Palzoun & SpinVector, 2010), have "pass and play" features that support many players on one device. *Reiner Knizia's Ra* (Codito Development, 2010) and *Small World for the iPad* (Days of Wonder, 2010) can be played by several players on the same device. *Scrabble* allows players to use their iPads as the game board and their iPhones as their tile racks! NewToy intentionally excluded AI from *Words with Friends* so players would recruit friends into playing, turning every player into a salesman for their game. (Resulting in their 2010 acquisition by Zynga for $53 million!) Days of Wonder emphasizes pass-and-play over mobile/social multiplayer because they want their games to feel like board games no matter what platform they are for. Don't be afraid to innovate. Perhaps you will come up with the next great feature in board game design!

Card Games

Traditional card games are omnipresent on mobile devices. Other than *Snake, Solitaire* is one of the most commonly found games on computers and mobile devices. More than 300 blackjack games are available on the iTunes Store. Scores of poker games were created in the wake of the great *Texas Hold'em* craze of the early 2000s. At first glance, it would appear that there are just too darn many card games available on touchscreen devices. Is there anywhere left to go? What will make your own game get noticed? What's a game designer to do? Fortunately, there's still a little room for your game in the world. Here are some ways to help your game stand out from the crowd:

○ **Offer something new:** I can hear you now: "These are *card games*. Hasn't everything already been invented?" Think again! With a little creativity, you can bring something new to the party. For example, *Sword & Poker* (GAIA Co, 2010) is a poker RPG! *Landlord Poker* (iSN solutions, 2011) has boss fights! *Absolute Space Poker* (ITIW, 2009) mixes *Galaxian* with poker! *Kenny Rogers Video Poker* (PlayScreen, 2008) has Kenny Rogers[6]!

○ **Offer variations:** Even the simplest card games have many local, historical, and cultural rule variations. *Solitaire,* for example, has *Klondike, Spider, FreeCell, Cascade,* and *Boardwalk.* Some of these change how cards are dealt; others have to do with how cards are played. Explore these options and add them to your own game. The more you offer, the more customers will think of your game as a "one-stop shop."

○ **Offer social interaction:** Card games are social games. This is why poker night is so popular. It isn't just the game, it's the company. Offer your players a way to socially interact with friends or strangers. Come up with more than chat and pushes to social media. Stretch your brain a little and come up with some truly novel ideas. Here is mine—a cowboy-themed poker game where players can cheat while playing and shoot each other dead if they're caught[7]. Sounds like fun to me!

○ **Offer location:** Where does your card game take place? A swanky casino? A dusty saloon? A rickety card table in someone's basement? Think about the type of environment you want your players to feel like they are in. Then use visuals, sound effects, and theming to make that atmosphere come to life.

○ **Offer licenses . . . or originality:** *Bicycle* and *Hoyle* brand playing cards are a familiar sight to most card game players, but that doesn't mean you can use them in your own game. These cards are copyrighted images. Avoid a lawsuit and either pay for the rights to use these images or . . . create your own artwork. The benefit of licensing is, for a fee, you get access to something that potential customers already are familiar with. They will be more likely to buy your product with a brand name they trust. Copyrights and trademarks are good things; they protect creative people so they can profit from their good ideas and hard work. However, be sure you think long and hard before you commit to obtaining a license. Carefully consider the added value against revenue you will lose through licensing fees. When evaluating licenses remember to make sure you are licensing the right thing: licensing the likeness of known poker players might connect with fans more than having a playing card company endorse your game.

---

[6]Lots of Kenny Rogers. So much Kenny Rogers . . .

[7]I think I just invented my next game.

○ **Offer gambling:** Simulated gambling or the real thing? For some designers, it's a no-brainer. For others, it's an ethical question or even a business decision. After you get past that, you will have plenty of infrastructures to build. How do players pay in to play? How do payouts work? What else can players spend their virtual money on? Keep in mind that Apple and Android don't allow apps to be sold in the App Store/Marketplace that directly allow gambling[8], but they do allow their devices to access mobile casino websites. Since Apple products don't support Adobe Flash (at this time), savvy entrepreneurs have created mobile-friendly sites to allow access to their casinos. Also be aware that in the United States, some states ban gambling online as do some countries around the world. Check your local, state and county laws to avoid getting into trouble.

In addition to these ideas, always apply the design pillars I've already mentioned: simplicity, tactility, and clarity. Those, coupled with a unique twist, might give your game a shot at success!

Real Time Strategy Games

Real Time Strategy (or RTS) games are strategy games played in real time. This is different than, say, *Chess* or *Highborn*, which are turn-based strategy games. It can be a bit confusing, however. I mean, most video games happen in real time, so why do RTS games get their own special title? You don't hear about Real Time Arcade (RTA) games or Real Time Sports (RTS[9]) games. I guess there is a Real Time Driving (RTD) game—the infamous *Desert Bus*[10] (Amateur Pixels, 2011)—but why other genres don't add the "Real Time" designation to their titles is a real head-scratcher.

---

[8]Yet.

[9]That would just be confusing.

[10]Originally part of the unreleased 1995 Sega CD game *Penn & Teller's Smoke and Mirrors, Desert Bus* became a gaming industry legend when a build made the rounds through the game reviewing and development communities. In *Desert Bus*, the player drives from Tucson, Arizona to Las Vegas, Nevada, at 45 mph in real time. That's 8 hours of driving time. There's very little for the player to look at as the desert scenery doesn't really change much as it scrolls by. There's no way to cheat around the experience, either (like setting the controller down and walking away) as the bus constantly pulls to the right. An unattended bus will drive off the road and cause the game to be over. Once the bus reaches Las Vegas, the player is awarded one point and given the option to make the 8-hour return trip. Players of the game have used it as an endurance test to see how many points they can score. In recent years, annual *Desert Bus* marathons have been held to raise money for the video game related charity Child's Play. To make a donation and get more info, please visit www.childsplaycharity.org.

[11]After all, it's what's best in life!

RTS games involve marching your armies around, crushing your enemies, seeing them driven before you, and hearing the lamentations of their women[11]. This gameplay remains the same no matter if your RTS is traditional, like *Z the Game* (Kavcom, 2011); displayed in side view, like *Super Wars* (Triniti Interactive, 2011); humorous, like *Robocalypse* (Vogster Entertainment, 2009); or casual, like *Ant Raid* (Prank, 2011). All RTS games require the following design features:

○ **Defense:** It doesn't matter if it's a home base, a landing pad, or a power source; you've got to give the player something to defend. Defense is almost always part of the victory condition: Take over the player's base or capture all the specific points on the map. That's where the strategy and the ebb and flow of tactics come in.

○ **Economy:** It's a balancing act to create a workable economic system. Trust me; it will take many passes to make the economy feel just right. Fortunately, a designer has many ways to create a balanced economy: time (time to build troops and buildings, time to recharge or restock), resources (like precious metals or power sources), money (the more money the player earns, the more expensive things get), and assets (players have to find equipment or materials to build troops, buildings, and so forth). Never make a resource have dual functionality (like energy both creates troops and powers weapons). Keep things simple.

○ **Fog of War:** Another feature common to RTS games is the "Fog of War," which obscures areas of the map that the player isn't in. This helps create a feeling of suspense and surprise. The fog can be literal (a dense fog that blurs out the rest of the map), or an exclusion of information so the player can't see what defense and troops the enemy is building. Determine how far into the fog the player can see and whether you want the player to have the ability to create technology that minimizes or totally removes the fog of war.

○ **Balancing:** Every RTS game is essentially the game of *Rock, Paper, and Scissors*, where one unit is stronger against another unit, but is also more vulnerable to a different unit. The best way to start designing units is to give them a ***singular function.*** More often than not, the functions are divided between attack, health, and speed. For example, a goblin scout may have a high speed, but have low health and a short attack range. An ogre unit on the other hand, could have high health and cause high damage, but attack less frequently and move slowly.

○ **Pacing:** After your economy is roughly in place, determine the pace that players can build and upgrade their technology. The tool that will help you plan this is called a technology (or tech) tree.

How to Create a Tech Tree

Video games have lots of moving parts. Managing these parts gets complicated quickly unless you have a good way to track them. That tracking tool is called a **tech tree.** Let's create a sample RTS. Start by listing all the elements in your game. List all the available buildings, vehicles, and upgrades.

Look at **dependencies:** technology that requires other technology for it to work. For example, a super-laser turret can't be built until the player has first built a laser turret.

Buildings	Troops	Turrets	Vehicles

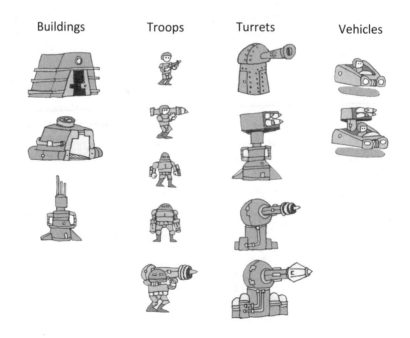

Now that you know the technological dependencies, determine **progression,** the order in which the player will be able to unlock and build items over the course of the entire game.

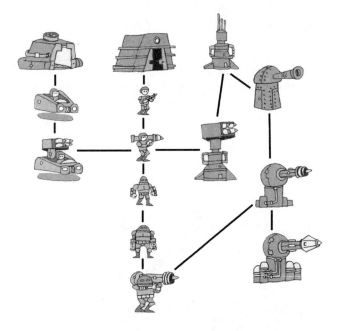

Next, create the build rate of technology. Some items take minutes to build, others take seconds. Is there a benefit or disadvantage for building multiples? Can a player spend real money to unlock or speed up the build rate? How does the gameplay change if the player can affect the game's progression in this way?

There you have it: a basic tech tree. Of course, most tech trees are much larger than this. Keep from getting overwhelmed by taking things one step at a time.

If you think designing RTS games can get overwhelming, what about playing them? RTS touchscreen games can get quite complicated for players to control, as if they are spinning several plates at once. You can reduce this confusion by grouping commands like building units or moving troops together. Minimize the number of steps it takes for a player to select a unit.

Give players a quick "find this unit/building" function or map to transport players quickly to the selected unit. A HUD should display a unit's timer, showing the remaining time until a unit comes online. Or you can just create a simplified version of your game . . . known as a **tower defense** (TD) game.

Tower Defense Games

While forms of the genre existed as early as the 1990s, the first true tower defense games were mods created by fans using RTS game editors. In a TD game[12], players defend their tower against waves of approaching **"creeps"** by placing weapon emplacements and obstacles in the enemy's way. The genre came into its own with the browser title *Desktop Tower Defense* (Paul Preece, 2007). When *Desktop Tower Defense* migrated over to mobile gaming, other developers followed suit. Notable TD titles include *Plants vs. Zombies* (PopCap, 2010), *Army of Darkness Defense* (Backflip Studios, 2011), *Tiny Defense* (Picsoft, 2011), *Fieldrunners* (Subatomic Studios, 2008), *Samurai Bloodshow* (Sega, 2011), and *GeoDefense* (Critical Thought Games, 2009).

---

[12]Be aware that publisher Com2uS has exclusive rights to use "Tower Defense" in the titles of their games. Other descriptors such as Defense, Defender, and Defend are still okay to use.

When designing a TD game, start with the path. While a RTS often has multiple paths and a fog of war, a TD game is very straightforward with a single path. This single path allows the player to concentrate on preplanned strategy rather than reactive strategy. While many TD games are viewed from a top-down or isometric camera view, others have unique paths, like *The Creeps HD* (Super Squawk Software, 2011), where the creeps move toward the camera, or *Star Defense* (ngmoco, 2011), where the path is on a scrolling globe. The camera view is essential to determining the style of gameplay. For example, a "five channels" style or side-scrolling defense game like *Legendary Wars* (Liv Games, 2011) is obviously going to be designed very differently than a "desktop" or top-down style game like *Anomaly Warzone Earth* (Chillingo, 2011).

Picking the camera view goes hand in hand with determining your path. Will your camera be fixed or scrollable? Will the player have to move the camera to see the entire map? Traditionally, TD maps are displayed on one screen. New maps usually equal additional levels. New maps take more work to create, but give your game more variety and longevity.

A well-designed path features both straightaways and curves. Straightaways allow creeps to move quickly, causing tension for the player. Curves allow players to capitalize on the creeps' switchbacking, giving turrets more opportunities to attack. Or if you want to get fancy, play with elevation changes. Just make sure the player has the defenses to deal with them.

* This drawing's original caption was deemed too offensive so I held a "rewrite the caption contest." The winning caption was written by Paul Kankiewicz. Thanks and congrats!

Speaking of defenses, let's talk **turrets.** These are the base unit of the TD player. Turrets can look like anything you want—gun emplacements, plants, laser turrets, or even people. Or they could be a convoy of moving vehicles, like in *Anomaly Warzone Earth*. No matter what their appearance, each turret can represent a single function that players can level up to gain new functionality as the game progresses. Not every turret has to shoot. Some turrets can be defensive or support the functions of nearby turrets.

Another design decision is how to limit the player's turret creation. *Plants vs. Zombies* use a pick-before-you-play system where the player can use a limited number of seed packets. *Anomaly Warzone Earth* uses a "pay as you go" system. As always, remember to design the functionality of your game and elements before determining the visuals. Here are some of the more common turret types to get you started:

- **Attacking:** Turrets that shoot (or melee) creeps when they enter an attack range or radius. These turrets can have singular functions or be upgraded to do more damage, have a longer range, fire faster, shoot more projectiles, recharge faster, and have more health.

- **Radial:** These turrets affect areas rather than a single target. They create radial areas of damage, heal or buff nearby towers, or stun groups of creeps.

- **Multi-directional:** These turrets can shoot at two or more creeps at once, helpful not only for destroying more enemies, but also for shooting at enemies that have managed to pass by other defenses.

- **Elevation:** These turrets are useful against flying creeps that can only be shot with floating or aerial shooting turrets. Another way to think of elevation is to have turrets that lob shots over defenses, creeps, or greater distances to hit where and when a direct shot cannot.

- **Enhancing:** These towers enhance the power or damage of an already existing tower. They usually have to be placed next to another tower for the effect to work. For example, *Plants vs. Zombies'* Torchwood ignites any projectile that passes through it and causes additional damage.

- **Barricade:** Nothing slows down a slowly advancing creep like a good wall (or wall-nut).

- **Deadly barricade:** Like a barricade but deals damage to or outright destroys a creep when one is encountered. Usually very effective but either expensive to create or slow to recharge . . . or both.

- **Stunning:** These turrets and barricades slow down or stop creeps right in their path, leaving them open to be blasted apart by other turrets.

- **Generator:** A very common turret (and usually one of the first available in most TD games) that doesn't attack, but rather generates the mana, power, money, health, sunlight, and so forth, to keep the player going. The more of these you plant, the more turrets you can get into play.

- **Smart bomb:** The final word in defense. If you can afford it, use it. Set this sucker off and pretty much all the creeps around it go bye-bye.

I want to give you a warning before you start designing a TD game. Some consumers feel that there are already too many tower defense games on the market. However, they've never played a tower defense game created by **you!** Of course, it doesn't hurt to have an appealing art style, an engaging mechanic, or a compelling hook to really make a splash in this genre. Good luck!

God Games

These days when people talk about casual gaming, they are usually thinking of simulation games like Maxis/EA's *The Sims* series, the *Theme Park* or *Roller Coaster Tycoon* series, or Zynga's line of "Ville" games[13]. These titles are all part of a bigger genre called *God games*. In God games, players are cast as an unseen deity/cosmic sociologist/puppet-master/tormentor[14] that is building, experimenting, improving, and destroying the lives of the residents of fictional homes, farms, cities, theme parks, and so forth. Much like in RTS titles, balance and economy play a big part in the game design. Players usually strive to keep the populace happy, keep power and production flowing while they expand their territory. The God genre migrated early over to touchscreen with Will Wright's *The Sims 3,* which was featured in Apple's promotion of the App Store.

---

[13]The -Ville suffix comes from *YoVille,* Zynga's first successful social game. Subsequent titles included *FarmVille, FrontierVille* (aka *The Pioneer Trail*), *CityVille, CityVille Hometown, CastleVille, PetVille,* and *FishVille.*

[14]Depending on the way you play the game.

However, the genre has split into two forms: the isometric "build a world and watch what happens" model, like Kairosoft's library of games (*GameDev Story*, *Grand Prix Story*, *Mega Mall Story*, *Pocket Academy*, *Hot Springs Story*, and *Oh! Edo Town*), and the side view "torment the little people and watch what happens" model seen in *Pocket God* (Bolt Creative, 2009), *Pocket Elves* (RetroStyle Games, 2009), and *Pocket Ants* (Concrete Software, 2011)[15].

Isometric view

Side view

When you are allowing players to create their own space or build their own cities, make sure that moving is an easy-to-find, easy-to-select, and easy-to-do activity. Be careful of overlapping elements; turn a foreground element transparent or allow the background elements to become more pronounced so it is easier for the player to grab hold of it and move it if need be. Highlighting elements, dragging and dropping, and quick pop-up menus that allow players to change or delete elements helps the players manipulate elements with ease. If it's no fun to manipulate the world, then it isn't going to be fun to play in it.

A key design component of any simulation game, like *The Sims 3*, *Artist Colony* (I-Play, 2010), or the *Virtual Villagers* series (Last Day of Work, 2011), is **customization.** Let me qualify that: a key design component of *any* game is customization, but since this part of the book is specifically about God games, that's the context I'm going to be using. What's the key take away? Customization = good for the player.

---

[15]I guess if you want to create a God game, it should be called "pocket" something!

Customization is a great way for the player to get emotionally invested in a game. Some games offer a wide variety of choices, from the appearance of the player's avatar to items that can be bought to furnish virtual property. The player is building a virtual dollhouse, and a house needs stuff! Little couches, TV sets, rugs, beds—you name it, it's available—can all be purchased from the game's store. There are many ways to offer customization for players:

- **Name:** Giving players the ability to name their own characters can be very powerful. If the soldiers in your army or the workers on your farm are generic no-named characters, you really don't care what happens to them. However, if you name them after your friends (or if they happen to actually *be* your friends), then you will be more inclined to help them succeed (or keep them alive).

- **Avatar:** If changing a name is exciting for the players, imagine how awesome it is for them to change their clothes! Or hair color! Or facial features! Why, you could play as your favorite character or even yourself. (There's something wrong about seeing yourself die over and over.) At the very least, let the players change their hair and skin color. After that, there's a huge range of customization that can be done. Just make sure your customization tool isn't more interesting than your game.

- **Weapons or vehicles:** I'm not just talking about changing a mace to an axe or choosing between a car and a car with a spoiler. What if you could design your weapon? Paint it or redesign your vehicle? Give it a name? You would take better care of it, wouldn't you? Just like with Batman's batarang or batmobile, weapons and vehicles should be an extension of the player's character. Some weapons and vehicles are so distinct that you only need to see them to know who uses them. Theming them to the character creates a stronger bond between players and their characters.

- **Abilities:** Giving the player several abilities to choose from is an interesting option. The player now has lots of ways to play your game, all of which require design work and lots of testing to make sure they play correctly. If you give players more options than they can use during one play session, then they have a reason to play again.

- **Decorative elements:** What do Superman, Batman, and Hugh Hefner have in common? Sweet man-caves. Hey, decorating houses isn't just for women. As *The Sims* creator Will Wright once said, "Pretty much everyone wants to play house." Give your players lots of ways to personalize their bases, lairs, and caves. Trophies of adventures are great ways to liven up a dreary space station or castle. Why not let the players pick the color of the curtains while you're at it?

- **Colors:** See? Colors. Didn't I just mention that in the preceding bullet point? Everyone has a favorite color. Including your players.

- **Music:** Some games let players select their own music from a CD or iTunes catalog; others let players program in a jukebox of the game's music.

There is, however, such a thing as too many choices. In the noted *Scientific American* article "The Tyranny of Choice[16]," researchers discovered there are two types of consumers: those who are satisfied with limited choices (known as satisficers) and those who check out every option from a wide variety before choosing a purchase (known as maximizers). The satisficers are always happier with their purchase than the maximizers, who feel like there is always something better available than what they ended up with.

Ultimately, it's better to offer your players **worthwhile** items than an excessive amount of items. You can start by making each item useful and unique. It's better to offer a +3 sword that does cutting damage and a +3 mace that does crushing damage than a +1, a +2, and a +3 sword. The differences should be large enough to make a difference to the player. Even better, the different items should look different, have a different effect (like fire or icy particles), and, if possible, feel different when playing. The vehicles of *Jetpack Joyride* are a good example of how different similar operating items can look and feel differently.

Customization leads to the simulation game's other signature mechanic, **monetization.** *The Smurfs' Village* (Beeline Interactive, 2010) and *Snoopy's Street Fair* (Beeline Europe, 2011) are free-to-play games, but charge real money for additional in-app content. **In-app purchases** (IAPs) have become a growing part of many developers' revenue plans. In 2011, 65% of free-to-play games made their profit with IAPs, up from 39% the prior year[17]. It's becoming clearer to developers that IAPs retain users who feel that the incremental charges are worth paying for, especially since the initial download was free.

Should you include IAPs in your game? Good question. If you have a content plan to support IAPs (and these are things like additional missions and content, new weapons, or modes of play that change the game's experience), then it might be the correct choice. Gamers are expecting developers to support their products for longer cycles than the old "release and done" model, so you'd better start designing your IAPs before you finish making your game!

---

[16] http://www.swarthmore.edu/SocSci/bschwar1/Sci.Amer.pdf

[17] http://gigaom.com/2011/07/07/freemium-titles-generate-two-thirds-of-app-store-gaming-revenues/

When charging players for items, you want to make sure you have an **in-app store** so it's easy for the players to buy your IAPs. When designing your store, label your items clearly and show images of the items. There's nothing consumers hate more than a blind buy. Show what makes your item worth buying, how it will improve their current game, or help the player win faster. When a player does buy it, have a way to indicate to the player that he now owns it. Unless it's a consumable item, a player shouldn't have to buy it twice.

And finally, make it super-clear that these items cost real money. Nothing is worse than not realizing that special item you just bought wiped out your bank account! Many players don't want to spend real money on virtual goods. Even worse, many players don't want their kids to spend real money on virtual goods[18]! In 2011, the Federal Trade Commission started an investigation into the practices of in-app purchases. While users can prevent inadvertent purchases by changing their device's settings to restrict downloading and making transactions, we developers can (and must) do our part to help:

○ Require a password for all in-app purchases. This is a default requirement for Apple's iOS. The user's password must be entered before iTunes will process a payment (or a password must have already been entered within the last 15 minutes). If the game utilizes game currency then no password or confirmation is required, which is how players (and kids) can get into trouble spending money within the game.

○ Use different visuals to differentiate between real and in-game cash. Zynga games use stacks of dollar bills to represent real cash and coins for in-game money.

○ Make it clear to the player which items cost real money to buy.

○ Give the player a chance to stop the transaction before the final purchase is submitted (aka the "Are you sure?" prompt).

Of course, there are other alternatives to shopping. The player can **grind** (perform activities that become daily and often boring routines, such as weeding gardens or chopping wood) to earn **in-game currency.** In the spirit of fair play, players should be able to earn most (if not all) of the items available in the game with hard work, although it is a common practice to make some exclusive items available for purchase only with real-world currency (and make rare in-games ones that bit more expensive to ensure they retain their desirability). Show the player the effort it will take to grind for the reward. This way, the player can make a decision to either grind or take the quicker route and spend real cash instead. Often, players realize the latter is the better option if they want to advance quickly in the game[19].

---

[18]http://www.washingtonpost.com/wp-dyn/content/article/2011/02/07/AR2011020706073.html

[19]And come to think of it, it's a better option for the developer, too!

Sports Games

Sports have been inspiring video game designers since the dawn of video games[20]. The upside to creating a sports game is that most of the heavy lifting has already been created: The rules, the physics, the environment, even what the avatar will be wearing already exist in the real world. There's no need to make stuff up. You can copy it all from reality and no one will accuse you of plagiarizing[21]. The only real decision the designers need to make is whether they are making an ***abstract*** of a sports game or a ***simulation*** of a sports game.

Abstract sports games, also known as arcade sports games, are the real-world games reduced down to their most fun elements. For example, *.Air.Hockey.HD* (Glauco Castro, 2011) boils hockey down into its essential elements: two player paddles, one puck, and two goals. Even the rules are simplified: Each player has to keep to her side and her reach cannot extend past the center line. If the puck gets into the goal, the player earns a point. Whoever scores a predetermined number of points wins the game. *.Air.Hockey.HD* still plays like hockey, but without icing, off-sides, fights, shoot-outs, and all the other rules that slow the game down.

---

[20]Remember, the first video game was *Tennis for Two*.

[21]Unless you really did plagiarize from another game, then shame on you.

Abstracting a sports game is easy. Just ask yourself, "What is the sport's primary action?" In the case of hockey, the primary action is shooting the puck to score. But you aren't limited to one choice. The designers of *Hockey Fight Pro* (Ratrod Studio, Inc., 2011) made their primary action the fights that break out during a match. It's a hockey game where you never play hockey.

Simulations tend to use real players more often than abstract games. When creating realistic characters, you should beware the **uncanny valley.** This is when a computer-generated character looks super realistic, but still not enough to convince the viewer that it's real. The end result is that the character looks creepy and unnatural. Watch out for "dead-eyes" that never blink, hands with "welded fingers" because the character doesn't have enough bones for articulated hands, or ridiculously detailed skin textures that look a little too plastic. Characters that live in the uncanny valley are very distracting for players, so attempt realism with caution.

If you don't want to attempt realism, **personality** goes a long way with characters in abstract sports games. The *Homerun Battle* series features over-the-top hit reactions like slo-mo and exploding signage when a homerun is scored. In *Homerun Battle 2*, the player's avatar can be customized into a wide variety of decidedly non-baseball themed characters, including pirates, kung-fu masters, and demons. In *Flick Home Run!* (Infinity Pocket, 2011), it's the balls that have the personality—mad-faced balls taunt the player and cross-eyed balls drop suddenly.

You need to abstract your controls as well. There are many ways to skin this cat . . . or whack the ball or slap the puck . . . you get the idea. For example, players flick at incoming balls in *Flick Home Run!* but tap into a hit zone to swing at the ball in *Homerun Battle 2*. Both result in the same action, swinging a bat, but they use two different approaches. It really doesn't matter which method you use, as long as the impact of the bat hitting the ball feels *physical*.

Physicality is a very important part of any sports game, be it golf, or boxing, or bowling[22]. Since many people have played these games in the real world (compared to piloting a battlemech, flying a hover-bike, or fighting a dragon), they have a frame of reference with which to compare the gameplay. And if you get the physicality wrong, players will notice. In other words, go bowling before you design a bowling game[23]. Concentrate on these aspects to make your game feel more real:

---

[22]It's an important part of any game, really.

[23]I suggest you do this for any game you design, within the realms of possibility of course! Shoot a gun if you are creating a shooter. Ride a motorcycle if you are designing a motorcycle racing game. The experience of doing the action will give you more insight into creating the game version of the experience. (And if you can't go out and do something, at least talk to someone who is very familiar with doing it to get an "insider's perspective.")

○ **Response:** In order for players to feel like they are in the action, animations have to happen quickly when the controls are pressed. One way to make your animation feel quick is to keep things short: no long "lead times" after the "button is pressed"[24]. One hundred frames of animation for a swing might look silky smooth, but it's going to take time to play that animation. And that's time the players don't need to spend watching the swing. They just want to hit the ball! Another way to provide a quick response is to keep your frame rate above 30 frames per second. While the human eye cannot keep track of individual frames of animation at this speed, anything that runs below this frame rate looks "stuttery," where you can see individual frames of animation that play like a flip book. The best games run at 60 frames per second, which makes them look cleaner, smoother, and more realistic.

○ **Realism:** Since we all live on the planet Earth[25], real-world physics is the one yardstick everyone knows. If the physics in a game don't feel right, if the character controls feel too "floaty" or "slidey" or too "loose," the player is going to feel it and will be frustrated. If a soccer[26] player kicks a ball and that ball sails too far or doesn't sail far enough or doesn't feel like it has inertia or the proper friction or gravity, then it is going to ruin the feel of the play of the game. Since most sports games center around a ball of some sort, it is essential to make the physics of these objects feel realistic.

○ **Audio feedback:** A good, solid "whack" really sells the action. A bat hitting a ball, a stick hitting a puck, a player catching a ball. Sound effects are important to games. Without them, the player has one less piece of information. Don't leave this to the last minute. In fact, get key sound effects (mainly hit and player reactions) into your game quickly to give play testers a point of reference. Use placeholder sounds before you even bring in a sound effects artist. You can find plenty of online, cost-free sound effects, or you can license/buy them through sound effects libraries like the Hollywood Edge or Revostock or Sound-Ideas. Or grab a microphone and go record them yourself!

---

[24]Or finger is swiped. You get the idea.

[25]If you aren't from Earth and are reading this book, then let me say "Welcome" to our new Alien Overlords!

[26]Apologies to my international readers.

Simulation sports games strive to realistically re-create a game. You often find this kind of game on gaming consoles where the player has more controls. There are some examples of realistic games on touchscreen devices though: *2K Sports NHL2K11* (2K Sports, 2010) and *NCAA Football* (EA Sports, 2010) emulate the "in-the-game" experience with third-person cameras, complex player interactions, and programmable play patterning. Gauging by the number of these games available on touchscreen devices (not many), one can gather that the majority of this audience is still playing this type of title on their consoles.

If you want your game to score with simulation sports fans, you will need to obtain a ***license.*** For a substantial fee, a license will let a developer use the official logos, music, sounds, player names and numbers, and playfields owned by a licensor for a designated period of time[27]. However, licenses often come with limitations, restricting what the developer can use for his game. For example, Com2uS' Major League Baseball Players Association (MLBPA) license only lets them use the players' names, but not the ballparks or the team names and logos, for their *9 Innings Pro Baseball 2011* (Com2uS, 2011). This can be a deal breaker for many sports fans who feel that a game without the authentic sounds, sights, announcers' voices, and stats from their favorite sports just isn't the real thing.

RPGs and MORPGs

---

[27]If you want to know what you are getting yourself into, check out this MLB licensing contract: http://contracts.onecle.com/topps/mlb-license-2006-01-01.shtml.

Every good game designer should play *Dungeons and Dragons* at least once. Let me amend that. Every good game designer should not only play *Dungeons and Dragons,* but should also run a *Dungeons and Dragons* adventure once in his/her life. Thanks to *Dungeons and Dragons*[28], we now have whole generations of game designers raised on pen and paper role-playing games (aka RPGs) who are creating RPGs and multiplayer online role-playing games (aka MORPGs) on mobile and touchscreen devices. There are many foundations of great game design to be learned from game mastering a RPG, including:

- **Creating maps:** Even if your game doesn't take place in a dungeon, learning to get your ideas on paper is pivotal for a game design. Like I always say, "You can come up with the design, but can you do the paperwork?" Map making is an essential skill when planning and building your game world, from creating references for artists to work from to assembling levels and screens in design and art tools.

- **Populating a world:** As the creator of a world, you need to fill it. Fill it with what? Not just people, but interesting places, challenging creatures, engaging scenarios, fabulous treasures, and moments that make the players stop and wonder or at least use their imagination. Create a beat chart to determine when things will appear in your game. Determine the pacing of these elements and events so that the player will encounter something amazing even if they're only playing for 3 minutes at a time.

- **Creating non-player characters (NPCs):** Creating interesting NPCs is hard. They need to be treated like any fictional character. They need a motivation, a background, and a personality. This is just as true for enemies. Sure, you can have an Orc attack the players, but an Orc who is afraid of magic is much more memorable. There are lots of games out there with simple characters, but it's the characters that have character that players fall in love with.

- **Telling a story:** The best role-playing games resemble campfire stories with dice and maps. Always "err on the side of drama" and make things epic, exciting, and scary. You are creating escapism, after all. Make those stories punchy, quick, and interesting. Your touchscreen gamers only have a short time in which to be drawn in. The clock is ticking, so make it count!

- **Reacting to unpredictable changes in your game:** Players break games. They don't always do what you want them to do. That well-thought-out story you wrote? They'll skip or ignore it. Those mechanics you designed? They'll find a way to break them. Sometimes they completely by-pass that dungeon that you spent 3 days designing. Be ready to roll with the punches. Have a plan B, C, and D in mind, just in case. Be prepared[29].

---

[28]And *Gamma World* and *Paranoia* and *Champions* and *Call of Cthulhu* and *G.U.R.P.S.* and *Vampire the Masquerade,* and a hundred other great RPGs.

[29]It's not just for Boy Scouts anymore.

○ **Rewarding players:** Like I said, players break games. As a result, it's easy to adopt a "crush the player" mentality. But this is bad game mastering. The players are there to have a good time. So instead of trying to destroy them, take my advice and "love thy player" instead. The more help and love you give your players, the longer they will want to play. The longer they play, the more fondly they will regard your game. The fonder of your game they are, the more friends they will recommend it to. And those friends will buy your game, too. It's in your best interest to love those little game-breakers.

Now that you know how to be a good game master, you need to design your game to appeal to what your players consider important:

○ **Story matters:** Story is what keeps the players coming back, especially if it's a story that makes the players care about continuing to play. I don't mean a story where the player's brother is killed off in the first 3 minutes of the game that gives the player nothing to care about because the brother means nothing to him. In order to make the player care about your characters, they need to mean something to the player. Don't kill a character just for shock, give it a gameplay reason. Aeris' death in *Final Fantasy VII* was shocking not just because she was the hero's love interest, but she was a useful member of the party. The loss meant something to the player.

○ **Personalization matters:** Why do people spend more than $100 on 3D models of their *World of Warcraft* characters?[30] Because the way their character looks matters to them. Their character *is* them in the online world. They wear armor and weapons that have been hard-fought for in raids and on adventures. What they wear are trophies of their level and progress. It's important to give players the opportunity to craft their own identity even if the characters are from templates. Armor, clothes, weapons, pets, decorations, and trophies. These are all things players love.

○ **Progression/stats matters:** A big part of any RPGs is statistics, or stats. Leveling up systems aid the players in determining how much further they have to go before they reach the next level of progression in the game. Incremental changes to the player's performance or odds of outcome are all part of the fun. Give the players plenty of opportunities to gain experience that can be used to increase statistics (always remember the six cardinal stats . . . come repeat them after me . . . strength, intelligence, wisdom, dexterity, constitution, charisma), or tweak saving throws, or buff up spells, or max out weapon damage. There are plenty of ways players can use experience. Take advantage of them all!

---

[30]http://www.figureprints.com/

○ **Randomness matters:** Depending on how random, how often, and what you are randomizing. Let's look at three different RPG tropes that should be randomized: Travel, Dungeons, and Loot. The random encounter started with *Dungeons and Dragons* (Dungeon Masters would roll from a chart listing monsters of varying difficulty and quantity) and became a staple of RPGs, especially Japanese-developed RPGs like the *Legend of Zelda* series. This ensures that players will always encounter something interesting during the mundane task of traveling through the world. However, if you encounter enemies too hard or too often, players will feel like they are being set upon by the designer. Randomizing dungeons gives the players a reason to revisit a location more than once. It requires a lot of thinking ahead of time to create a randomized dungeon system. It is a giant puzzle with many pieces that can fit together in many configurations and with many different denizens. In MORPGs, these are called **instanced dungeons.** They allow the designer to get more bang out of a smaller scaled world. Look at the *Diablo* and *Torchlight* series of games for great examples. Randomizing loot is a must for any RPG. It is so important, in fact, that it deserves its own bullet point:

○ **Loot matters:** OMG, does it matter. Give the player a large selection of loot that can "drop" at any time. And not just great loot, but rare loot. A rarity scheme is a huge motivator to keep players playing as they scour the ends of your earth or anticipate the next item drop from a defeated enemy. Offer the players a wide variety of loot, from useful but quickly made useless common items to powerful (but not too powerful— you don't want to break your game!) and rare items that let them take on the toughest monsters without breaking too much of a sweat. The magic starting formula of rarity is 10 common items, 4 uncommon items, and 1 rare item. If you are including ultra-rare items, then they should drop once every 50 or so times. You can also create a dynamic loot dropping system to help the players when they need it the most. Are they low on health? Give them a health potion instead of gold. If they are having trouble with combat, drop a better weapon. Award prizes that influence the random drops: for example helmets in *Infinity Blade* that award more loot to the player. *King Cashing* lets players buy power-ups that influence the percentage of occurrence of enemies, weapons, and treasure that appear in the game. Allow players to nudge randomness in their favor. Err on the side of helping your players whenever possible. It will make them even hungrier for more loot.

○ **Rewards and empowerment matter:** In her book *Reality Is Broken,* author Jane McGonigal proposes that the reason people play so many hours of online games is that they are getting something in these virtual worlds they aren't getting in their real lives: positive feedback. All I know is that it feels good to get better at something and it feels great to get acknowledged for succeeding. Make sure you let your players know that they are doing great. Everything from in-game text messages to exciting Vegas-like sound effects to fireworks-like particle effects to NPCs remarking on how heroic the players are as they pass by. All these things make players feel good about their experience. Of course, you don't want to lay it on thick; otherwise, the player will get jaded and start to ignore or even resent all the congratulations, no matter how sincere it is meant to be.

○ **Socialization matters:** Mobile gaming has quickly evolved from a solitary activity to a shared one[31]. Players love to play together, and they love to communicate with each other. Look at all the available communication systems: chat, texting, social media stories, photography, and video messaging systems like *Skype*. Embrace these tools now because they will be the building blocks of games moving into the future.

The Crown Jewel of Casual

Whew! That was a lot of game genres to cover! However, I've saved one for last. If any single genre epitomizes the "birthed by browser" games that have made the jump to mobile and touchscreen devices, it is **match three** games.

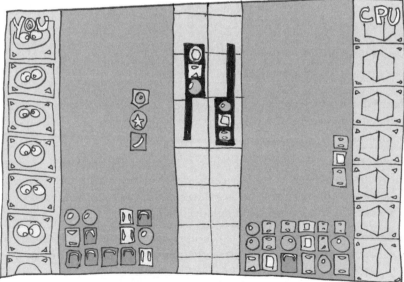

Columns

---

[31]Which is odd considering phones are social-enabling devices to begin with.

A contemporary of *Tetris*, *ChainShot!* (Morisuke, 1985) introduced the mechanic of matching five colored squares to clear an area. *Columns* (Sega, 1989) changed the visual to **gems**[32] and reduced the number of matches required to three. When a match was made, the gems would shatter, which contributed to the genre's other name: **"breaker"** games. Other match three titles appeared: *Dr. Mario* (Nintendo, 1990), *Magic Jewelry* (Hwang Shinwei, 1990), and *Puyo Puyo* (Sega, 1991). After capturing the attention of console gamers, the match three genre migrated over to browsers. Programs like *Flash* (first Macromedia, later Adobe) made it easy for developers to create match three games for browsers, and they multiplied exponentially. Titles like *Rise of Atlantis*, *Jungle Jewels*, and *Jewel Quest* became popular browser games. But none of them were as popular as *Bejeweled*, which has gone on to become one of the most played casual games of all time.

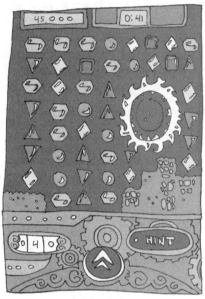

Bejeweled

In his own exploration of the match three genre, Professor Jesper Juul has boiled the match three genre down to four design foundations:[33]

- ○ **Manipulation:** When and how the player can manipulate the gems makes a difference in how the game is played. Players can manipulate gems as they fall or when they have fallen.

- ○ **Match criteria:** There are many ways to create match criteria. Matching can be limited by direction, the number of gems required to make a match, or the shapes or colors of the gems. These criteria can be greatly expanded when theming (where the gems are now objects or characters) is introduced into the game.

- ○ **Obligatory matches:** Can players perform a move if it doesn't result in a match? *Tetris* says yes. *ChainShot!* says no. It's a question you are going to have to answer as it affects your gameplay.

---

[32]As gems are the most commonly seen objects in match three games, the objects in match three games are often referred to as "gems" no matter what they look like.

[33]Juul, Jesper. "Swap Adjacent Gems to Make Sets of Three: A History of Matching Tile Games." Artifact journal. Vol. 2, 2007. London: Routledge.

○ **Time:** Time equals pressure on the player. It can manifest as a ticking clock or the time it takes for the next row of gems to drop. Remove time and you make the game a much more Zen experience. The developers of *Bejeweled* admit that it is the inclusion of the untimed mode that helped make their game a success. Allowing the player all the time they needed to keep looking for a match allowed players to search at their leisure. Without a fail state, the players kept playing.

Match three games and touchscreens are proving to be a match made in heaven[34]. *Trism* (Demiforce LLC, 2008) developer Steve Demeter earned $250,000 in profit within the first 2 months of the game's release[35]. And there's a reason for that success. The physical act of using one's finger to move gems feels good, as long as it is responsive and simple.

Looking at *Trism* today, would it stand out among all of the other match three games on the App Store? Unlikely, but it was that combination of market timing and gameplay simplicity that helped it be the "right game at the right time." Nowadays, the match three genre is heavily saturated on the App Store and developers really need an interesting angle to their game and a solid monetization plan before they potentially waste their time with this genre.

Another advantage to creating a match three game is that they have proven to be surprisingly flexible when merging with other genres. The *Puzzle Quest* series mixes RPGs with match three gaming. *Containment: The Zombie Puzzler* (Bootsnake Games, 2011) combines horror and color matching gameplay. *Dungeon Raid* permits multiple items matching, adds a line-drawing mechanic, and has RPG elements. The genre is limited only by the developer's imagination. What other genres can be mixed with match three gameplay? Driving? First-person shooter? Rhythm games? I look forward to seeing what you come up with!

To Clone or Not to Clone?

Despite all this success translating browser and console style games to the touchscreen market, there is a dark side. Okay, maybe not a dark side, but a side that feels pretty cheesy. I am talking about cloning. Cloning is where you copy a game's gameplay so closely that it could be mistaken by the uninformed for the real thing. Clones ran rampant during the arcade and early PC days. If a game didn't appear on a certain computer, a programmer would just make his own version. Since then, copyright laws have become stricter, but it doesn't mean this practice doesn't still happen. Of course, cloning popular games is nothing new. It could be argued that *Pong* was a clone of *Tennis for Two*. *Space Wars!* was a clone of *Computer Space*. Cloning has been with developers since the beginning of gaming . . . but it doesn't mean it's always appropriate.

---

[34]Sorry. Couldn't resist.

[35]`http://articles.cnn.com/2008-11-18/tech/iphone.game.developer_1_trism-iphone-app-store`. Granted, Demeter had the first good puzzle game available on the App Store when it opened, but it was still enough money for him to semi-retire from gaming.

There are two sides to every argument. The pro side says "it's a popular genre of game that isn't represented on the platform." Some people call it "business opportunity"; others call it a "rip-off." The con side says "come up with something original!" But the truth is that it's hard to create a truly original game[36]. If you *are* driven to create a clone, I recommend that you:

- ○ Come up with an original story. Gamers can smell a copycat from a virtual mile away.

- ○ Stop trying to rip off the lead character from a famous game[37]. Gamers can spot a copycat from that same virtual mile away.

- ○ Add something new to the gameplay or at least make some attempt to improve what didn't work in the original game.

. . . Or instead of ripping off old games, why not make up something new instead? Turn to Chapter 10 to look at some of the "new genres" of games by developers who did just that!

---

[36]Then again, I believe that just by the nature of YOU making YOUR version of a game is a big step in making something unique. I'm so conflicted!

[37]No one is fooled when you name your tormented, monster-fighting Spartan hero Argos, which sounds a lot like Kratos. Just sayin'.

DEVELOPER INTERVIEW 5

Sam Rosenthal

Developer profile: I first met Sam as a student at USC's interactive media program. His first job was at Disney Mobile as a game design associate on *Where's My Water?*, which dethroned *Angry Birds* as the top-selling game on the App Store. Not a bad start to a career!

Last completed/published project: *Where's My Water?* (iOS)

Company website: `disney.go.com/wheresmywater/`

Sam, thanks for taking time to talk with *Swipe This!* What was your inspiration for *Where's My Water?*

We found a bit of inspiration for *Where's My Water?* in *Cut the Rope,* and I think that's somewhat apparent in the final design (except Swampy's way cuter than Om Nom; just sayin'). *Cut the Rope* is a physics puzzler that does a great job taking advantage of the touchscreen with its incredibly creative mechanics. It is a bit shallow on the story side, which is not necessarily a fault, but an aspect we tried to spend more time developing in our game.

I play tons of mobile games. In fact, I think I've bought every single iOS Game of the Week since I bought my iPhone. My favorites always tend to be those that take advantage of the device's capabilities in a creative manner, such as *Fruit Ninja, Mirror's Edge, Infinity Blade,* and *Sword and Sworcery EP.* Once in a while, I like to play rereleases on iOS, like *Another World,* as long as the touch controls are handled well.

What gameplay and control challenges did you face when designing your touchscreen game?

We often had a hard time cramming a level onto a single screen, which was made more difficult because our spoiled alligator apparently demanded a pretty massive bathtub that took up a significant amount of screen real estate. The most obvious response to this problem can be seen in our multiscreen levels, but like every new addition, they created more challenges. We also ran into the same problems that plague every touchscreen game. How do you make sure the player's finger does not obstruct the gameplay? How do you present the same level on both an iPhone and an iPad even though they have different screen resolutions? Every solution was carefully tested and revised until it felt just right.

"Direct finger" vs. "virtual joystick": Which do you prefer and why?

In my opinion, the "direct finger" control scheme is unquestionably better. I am a firm believer in designing *for* a particular platform's affordances, not around them. The most fun touchscreen games would simply not play as well on any other type of device. I have yet to see a game that uses a virtual interface that would not function better on a device with buttons.

What were some of the challenges you encountered designing physics puzzles?

The problem with physics is that they can be hard to predict! A lot of my ideas that sounded great on paper just did not translate well when I implemented them in the actual game. Several concepts, such as jumping the water over a gap, required constant play testing and tweaking until the level design guaranteed a high rate of success. We also required a certain amount of particles to enter the bathtub to complete a level, which made it harder to implement some of our later mechanics that were designed to deplete the player's water supply.

What advice do you have for game designers who are creating their own puzzle games? What can they do to keep things fresh and interesting over the course of many puzzles?

Come up with a unique mechanic that can lend itself well to a variety of different puzzles. The core "digging" mechanic in *Where's My Water?* immediately made sense to players and gave us a lot of flexibility when designing levels. One of my golden rules of level design is to never create a level with an identical high-level concept to an existing level. No one wants to solve the same riddle twice, no matter how it is expressed. Always be aware of the concepts the game is already testing, and test different combinations of mechanics to create different types of player interactions. If all else fails, make more mechanics!

With so many puzzle games available for tablet gamers, what drew you toward this genre?

The team actually came up with the idea before I was brought on, so this might be a better question for them! Physics puzzles are popular on touchscreens because they are instantly accessible. As my supervisor would say, every human who has been alive for a couple of years has the necessary basis to understand a physics game. Like I said before, much of a puzzle game's overall success lies in the strength of its core mechanic. Additionally, it is crucial to make sure a solution feels satisfying rather than accidental. If a player reaches the solution without understanding the process, the level is not yet ready for prime time.

What is your prediction on the future of touchscreen gaming?

The future is always hard to predict in this industry. Just a few years ago, there was no App Store, and now it is one of the most successful game platforms in history. Any platform could emerge at any time and shake up the entire video game industry, and no one can say with certainty which platforms will continue to be successful even just a year down the road. I have long considered traditional video game consoles to be this industry's equivalent to the film industry's notoriously failed studio system, and their collapse may already have started, judging by the abysmal sales of dedicated portable game systems. Today, we want our games to be with us everywhere, but we do not want to be confined to a bulky device that can only play games or to a giant box that plugs into our television set. I am not sure which method of consumption will overtake consoles to become the standard, but whether it is mobile, cloud, or something we have yet to conceive, I am confident that it will come sooner rather than later. The video game industry is changing fast, so hold on to your hats!

chapter **10**

The New Genres

WE NOW STAND on the observation deck of the present, gazing at the viewport of the future of touchscreen gaming. It's a great view. The horizon is wide, full of possibilities. There are many bright stars, pinpoints, and supernovas. But looking at these stars is like staring at a lit Christmas tree with your eyes squinted. It's beautiful, but nothing is clear. If I could see this future clearly, I would be working on the next *Angry Birds* or *World of Warcraft* or *Minecraft* and spending the rest of my days rolling around in a swimming pool full of money[1]. No one can truly see the future.

But there is one thing we *do* know about the future: For each new technology that is created, new genres of games emerge—games that cleverly play to the strengths of the technology. And because you are smart (and you have read this book), you know those strengths are . . .

- ○ Portability
- ○ Short play experiences
- ○ Touch controls
- ○ Built-in camera(s)
- ○ Accelerometer
- ○ Gyroscope
- ○ Connectivity

---

[1]If this book sells well, there is still a chance this could happen!

Over the course of this book, you've seen many genres translated from other systems onto touchscreens. Now let's put on our monocles and examine genres that have naturally evolved on touchscreen systems. These are the new genres.

Micro-games

Miniature games (or mini-games) have been part of gaming since the early arcade days. While *Gorf* (Midway, 1981) and *Tron* (Bally Midway, 1982) were compilation games that included several short game experiences, it was *Major Havoc* (Atari, 1983) that created the first true mini-game: a *Breakout* game that granted extra lives and a *Lunar Lander*-style game where the player docked her spaceship at the star base levels.

Mini-games are common in console and computer gaming, interjecting much needed variety into longer gameplay experiences. I have played mini-games where the player plays a mini-game to lock-pick open chests, shoot cannons, hack computers, paint a picture, wrestle a minotaur, throw batarangs, jump rope, and perform a hundred other mundane activities in fun game form. Mini-games confirm my belief that anything can be a video game, given the right context and controls. (Want to have some fun? Think about what you did today and devise a way to turn it into a mini-game.)

Micro-games first appeared on the GameBoy Advance title *WarioWare Inc. Mega Microgames!* (Nintendo, 2003). Another *WarioWare* game came out for the Gameboy Advance, but the micro-game genre leapt forward with *WarioWare Touched!* (Nintendo, 2004). The DS's touchscreen controls made *WarioWare*'s micro-games feel faster and more frantic than its earlier incarnations. The key difference between mini-games and micro-games is duration; each *WarioWare* micro-game lasts no longer than 5 seconds (!), making them a completely pure expression of gameplay. Half of a micro-game's gameplay involves the player figuring out how to play the game. Since the player only has seconds to learn the game and pull off the correct move, primary actions should be kept extremely simple. *WarioWare* simplified the instructions brilliantly and described the player's goal in one of several single words: Pop, Slice, Tap, Rub, Pick, and so forth.

Variety is equally important when designing micro-games. Brainstorm as many wacky ideas as you can. Don't hold yourself back: The stranger the idea, the better. *WarioWare: Touched!* has players picking noses, carving classical statues, extinguishing fires by peeing on them, and rotating records to hear hidden messages. The game applies this strategy to art styles, too. The art in the *WarioWare* series varies from beautiful to surreal to crudely drawn. Keeping things weird will keep things interesting, and keeping things interesting keeps the player playing.

The last important component of micro-games is **quantity.** *The Moron Test* (DistinctDev, Inc. 2011) and its sequel[2] offers hundreds of logic and follow-the-direction puzzles, none of which last more than a few seconds to solve. Design as many micro-games as you can. It is going to take a lot of work to design, code, and create art for these games, but it's always easier to cut content than to shoehorn it back in. Even though micro-games are short, it doesn't mean your entire game should be.

Gesture Games

It's hard to believe how new touch-controlled games are compared to other game genres. Gesture games like *Angry Birds, Infinity Blade, Fruit Ninja, Cut the Rope,* and *Flight Control HD* are already making a big impact on the gaming world. It feels like they've been around for a long time, not a short time. I think that has something to do with how comfortable we feel playing with our fingers.

Now, I've hit the topic of gesture game design pretty hard over the course of the book, and I would be remiss if I didn't have some advice for you here. But since I just wrote nine chapters on the topic, I don't. Instead, here's some advice from the smartest person I know, *Star Wars'* Obi Wan Kenobi:

---

[2]The Moron Test 2. Duh.

". . . don't give in to hate – that leads to the dark side."

Obi Wan warns us that a great designer shouldn't desire to crush the player, but to create an enjoyable experience. A designer should be the invisible hand on the players' backsides, pushing them ever upward. Don't be a hater. Love thy player. Give players enough time to react between gestures. Surprise them as often as you can. Reward them as often as you can. Due to the "disposable" nature of touchscreen gaming, they will abandon a game as quickly as they pick it up. Nothing will make a player quit faster than a game that's too difficult.

"Let go your conscious self . . . and act on instinct."

This is good advice from the Obi Wan. If you have an idea for a great game, then make it! If your game feels too hard or too boring, then it is! If your gameplay is going in a direction that you don't think is right for your game, change it! Learn to trust that little voice in your head. It will give you some of your best (and craziest) ideas.

"In my experience, there's no such thing as luck."

Obi Wan is warning us that gesture controls should be tight enough to be responsive but loose enough to allow the player to make a mistake. Your players should never feel like it is the game's fault that they failed or it was dumb luck that let them succeed.

"Who's the more foolish, the fool, or the fool who follows him?"

Obi Wan reminds us that the most important thing about your game is that *you* are making it. Don't give in to trends when designing your game. Bring your own interests to your design. If you love archaeology and singing and sports, then find a way to work them into your game. Not only will your game be more authentic, but it will also keep your interest while you make it.

"Stretch out with your feelings."

Hmmm. Feelings. Like feeling with your fingers. Like feeling with gesture controls. Sure, that works! I think Obi Wan is reminding us to simulate real-world motions when designing gesture controls. Don't overcomplicate gestures. Keep them simple. Keep them real . . . or at least a reasonable facsimile.

"The Force will be with you. Always."

I have no idea what Obi Wan is referring to here. Something about the accelerometer, maybe?

Ah, I finally thought of some good advice for designing gesture games. Don't overcomplicate the number of gestures. Start with the game's primary action and let it be the foundation for all the player's gestures. (You don't have to be a Jedi Master to know that one.)

The Art of Art

There's something else the most successful gesture games share in common . . . and that's beautiful art. Don't kid yourself; game art is very important. Visuals are the player's gateway to your game. As I always say: "Great art lures 'em in, great controls hook 'em on, and great design keeps 'em playin'." As the touchscreen market grows more competitive, your game will require professional art. If you can't create great-looking art yourself, then you will need to partner up with someone who can. We'll solve that problem later, but how can you tell if something is great-looking art? Well, as the old saying goes, "I may not know art, but I know what I like."

Start by finding an art style you like. It might be a high-detailed realistic style. Or it might be a cartoony style. Or it might be a retro 8-bit style. Start by finding a game (or comic or cartoon or painting or drawing or photograph) that you like and get cracking on Google image search or . . . you could go old-school and do some research at the library. I think research is becoming a bit of a lost art. You can spend hours or days looking for images, but using the right search **keywords** will save you time and effort. Here's where having a good vocabulary helps. Let's say you are looking for a steampunk robot. Obviously *steampunk* and *robot* are good words to start with. If you enter *steam powered robot,* it yields very different images. Now try *clockwork robot* or *mechanical man.* Once again, each shows a very different type of robot. *Automaton* and *wind-up robot* and *Victorian robot* all yield very different results. When you find an image you do like, search that website for more keywords. If you can't find exactly what you want, use the images you do find as the basis for an image you create in *Photoshop* or some other photo manipulation program. Or use them as references for a drawing. At the very least, you can send these images to an artist to give her inspiration to create her own original work. Any image is better than no image when it comes to communicating your ideas to an artist.

While we're talking about art, let's talk about **cinematics** (also known as **cutscenes**) and **puppet shows.** Cinematics are pre-rendered movies that are created using computer graphics, flash animation, or any other method that you can animate. These cinematics can be created exclusively for your game or you can use pre-existing footage (if you are making a game based on a movie, for example). Puppet shows are cinematics that use in-game assets like character models and effects.

While cinematics are an easy way to tell your story, there also are disadvantages to having cinematics in your touchscreen game:

- ○ If not optimized for smaller screens, they can be tough to see.

- ○ The player can't do anything while a cinematic plays (if it is unskippable), which is annoying when your cinematic is longer than a minute or two.

- ○ Cinematics take up a lot of memory space, even when compressed.

- ○ Cinematics are time consuming and expensive to create. Even a few minutes can cost thousands (if not millions) of dollars to create, and that isn't counting voiceover, music, or sound effects.

An alternative to preloaded cinematics is to post a video on YouTube since all iOS devices come pre-loaded with a YouTube app. You can have your game call that app and launch the video when needed. The downside is that your video will not be available when the device can't connect to the Internet. While this method literally takes the player out of the app, the upside is that it is on YouTube, helping to promote your game!

Ultimately, you are going to have to decide whether or not to have cinematics or cutscenes in your game. The best advice I can give is that it totally depends on the game you are trying to make. There's no right answer, just the answer that's right for you. *"Trust your feelings, Luke."* Oh wait, that was the last section.

Tilt Games

When **accelerometers** were added to mobile devices, tilt games became the new hotness. Early hits like *Labyrinth* (Codify AB, 2008), *Rolando* (ngmoco, 2008), and *Motion X Poker* (Full Power Technologies, 2008) were not only great games, but they were great for showing off your brand new smartphone or iPad. Now, there's one thing video game developers do well . . . and that's capitalize on a trend. Soon games like *Doodle Jump* (Lima Sky, 2009), *Sky Burger* (Nimblebit, 2009), and *Tilt to Live* (One Man Left, 2010) introduced new paradigms to accelerometer play and controls. We covered accelerometer (and shake controls) pretty thoroughly back in Chapter 3, but I have a few more thoughts about accelerometer gameplay. For such a simple device, they offer some robust design options:

○ Control the world and not just the avatar. Play with the full range of rotation the accelerometer provides. How can turning your game world 45 degrees change the gameplay? 180 degrees? 360 degrees?

○ "Controlled uncontrollability" is when the player is racing out of control, but is guided by the environment. Tilt the device forward to go faster. Franticness can be fun! How fast and furious can your game get?

○ What a difference a shake can make! Use a shake move to let the player roll some dice, reload a gun, toss some bad guys around, or even jump.

Warning! Extreme device tilting can lead to the following: Changing perspectives. Obscuring glare. Disorientation. Foolish feelings. "Gamer wrist." Burning rash. (That last one might be caused by something else.) All of these can impact the player's experience over time. The initial novelty of tilting the screen can give way to fatigue and anything more than a slight wrist-tilt (as in *Doodle Jump*) can get old fast. Also, the ergonomics of tilt controls vary from device to device: Tilt controls on a larger iPad will require different tuning than a smaller iPhone or iPod touch to achieve the same results.

Endless Runners

One of the most intriguing new genres is the ***endless runner*** or ***distance game.*** The player controls a constantly moving avatar that jumps, dodges, ducks, flies, and climbs as far as it can while avoiding hazards and enemies. Success is measured on distance. Death comes quickly as these characters are (usually) one-hit wonders. The genre's roots lie in arcade side-scrolling shooters like *Scramble* (Konami, 1981) and *Moon Patrol* (Irem, 1982), and "chase" sequences found in platform games like *Disney's Aladdin* (Virgin Games, 1993) and *Crash Bandicoot* (Naughty Dog, 1996). Why aren't these called "jumpy scrolly games"? The chief differentiator is the word "endless."

The first true endless runner, *Canabalt* (Semi Secret Software, 2009) was praised for its combination of fast-paced movement, super-simple control scheme (one button to jump), and highly addictive "one more go" gameplay. It was a perfect fit for mobile devices. Seeing *Canabalt*'s success, more developers joined the race. Today there are many examples of the genre, including *Tiny Wings* (Andreas Illiger, 2011), *Whale Trail* (ustwo, 2011), *Ninjump* (Backflip Studios, 2010), and *Temple Run* (Imangi, 2011).

While the endless runner has a simple concept—"how high/far can you get?"—they don't need to all feel the same. Make your endless runner different just by adding a single gameplay mechanic . . . like any of these:

- **Hazards aplenty.** You don't need a lot of hazards for an interesting game. A limited tool set is often better to work with than a complex one. *Last Ace of Space* has just four types of hazards and enemies (jump, shoot, flick, and slide), while *Jetpack Joyride* has three (barriers, rockets, and laser beams). Sure, there are variations within these hazards (moving beams, long and short beams, multiple rows of lasers), but interacting with them remains consistent throughout the game.

- **We've got the beat.** As players react to jumps, obstacles, traps, and enemies, they fall into a certain rhythm. Your goal as the designer is to create this rhythm (or flow), but how many hazards do you need to create it? The best way is to start mathematically. Groups of threes and fives create nice blocks of rhythm. Place the obstacles, and then give the player a short breather. Of course you will want to change the patterns to keep things interesting and less predictable. A trick I use is to design to music. Try to get the player to "jump to the music." Even if you aren't playing the song, the player will feel the rhythm.

- **Fast or really fast?** The world of the endless runner is constantly scrolling, but how fast is too fast? Consider the player's reaction time when determining the player character's speed. You have to give the player time to react; otherwise, it just isn't fair. Amping up the player's speed creates pressure on the player and excitement. There are ways to give the player a break. *Jetpack Joyride*'s character speeds up as it travels further in the game, but vehicles will slow things down for as long as the player can keep the character equipped.

- **Which way?** Just by changing the direction of the player, you change the feel of the game. Players move from left to right in *Jetpack Joyride,* up in *Ninjump,* and into the screen in *Falling Fred. Mirror's Edge* makes the player go in all directions: up, down, backtrack, left, and right. Be aware that each direction presents its own challenges. Game world elements might be covered up in a game where the character falls into the screen. Players might not have enough time to react as they rush from left to right. Moving right to left has a physiological effect on Western players; it makes them feel like they are moving "against the flow" and not moving as quickly.

○ **Save the player or save the world?** The charming distance game *Bumpy Road* (Simogo, 2011) has the player pulling up and pushing down the road to make the player's car hop over hazards and collect items. In *Bed Bugs* (Igloo Games, 2009), the player doesn't even control the main character, but rather, protects him from bugs as he sleepwalks his way through the game.

○ **Music makes it awesome!** The secret to music for a distance runner is to keep it fast-paced. Whatever song you use should be more energetic than the action on-screen. The music never changes during the gameplay of *Last Ace of Space*, *Jetpack Joyride*, and *Bumpy Road,* but it's the choice of the *right song* that makes the difference between enjoying these games and being driven crazy by the same song playing over and over again.

○ **You only live once. Or do you?** One of the signature traits of endless runner gameplay is the "one hit = death" system. And while that adds an exciting sense of impending peril that keeps the player on edge during the game, sometimes it's okay to give the player a break. Whether it's *Lame Castle*'s hit points, *Robot Unicorn Attack*'s invulnerability, *Banditoo*'s time dilation, *Monster Dash*'s vehicles, or *Whale Trail*'s Frenzy which lets the player turn the tables on the enemies, *Pac-Man* style, give the player a breather and a fighting chance to better his score and play just a little more.

○ **The end . . . or is it?** They *are* called *endless* runners, but that doesn't mean they can't have an ending. Designing an ending for your endless runner gives the player an opportunity to take a break. The player is going to stop playing at some point, so you might as well have it be at a logical break in the game rather than after the character dies for yet another time. *Tiny Wings* builds the level's end into its gameplay: The little bird will fall asleep when it becomes night, but it's up to the player when night falls.

All these mechanics are great additions, but sometimes the simplicity of the player vs. the world is enough. Even with two or three mechanics, there can be plenty of gameplay to keep players engaged for weeks if not months or years. And the mechanism that does that the best is achievements.

Achievements are high scores with personality. They are missions, sometimes trivial and sometimes epic, that throw down the gauntlet to the player and say, "I'll bet you can't do this . . ." Originating on console systems (particularly the Xbox 360), achievements quickly spread to all gaming platforms. The truth is, achievements have always existed in games, but it was always the players bragging about them to each other. Now we have a formal system to back up those brags!

Current games offer several achievements to the player in addition to the "main" gameplay, offering interesting diversions to the player. Achievements work best when the player has some prior knowledge about them. It's why console game developers release the list of achievements prior to the release of the game.

iOS designers will have a system-imposed budget for the number of achievements they can offer and how many points each achievement is worth. Make sure to reserve some of your "achievement budget" for updates.

There are many different ways to create achievements. Often many of them are created during the course of the game's development as the team members think of ways to challenge themselves or just try to break the game. When creating achievements, I have found that achievements fall into the following criteria:

○ **Time:** This achievement has the player trying to achieve something within a set time period. Or a set number of times. Time achievements create suspense as the clock ticks down while the player scrambles to complete the task in time.

○ **Completion:** The player uses every object or weapon, plays every level, finishes all the missions, or rides every vehicle. Completion achievements expose the player to all the cool things you have designed in your game with the goal of getting the player to use them more often. In the end, players appreciate all the great content you've put in your game.

○ **Collection:** The player collects a set of prizes, captures all the enemies in the game, or finds every secret. This achievement rewards players for their compulsive behavior, making them feel that all that time they wasted trying to get every collectable wasn't such a waste of time after all.

○ **Social:** This achievement type rewards players when they interact with each other. You can earn achievements by inviting friends to play your game, reward players for giving away prizes to other players, or for simply participating in multiplayer games.

○ **Specificity:** The player earns an achievement for killing a specific number of enemies, receiving a specific score, or collecting a specific number of coins. Or he can earn an achievement for jumping over a bear wearing nothing but a top hat and underwear. Beware, as these achievements can feel "grindy" unless there is a worthwhile reward attached.

○ **Distance:** This achievement is rewarded when the player travels a certain distance, leaps a certain height, or reaches a predetermined location. This achievement is similar to specificity achievements, but has an emphasis on measurable distance, usually stated in real-world terms such as miles or feet.

○ **Economic:** This achievement rewards players when they purchase a specific item or class of item. The economic achievement has its pluses and minuses. It's a good way to expose your players to a game's shop or to let them know about a specific item that will help them. Then again, it can feel like a crass way to get them to spend their hard-earned change.

○ **Failure:** Why do you have to succeed to win? Several games reward players for dying several times in a row, getting killed in unique and horrible ways, or just outright failing to do the simplest of skills. A failure achievement makes the players laugh about their mistakes rather than regret them.

ACHIEVEMENT UNLOCKED!!
You Discovered a Secret Achievement!!

○ **Secret:** Have a plot point you don't want to give away? Want to surprise the player? Want to make the player wonder how many secrets there are in the game? Then keep your achievement a secret from the player by not making it visible to them until they unlock it.

ACHIEVEMENT UNLOCKED!!
You Didn't Drop Dead Since
Reading This Achievement!!

○ **Wackiness:** The more creative and unusual the achievement is, the more memorable it will be. And players will do some of the stupidest achievements in a game if they know they can earn a reward for doing them. For example, *Jetpack Joyride* awards an achievement for opening and closing the main menu slider 10 times.

ACHIEVEMENT UNLOCKED!!
You Unlocked All of the Achievements!!

Congratulations! You've read this whole section! Great job! Even a little recognition makes the player (or reader) feel good. As author Jane McGonigal[3] writes, rewards are why people like playing games. Sadly, most people don't receive much positive reinforcement in the real world, so is it any wonder why players want to spend more of their lives in the virtual world?

Augmented Reality

Creating a true virtual reality has been a goal of technologists since the early days of gaming. They believed the solution lay in heavy headsets, complex haptic systems, and claustrophobic simulation pods. There might be a virtual reality in our future, but in the meantime, augmented reality has come to mobile gaming.

Augmented reality uses a mobile device or game system's built-in camera to merge the real world with the virtual world. It's as if the player were looking through the cracks of reality to the game world that was always there; it's just that the player couldn't see it before.

Three dominant styles of augmented games dominate the market as of this writing: **_overlay_**, **_interactive,_** and **_positional._**

---

[3]Read more about Jane's great theories on games and gamers in her book, "Reality Is Broken."

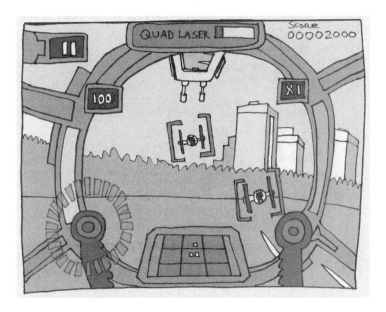

Overlay augmented reality games display digitally generated images over whatever the camera is looking at. The player views the world through a heads-up display (HUD), much like the title characters in the movies *Robocop* and *The Terminator*.

Games like *Star Wars Arcade: Falcon Gunner* (THQ Inc. 2010), *Mosquitos* (Makayama.com, 2009), and *Sky Siege 3D* (Simbiotics, 2010) use the real world as a background, while virtual enemies attack the player who fires (or swats) using virtual controls. However, not all overlay AR games are shooters. *AR Soccer* (Laan Labs, 2010) lets the player kick a virtual soccer ball, and *Par Tee* (Silvertech Studios, Inc., 2011) uses the accelerometer, compass, and GPS tracking to create a virtual golfing experience.

When creating an overlay game, be aware that depth perception can cause a problem for the player. Since the displayed object isn't affected by real-time lighting or atmospheric effects, it can look closer than it is in the code. Artificial objects can move faster than players can respond, so make sure to put some lag or rubber-banding into their movements to give the player a fighting chance. There is no law that you can't have cartoony objects in your AR game, but objects will feel less jarring to the player if some attempt is made to model reality.

Interactive augmented reality games use the camera and a preprinted digital pattern to display a virtual creature or vehicle that can be viewed and manipulated in three dimensions. Players maneuver around to see the object as long as they keep the printed digital pattern in view. If the view with the pattern is broken, then the image disappears. In *ARDefender* (int13, 2010), the player has to maneuver around in real space to aim and shoot at incoming creeps. In *Ar! Pirates* (HPN Associates, 2011), players sail and battle their pirate ships on desktops, floors, or any other flat surface. The illusion can be quite convincing given the right gameplay and interaction.

Another key feature of interactive AR games is interaction with virtual creatures. Games like *EyePets* (Playlogic Game Factory, 2010) allow players to "touch," guide, and play games with their virtual animal as viewed through the mobile device's camera. Once again, give the creatures AI; the effect can be quite realistic with the virtual critter reacting to the player's movements.

Remember when designing for interactive AR games, space can be quite limited (unless the player prints a large copy of the digital pattern). Try to keep the experience localized; otherwise, the players will spend all their time re-synching their cameras to the pattern.

Positional augmented reality games use the device's **global positioning device** (or **GPS**) to determine the player's location for use in gameplay. "Check in" games like *Foursquare* (Foursquare Labs, Inc., 2009) and *The Hidden Park* (bulpadock, 2009) turn the player's position and their frequency of location visitation into a game mechanic. *Paranormal Activity: Sanctuary* (Ogmento, 2011), *Parallel Kingdom* (PerBlue Inc., 2009), *Zombies, Run!* (Six to Start, 2012), and *World Siege: Orc Defender* (Kineplay, 2011) all use the player's position in the real world as the location that the play occurs in. It's actually pretty cool to see the street you are standing on or a building you are in be used as the setting of the gameplay. Something to be aware of when using a mobile device's GPS, though: Current GPSs use a lot of battery life. Until this hardware problem is solved, don't expect players to spend many hours playing your game. Give them (and their batteries) a break every so often so they can recharge before re-entering the action.

One last word of advice on AR games: If your player is going to move during your game, break up the experience into short bursts. The last thing you want is a player who is head-down in her device while playing your game walking into a wall!

Now Is the Future!

It just took a few amazing new features added to the gaming system's hardware to create a brave new world of gameplay concepts and genres.

Let's stand again on the observation deck of the present, gazing at the viewport of the future of touchscreen gaming. It's still a great view. The horizon is wide, full of possibilities. There are many bright stars, pinpoints, and supernovas. But those stars are all closer than they appear. All you need to do is reach out and grab one for yourself. Go ahead and make the future a reality!

GAME DESIGN SPOTLIGHT 5

No, Human

Format: iOS (Universal)

Developer: vol-2

Designer: Rolf Fleischmann

No, Human is a physics-based action-puzzle game, taking place during the latest conflict between mankind's puny struggle for meaning and the universe. With your skillful finger, a delight in destruction, and some patience, you will demobilize the human presence outside of planet Earth in a joyful way.

No, Human is a physics puzzler where space-faring humans strive to conquer the far reaches of space ... but the universe isn't having any of that. Although God may not play dice with the universe, he apparently does play bumper pool. The player, cast as a malevolent universe, flings asteroids into humans' spaceships, satellites, and space stations. The destruction of spaceships has never been so entertaining.

No, Human opens on asteroids spinning silently in space to Chopin's *Prelude, Opus 28, Nr. 4.*, which aptly sets up the game's self-important *2001: A Space Odyssey*-esque tone. An opening cutscene shows a bearded astronaut challenging the universe, "I will colonize you!" In turn, a toothed universe answers, "Oh, yeah?!" The game's droll narrator (and constant commentator) tells the player that "then the universe threw a fireball at the human." The player soon realizes that the narrator is talking to *her* as the tutorial begins. It's an extremely clever way to pull the player into the game quickly by making her part of the story. After the brief tutorial, there's very little in way of instruction—the new mechanics are pretty self-explanatory—or cutscenes—other than a slo-mo shot of the last ship being wiped out, giving the player a chance to relish her moment of victory.

Graphically, *No, Human* is extremely stylized and austere, like a photograph taken on the surface of the moon. Text is in simple and clean Helvetica. In-game navigation is equally uncluttered. Particles are used sparingly to highlight a fireball that can be thrown, and a meteor that can be ignited to indicate a shield has been struck.

3D characters, objects, and vehicles are lit but texture-free[1], reminding me of late 1990s games like *Out of This World* and the original *Alone in the Dark*. It's a great choice as there's no mistaking a screen shot of *No, Human* for any other touchscreen game.

If there is a common thread emerging from all of these analyses, it is that all these games' controls are **simple.** And *No, Human* is no different. The player flings his fireball with a single flick. The fireball has actual weight that comes into play when solving puzzles. A gentle fling will send it spinning slowly; a fast flick will rocket it across the screen. If the player holds down on the fireball before flicking it and then draws a line (unseen by the player), it will fly along the invisible trajectory to the player's target.

Speed, direction, timing, and patience are tools in this game designer's toolbox. Logic also plays a large part in puzzle design. These are thinking person's puzzles, and the clear answer isn't always the best one. But when it is, it is hilarious. For example, the title of the puzzle where a hapless space station floats between one small and one large fireball is *Sometimes the Choice Is the Challenge*.

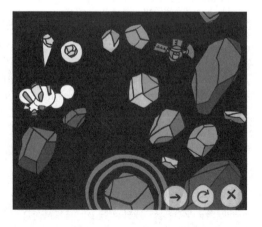

---

[1]Colored surfaces are technically textures, but that's beside the point.

Ricocheting fireballs against asteroids, using trajectories to make debris destroy the target for you, and cause-and-effect scenarios compose many of the puzzle's solutions. For every "nudge the fireball ever so slowly" puzzle, there are plenty of "fling the fireball right at the spaceship" solutions to satisfy the player's need for quick destruction.

A few simple mechanics add complication. "Inert" fireballs can be ignited when a "hot" fireball touches them or even passes close by. Positive and negative polarity asteroids push and pull fireballs around. Passing comets can be nudged out of their path to do the player's bidding. Chunks of magnetic ore follow in the wake of a passing fireball and often hinder as much as they help the player's plans.

You can take as long as you'd like to solve a puzzle (as long as the puzzle doesn't rely on timing elements) and for a game set in outer space, there's not a star grading system in sight. Instead, damage points (which I'll be damned if I know how they're calculated) and a bonus for using less than the offered elements are the game's only scoring systems. Although there are online leaderboards, in the end, score doesn't really matter: Just seeing the next puzzle is motivation enough to keep the player going. The game does allow you to skip a puzzle after seven failed attempts. This is an interesting twist on many puzzle games in which success is mandatory for progression. It's a good choice by the designer, who obviously wants you to enjoy the game, not be confounded by it.

As mentioned earlier, *No, Human*'s writing has a distinct personality. The narrator is cruel and wry. The puzzle titles give players subtle hints to their solutions: "Sacrifice One to Destroy Many" informs the player that both fireballs will serve different purposes. "Rejection Is an Opportunity" refers to using the negative polarity of an asteroid. I'll let you figure out the clue to what "Gravity, It's Attractive" means on your own.

Like the silence of space, *No, Human*'s sound effects are few and far between. There's a clunk when your meteor knocks into an asteroid, a distinctive blorp when the polarity of gravity mechanic is changed from positive to negative (and vice versa), icy asteroids crack when struck, and there is a delightful crash when a spaceship or station is knocked to bits. All this cosmic mayhem is set to the constant and gentle piano notes of Chopin and Edvard Grieg. If anything, *No, Human* is classy enough to give you only the sounds you *need* to hear, and nothing else.

So why is *No, Human* so good? I chalk it up to the following:

- ○ "Simple to play, hard to master" game play
- ○ A clean art style that makes it stand out from its competitors
- ○ Wit and personality in the presentation and writing
- ○ Increasing difficulty that never feels unfair

No, Human is available on iTunes.

DEVELOPER INTERVIEW 6

Andy Reeves

Developer profile: Andy Reeves had been working as a 3D artist in television and the theme park industry when he fell in love with the iOS market when it launched in 2008. An (almost) one-man operation, Andy designs, programs, and creates the art for his iOS titles, which range from casual endless runners to hardcore shooters.

Last completed/published project: *Die Zombie Die* (iOS)

Company website: http://www.3dsense.com

Andy, thanks for taking time to talk with *Swipe This!* Tell us how you got into making iOS games.

About 3 years ago, my wife got a job as a graphic designer/storyboard artist at a mobile app developer company. I was surprised to see how big the iPhone market, namely the iTunes App Store, got. I have extensive background in 3D modeling, animation, and design, as well as in 2D texturing, coding, and audio/music creation/design and editing. In 2008, my first iOS app was a photo-real, real-time 3D recreation of a known Hollywood landmark building and plaza. The app creation from concept to launch took about 5 months. It was an amazing experience and huge fun. Since this app, I launched two other iOS games: *Die Zombie Die* (a shooter) and *Dolphin Ride* (a casual side scroller).

What advice can you give to someone who wants to get into designing games for touchscreen/tablet space?

Learn graphics AND coding. Not just one or the other. With these two skill sets, you can do anything. If you are super skilled in 3D or 2D graphics, learn a little coding; it helps to come up with game mechanics and it helps the programmer. If you are a programmer, learn how to draw, how to use colors. You can even learn a little 3D and create your own 3D game. It always helps if you know a little about audio and music as well. Start with the iOS platform; it's the largest indie platform with good support and a good Software Development Kit (SDK) background.

Where do you start when coming up with a game idea: the gameplay mechanic or the visuals?

With an iOS platform, it's always the game-mechanics idea that comes first. With half a million games in the iTunes App Store, new games HAVE TO BE interesting, unique, and not just copycats of others. Visuals can come after the idea of the mechanics is locked, unless the game is about some cool new effect like flowing water or controlling smoke with a touch. In this case, the visuals are first, but actually we can call these effects game-mechanics as well.

How easy or hard is it for a beginner to learn how to create iOS titles? What software do you use?

Not easy, but not crazy hard. First, some coding knowledge is important. Unity3D is a good SDK to start with. Friendly user interface, a wysiwyg system, instant playback/testing, and platform-free compiler (output can be iOS, web, Android, PS3, Wii).

So the first step is getting a book on Unity, or Cocos2D. Do the tutorials, play with the source codes. Modify and understand the supplied code. Learn 2D graphics and change the textures in the code. Practice, practice, practice—and love what you are doing. You don't have to go to a fancy game creation school, but you have to read and practice a lot. Search for indie game forums and sign up, ask questions, and download other developers' free code samples and understand and use them. Never quit, and document your study. Get a textbook and write all the code snippets you learned; it will help later. Learn basic 3D, and create scenes and load them into your games. The rule is: Always enjoy what you are doing and it will come naturally. You might be stuck on a code that is not working for days, but eventually you will succeed. Never quit. Upload your creations to the App Store, even if it's free, and learn from the critiques. Gamers are mean on the iTunes App Store. There are always the ones who envy your creations and will diss your game, but don't be discouraged. You can learn even from those comments too. Game creation is one of the most enjoyable activities you can do on this planet, and you give enjoyable moments to gamers all around the world.

Do you think the "Freemium" model works, or will it cause trouble for the gaming industry in the long run? What gameplay features have you monetized in your own titles?

My 4 years of experience in creating iOS games and the research through my own titles show that gamers HATE in-app purchases. Some hate it so much that if they see that you are trying to sell them a level for 99 cents right on the opening screen, they will just quit the game and delete it (with a one-star negative review). They are okay with paying the 99 cents up front, and that's it. Ads in a paid game: a huge war. Ads in a paid game are a big NO-NO.

The best model is: Launch a free version so gamers can feel the controls and the gameplay. (Don't bother to put ads in the free version; the constant ping slows down the gameplay and the revenue is so small it doesn't really matter.) Don't give too much fun, just the right amount so they want the full version. The full version needs to have at least 50 levels (if not an endless scroller, or FPS style game). I would not put a "BUY NEW LEVELS" button at the end of the game. Create new versions of your game with 50 to 100 new levels, and launch it as a separate game. Update your games with 5 to 10 free levels every 2 to 4 weeks to keep up the interest and hype.

What are your predictions for the future of touchscreen gaming?

Huge. About a year ago, I thought mobile games would die soon. I changed my predictions completely. Touchscreen gaming will stay, and it will drive the game industry with power.

chapter **11**

Make Your Own *Star Wars*

WHEN VIDEO GAME designers get together, they often ask each other this question: "If you could design *any game you wanted*, what game would you make?" Every designer I know has an answer. I know I do, and I know you do! Go ahead and write yours below!

If I could design any game I wanted, it would be about:

_____

_____

Many years ago, my friend and fellow game designer Hardy LeBel asked me this same question. I gave him my usual answer: to design a *Batman* or a *Star Wars* licensed game[1] and I launched into my game design pitch on the world's greatest game.

 Hardy stopped me mid-pitch and asked: "Why would you want to do that?"

"Do what?"

"Design a game based on someone else's ideas? You're a creative guy; why don't you *make your own Star Wars?*"

MAKE MY OWN STAR WARS.

To be honest, the thought had simply never occurred to me before. I mean, I knew how to write a story and create good action scenes and design interesting looking characters[2]. I had all of the tools I needed to create my own universe of adventure, so why shouldn't I create my own *Star Wars*?

You don't need to follow someone else's idea. You don't need to play in someone else's universe. Your ideas are just as valid as anyone else's. All they need is to be brought to life.

The only thing stopping me was myself. And that's when I started coming up with excuses. It was easy to do. Making console video games back then was actually pretty expensive and complex. Here's what you needed to make one:

○ About 25–50 talented people

○ Many state-of-the-art computers

○ An office (and all its related paraphernalia)

---

[1] Keep in mind this was back in the early 1990s when there were very few good *Batman* and *Star Wars* games.
[2] If I do say so myself.

○ Thousands (if not millions) of dollars for development

○ Thousands for a developer's license and development tool kit

○ A publisher

○ Two or more years of your life

But fast-forward to today. In the world of mobile gaming, that list now looks something like this:

○ ~~About 25 - 50~~ 1–3 talented people

○ ~~Many~~ A couple of state-of-the-art computers and a mobile device

○ An office (and all its related paraphernalia)

○ ~~Thousands (if not millions)~~ Hundreds (if not thousands) of dollars for development

○ ~~Thousands~~ A hundred (or so) for a developer's license ~~and development tool kit~~

○ A publisher

○ ~~Two or more years~~ At least three or four months of your life

As you can see, there is a drastic difference in the required staff, equipment, time, and money between console and mobile game development. All those excuses? Too much money? Takes too much time? I don't have a team? I don't have a publisher? No longer relevant.

Current mobile game developers are more empowered, have their choice of cheaper and more powerful tools than ever, have access to more information and more potential teammates than ever before in the history of the medium. Teams are becoming smaller, more agile, and more flexible. Games are becoming quicker to develop. When it used to take years, now it takes months. You no longer need hundreds of thousands of dollars or even a publisher to sell your game. Listen: If you take away just one thing from this book, it should be this:

It has NEVER BEEN EASIER for YOU to create and sell your own video game.

In other words, stop making excuses and start making games! The game industry isn't going to send you an invitation to the game industry. I'm giving you permission to make your game. If you *love* games, then you will make the time to *make* games. If you can't make games full time, then make them in your spare time. Create your game in the evenings. On the weekends. Whenever you can. How to make games? By *making* them. It's the doing that matters.

I know this all can be scary. You might be nervous to start. You might not know where to start. Man, am I glad you are holding this book. It makes this next part much easier!

How to Start

Swipe This! isn't a book about iOS game production per se, but the least I can do is give you a push-start in the right direction. Assuming you are a game designer, let's start with a list of what you will need to make a game:

- ○ An idea
- ○ The Game Designer's Checklist
- ○ Wireframes
- ○ A team
- ○ Computers and software
- ○ A mobile device
- ○ The proper paperwork
- ○ Your submission categories
- ○ A monetization plan

Let's start with **an idea:** I know you already have an idea because you just wrote it down a few pages ago[3]. See? You've already taken the first step to making a game! (If you need more help, then read Chapter 2.)

The Game Designer's Checklist: Normally, a game designer would create a ***game design document*** (or **GDD**). This is a somewhat long document that lists everything in the game, from story to controls to mechanics and hazards. This document can get pretty long, but you don't really need a GDD to make a mobile game since many of them are pretty simple. My previous book, *Level Up! The Guide to Great Video Game Design*, covers GDDs in great detail. It even has a handy-dandy GDD outline to get you started.

However, rather than repeat myself, I have created the ***Game Designer's Checklist*** found in Appendix 4 of this book. The game designer's checklist (or **GDC**[4]) is a simple way to organize your thoughts and ideas. Remember that any game design document is fluid. It will always change as you develop your game. Make sure to share your design documents with your team members and anyone else who will read it. The more people you can show your ideas to, the more opportunities you will have to test them and see if they are sound. People are really good at poking holes in ideas. If your idea can hold up to repeated poking, then you have a strong idea!

---

[3]Go ahead and write in this book. That's what it's there for! If you're worried about ruining this book by writing in it, you can always go ahead and buy another copy. ☺

[4]No relation to the Game Developer's Conference.

One more thing about making a design document: I have learned that people respond well to pictures. A picture speaks a thousand words. Who wants to type a thousand words anyway (other than, say, book authors)? Draw a nice picture instead! People will look at your design document rather than toss it aside. The more pictures you include in your document, the better. Get them from comics, other games, Google images, or draw them yourself. Use whatever works to communicate your idea clearly to your reader.

Diversion #1: How to Storyboard Gameplay

The best use of pictures is to storyboard gameplay. It's like a comic strip that instructs the reader on how the player performs an action, interacts with a mechanic or hazard, or fights an enemy. In order to create storyboards, you first list all the ways the player can interact with a mechanic, then draw those scenarios. Simple! Make sure that you number your images sequentially so the reader can tell what order they happen in. Write any description text that will tell the reader what's going on.

Let's storyboard a hazard example. Say you want to design a hazard that is dangerous for your players to collide against, but if they jump on it, they can use it to defeat enemies.

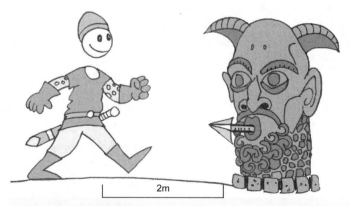

2m

1. Player approaches satyr spear column. When the player gets within 2 meters of the column, it will start to shake and make a "rattling" sfx.

1. Start your storyboard with the **setup.** Show how the hazard is encountered in context of the game.

2. After shaking for 2 seconds, the column will fire a spear that does
10 damage. This spear can be blocked by a shield.

2. Next show an ***interaction***—in this case, an image that shows what happens if the player collides with the hazard. Interactions often have several steps or different outcomes. Some interactions show negative results (for example, what bad thing happens to the player); others show the successful interaction (for example, how the player can defeat or avoid the hazard or enemy).

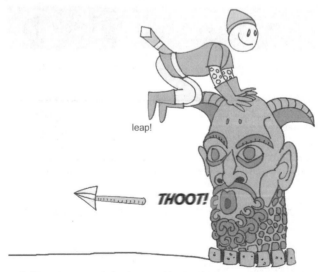

3. The column cannot be destroyed by the player.
The 2 second shake is just long enough for the player to safely vault over the column and avoid taking damage.

3. Since we've taken the negative interaction to its conclusion, let's draw the successful interaction—where the player safely jumps over the hazard.

4. The column may be used tactically if the player is pursued by an enemy...

4. Now, we see what happens when the player interacts with the hazard and enemies are around.

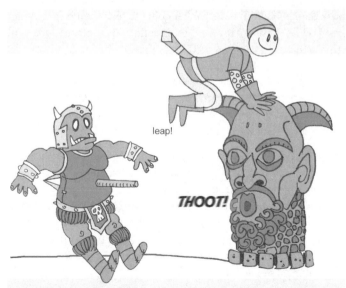

5. If the player can avoid being hit by the enemy and can vault the column in time, an enemy can take damage from the spear projectile instead.

5. And that's pretty much all there is to basic storyboarding!

Another type of storyboarding serves a slightly different function. It is called **_wireframing._**

Wireframes: Wireframes are storyboards that show how your player is going to navigate your game. The difference between storyboards and wireframes are that wireframes show navigation, not gameplay. Let's make our own wireframe example. Ready? Go! Since the developer's logo is the first thing the player will see upon starting the app, let's look at how to create the wireframe to show that.

logo

Diversion #2: A Word About Title Screens

Hey, wait a second! What's the name of your company? Let's take a break from wireframing to come up with a name. A **_developer name_** is just as important as naming your game . . . if not more so. It's the name of your identity as a game developer, so you really want to choose a good one. A bad name can also cost you real money if you are trying to sell your company. You might find it funny to call your outfit "Lousy Games," but how is a banker going to feel when he's signing a check made out to that name? While there are no rules to naming your company, you could follow this bad advice on things to avoid:

○ **Taken:** You could call your game company "Nintendo" or "EA" or "Rovio[5]" or . . . you could do your homework. Research existing names both in your own country and abroad. Sometimes a simple Google search is all it takes. You should avoid names that are even close. You don't want your company being mistaken for someone else's.

○ **Long:** You've just christened your company *Fantabulous Super-Awesome Ninja Monkey Novelty Factory*. Good luck fitting that name on a business card or your company letterhead. More importantly, think of how exhausted you are going to get answering the phone with that every day. All the more reason to keep your name short. Short = easier to remember, which is important when someone wants to hire you to make a video game or find you on an app search engine. I suggest a two-word or two-syllable name. It's simple and easy to remember and most importantly, short. People have notoriously bad memories, so be kind to them.

---

[5]I don't think you are that ignorant to name your company any of these names. Then again, think of how much business you'd have . . . for about 3 seconds!

○ **Jokey:** A developer friend once told me that if she knew she was going to be making serious simulation games, she never would have called her company "StupidSoft.[6]" You are a business. Your company name should reflect what you are making. If you are making games, then your name should sound like you make games, not novelty dog poop. Avoid a name that sounds too embarrassing. Sometimes names look great on the page but sound bad when spoken aloud. You should create a name that you would be proud of saying aloud. I call this the **"Batman rule."**

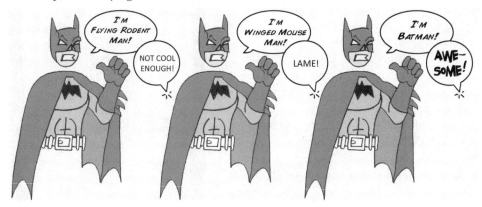

○ **Lazy/stubborn:** It's so much work to change a company name! Why should we change our name because all those dumb people don't get it? We have to print new business cards and design a new logo! Oh, the pain! Snap out of it! If you've created a bad name, then change it! *"Silicon and Synapse"* changed their company name to *"Blizzard,"* and last I heard, they turned out okay.

○ **Huh?:** I used to think that the coolest name for a game company would be *"Vaporware,"* which is industry slang for a game that people heard of but that has never come out for one reason or another[7]. However, that name is really only funny to me. Avoid obscure jargon or names made from a collection of abbreviations. A name like *"RogDevCo"* sounds like it refines oil, not develops video games. Don't make your name so obscure that people will be confused about what it means or why you chose it.

○ **Kwazy:** I have a rule when it comes to science fiction and fantasy novels. I don't read a book in which I can't pronounce the hero's name. I don't read a book where the writer uses apostrophes, substitutes the letter Y for other vowels, or uses "cutesy" or "wacky" spellings for the names of characters or places[8]. Characters with names like Fr'x or Sybllynne or Jenniferque. They make the reader wonder how to pronounce it. Avoid confusion and stick to proper English (or whatever your native language may be).

---

[6]Name, genres, and gender have been changed to protect those who made bad choices.

[7]I was going to insert a *Duke Nukem Forever* joke here, but that DNF had the nerve to finally come out after a 15-year delay!

[8]I might be a curmudgeon, but I know what I like.

○ **Not iconic:** Many video game developers use ***logos*** as shorthand for their company identity. Some companies (Apple, McDonald's, Nike) have icons that are so, well, iconic that they don't even need to show the name. A picture not only speaks a thousand words, but it also helps your customers remember who made your game.

Where were we? Ah, yes. Wireframing. Depending on the tools you use, your next wireframe screen might show the logo of code or a tool used to develop your game. This may be optional, depending on your licensing agreement. For example, if you use Unity basic, you are required by license to leave the logo/splash screens in place. The code will automatically include these screens. If you upgrade to their pro tools, you have the option to remove their logo. The tool developer often has options. For example: The Unity logo is available as normal, in a single color (black), inverted in light text (which works better against a dark background), or in a single color inverted (white). Please refer to the developer's identity guide for proper placement of the logo in relation to other elements on the screen.

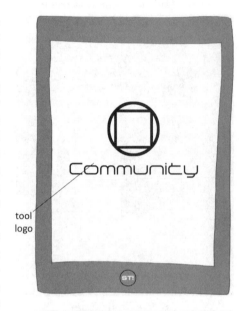

tool logo

The next screen the player will see is the game's title screen. Your title screen is one of the most important screens you can have in your game. It's your first impression, your debut to the world, and one of the most-seen screens in your game. It's a portal not only to your game, but also to other locations, such as social media and your game's store. A start screen is composed of many components:

○ **Name:** We covered creating your game's name in Chapter 4, but you still have to think about how it is presented.

title

links to social sites

start button

link to game center

What font do you use? Will it animate? Is it displayed large on-screen? It should be large on-screen. In fact, it should be the largest thing on the title screen . . . after all, it is the title.

○ **A compelling image:** Think of your title screen as the movie poster for your game. If you could sum up your game in one image, what would it be? Obviously, you want to show something cool but not something that gives away an important plot point.

○ **Copyright indicia:** The Apple and Android stores require a developer to register information pertaining to copyrights, but it's a good idea to include your copyright on your start screen. List the name of the copyright holder (usually the individual or company name), the year, and the copyright icon. You can protect your creation further by registering a formal copyright at the Library of Congress (or wherever is appropriate for your country of origin).

○ **Music:** Some developers don't think a mobile game should even have sound. It's pretty hard to hear sound on some devices, and almost impossible if riding on a train or subway. Why bother? Well, ear buds, for one. And two, music sets your game's mood. Think of the start screen as the overture to your game. If your game is scary, then get players into the mood with some foreboding music. If your game is action-packed, nothing says over-the-top like an exciting cinematic score. Or use music ironically. *Jetpack Joyride*, for example, starts with hoity-toity classical music: a stark contrast to the mayhem that is about to start. Even better, they changed the opening tune to "We Wish You a Merry Christmas" for their holiday release.

○ **Start button:** While your title should be the biggest thing on the screen, the start button should be the next biggest. The player shouldn't have to hunt to get into the action. Make sure it's clear, it's bright (red always helps), and it's easy to read.

○ **Difficulty level:** If you are going to let the player have a choice of difficulties, then the start screen is the place to indicate those difficulty levels.

○ **Link to in-app store:** While some designers might want to nestle the store in their game, I say "let it all hang out!" There's nothing wrong with letting your players see what they are in for over the course of the game. Even better, they will see the wide variety of things to buy and start strategizing how they are going to get them. There's nothing wrong with promoting a player's desire to get stuff.

○ **Link to social features:** If your game has connections to social networks like Game Center or Open Feint, or if you allow your players to connect via Facebook or some other sign-in system, let them do it on the start screen so they don't have to worry about it again for the rest of their playtime. Nothing is more annoying than a constant flood of reminders to link in and push stories.

Think of your wireframes as a road map for the player. Follow this road map and you won't steer the player wrong!

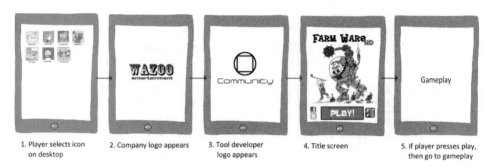

1. Player selects icon on desktop   2. Company logo appears   3. Tool developer logo appears   4. Title screen   5. If player presses play, then go to gameplay

Team Building 101

You've got an idea. You've got a design document. All you need now is some help to make your game. Who you gonna call? Try your friends. And if not them, how about some complete strangers? (Who, hopefully, will become your friends!)

That's not to say that you can't make your mobile game by yourself. It has been done. Over the years, "one-man teams" have indeed created successful games: *Prince of Persia* by Jordan Menchner, *Minecraft* by Markus "Notch" Perssen, and *Cave Story* by Daisuke "Pixel" Amaya are the standout examples. Those success stories, however, are few and very far between. It's easier to get by with a little help from your friends, as designer Casey Holtz recommends:

> *Making a game by yourself is hard and I would not advise it in most situations. When things get tough and you hit a wall, it is good to have some support and another mind to help solve problems. Always try to work with smarter, more talented people than yourself. Another set of eyes can also expose edge chases, design issues, and help formulate creative solutions to technical issues.*

Most mobile game teams are very small by gaming industry standards. The average mobile game team size averages five team members, though there can be more depending on the needs of the game. Unlike console developers, who perform very specific tasks, mobile developers need to wear many hats in order to get the game done. Those hats include:

Programmer: Someone needs to write the code to make the game work, and it might as well be you! Even if you aren't the math-y type, it never hurts to know how to write a little code. Fortunately, there are plenty of (relatively) easy-to-use development platforms, such as Unity, Cocos2D, Corona, and iTorque Game Builder, that make game creation easier. Familiarity with one if not several of these platforms is critical to creating your game. Without a code, you have no game! So, get to learning!

Development platforms come in a wide range of prices too, from free to thousands of dollars! Benefits to buying a tool range from access to additional plug-in tools to developer support. However, free is free! Free! Think about it: You can spend little to no money to make a real game! Pretty darn cool! The real question is where do you find these tools? Start with one of the following links:

- ○ **Cocos2D:** `http://www.cocos2d-iphone.org/`
- ○ **Corona SDK:** `http://www.anscamobile.com/corona/`
- ○ **Game Salad:** `http://gamesalad.com/`
- ○ **iTorque2D:** `http://www.garagegames.com/products/torque-2d`
- ○ **Shiva 3D:** `http://www.stonetrip.com/`
- ○ **SIO2:** `http://sio2interactive.com/`
- ○ **Sparrow:** `http://www.sparrow-framework.org/`
- ○ **Unity 3D:** `http://unity3d.com/unity/`

Are you getting used to that programmer's hat? Is it fuzzy and warm enough for you? Yoink! I just took off your hat! Time to put on a new one!

Artist: Art is as important as programming to game creation. Someone needs to create it, and that requires two things: talent and tools. Talent is something I can't help you with. What I can do is point you toward the right tools. You will need tools to create the three types of art used in video games: ***raster, vector,*** and ***3D polygonal.***

- ○ **Raster** or **Bitmap:** Images created using pixels. Bitmaps can be used to create ***sprites:*** single-frame images used to create game characters and objects that are animated, like a flip book. Bitmaps are also used to texture 3D models. The disadvantage to raster art is that they ***alias*** or look jaggy or distorted when reduced in size. Raster art can be created twice to four times as large as they are displayed on the device. This larger scale art is called **Retina** scale. Classic "retro" games use the distinctive bitmap art style.

○ **Vector:** Art that is created from points, lines, curves, shapes, and polygons. The production advantage of vector art is that it doesn't distort upon reduction and increasing of size, which is particularly important when creating art that can be used with both small mobile device screens and larger marketing or website images.

○ **3D Polygonal:** Using polygons, the artist creates a 3D model of an object, character, or world which then can be textured, lit, and animated if ***rigged*** by creating a skeleton that can be moved in the same manner as stop-motion animation.

Fortunately, you have at your disposal a variety of tools to bring your art, animations, and 3D models to life:

○ **Blender:** A free 3D modeling, texturing, rigging software program that also supports particle systems and compositing.

○ **Brushes:** An iPad painting app. Good for creating raster images. The developer of *Katana Jack* used this app to create his art assets.

○ **Adobe Flash:** A tool used to create vector and raster animations. Flash has audio tools and even code to create controls for browser-based games. Remember, if you are developing for iOS games, avoid Adobe Flash as it won't work on iOS devices.

○ **GIMP (or GNU Image Manipulation Program):** A free raster image tool that can also create animation.

○ **Illustrator:** An image creation and manipulation program that can convert raster images to vector images (among other things).

○ **Inkscape:** A free vector-based drawing program.

○ **Paint:** A simple painting program included with all copies of Microsoft's Windows operating systems. Best for creating low resolution, 8-bit style images.

○ **Photoshop/Elements:** A drawing and photo manipulation tool with many effects, plug-ins, and features. Great for creating bitmap images.

○ **Pro-Motion:** An inexpensive 2D program that is favored for 2D raster art and animation creation.

○ **Unity 3D:** Wait a moment, Unity is on both lists!? That's because Unity 3D is not just a game engine. It can be used to create and animate 3D assets. Through plugins, Unity offers the ability to manipulate or modify certain assets; but keep in mind it is definitely no replacement for a painting or modeling tool. The Unity engine is the same tool used to create many console video games and was first used in *Infinity Blade* on the iOS platform.

To create art for your game, you need at least a 2D art tool (like Pro-Motion or Photoshop) to draw sprites, create text (like fonts and logos), or create textures. You need a 3D tool to model characters, vehicles, levels, and so on. Odds are you'll need more than one person to create your art assets, so this is where you wear a third hat: **Art Director!**

To be a successful video game art director, you need to possess four abilities:

○ Select an art style and stick with it. These are styles like cartoony, realistic, retro, "just like (insert your favorite touchscreen game here)." The key is finding a style and sticking with it. If you change it, you are going to end up with a visual mish-mash.

○ Find or create examples of your art style. You can do this by searching online, in books, in other games, or in movies. Or draw it yourself! Whatever helps you determine your vision of what your game looks like.

○ Communicate what is important about this style to your teammates. To do this, you might need to create a style guide using the examples you found or created.

○ Offer constructive criticism and corrections to your teammates.

How do you do all this without being a total jerk? Like so: When you tell someone you don't like something, don't just say, "No." You should also give the "because." For example, you could say, "That model's hair sucks. Change it." And you would be a jerk. Or you could say, "You are doing good work, but I think the hair on your model should be less spikey because when the figure is viewed from far away, it will look more like spikes and less like hair. Here are some examples in the style guide for you to look at that might help." See? That was a much nicer way to give constructive criticism and feedback. If you are smart, helpful, and nice, you will go far in the world.

Alright, ready to wear the next hat? Let's try it on. I hear it's super popular with the ladies (and the dudes too).

Sound Advice

It's time to put on your **musician**'s hat. When I say musician, I really mean "the team member responsible for sound and music in your game." Being responsible for these assets requires many of the same skills that I previously listed for an art director. Just replace "art" in that list with the word(s) "music" or "sound effects."

That said, unless you are going to license someone else's music for your game (which can be a time- and money-consuming process), you still need to create and mix it. Fortunately, several tools are available:

- **Audacity:** A free digital audio editor that offers a wide variety of multi-track editing functions.

- **GarageBand:** A music creation tool that is available for purchase on the Apple App Store.

- **FL Studio**: Formerly known as "Fruity Loops", this digital audio workstation is a popular choice amongst non-musicians who want to make music.

- **Logic Pro:** A MIDI sequencer and digital audio workstation that is available for purchase on the Apple App Store.

- **Music Studio 2:** A music creation and mixing board app.

- **Pro Tools:** A multi-track tape recorder and mixer program.

- **Sound Forge:** Sound mixing and sampling software that supports a wide variety of formats.

I'm no musician, but I do want you to consider a few things when designing music and sound for your game:

- Remember that mobile gamers often play games with the sound off. Use visuals as well as sound to communicate your gameplay.

- Remember that most mobile devices can't support more than one music track and a few sounds playing at once, so don't design yourself into a corner if you want lots of sound assets to play simultaneously.

- Many video game songs loop, so don't forget to compose your music to be "endless." Remove silences at the beginning and end of your tunes and make sure everything "lines up" properly to make the transition from the end of the track back to the beginning smooth, without pops or jumps.

- Always test your final sounds or music on your mobile device before committing it to your game. That way, you can see if it's been mixed too low or too high.

○ Syncing music to a particular action is pretty hard for a game; just make sure your music is exciting regardless of whatever the player is doing. It's better to have fast-moving, exciting music when the player is doing nothing than have slow, boring music when the player is doing something exciting!

○ Most mobile devices allow players to enjoy games while listening to personal music libraries. Players will appreciate an interface that makes it easy for them to choose their own music.

The Three -ions

You have one last hat to put on, and that's the responsible hat of the **producer.** It might not be the most fun hat to wear, but it's necessary if you want to prevent your game's production from having problems. A successful producer possesses many skills: financial, organization, diplomatic, problem-solving, and people skills. The best producers are masters of the three -ions: ***preparation, organization,*** and ***communication.***

○ **Preparation:** A good producer is a prepared producer.

○ **Organization:** A good producer is an organized producer.

○ **Communication:** A good producer communicates regularly with his/her teammates.

Preparation: Be prepared! Start by making sure all pre-production elements—game design, pre-production art, and technical requirements—are complete (or at least to a state where everyone is in agreement). Knowing what tools your three disciplines (art, design, and programming) will need to get their work done and how to get them those tools quickly is a key task for a producer. Speaking of teammates . . .

Diversion #3: Where to Find Teammates

Dang! Those are a lot of hats! Too many hats for just one head. You're gonna need some help. Team building is one of the first major tasks a producer faces. It would be a lot easier if life were like *Dungeons and Dragons,* where you could recruit your teammates by finding them waiting for adventure in the local tavern.

Then again, maybe that's not too far from reality! Start with your **friends.** Have you ever sat around with your friends and talked about making a game? Stop talking about it and start doing it! Come up with a game design, clear some space off your kitchen table, set up your laptops, download some tools, and get to work! Remember that making games is a lot of hard work, so make sure your friends all know what they are in for before they start. You don't want to lose any friends due to disagreements you might have while making your game.

Schools are also a great place to build a team. If you are already enrolled in a game design program[9], then your team might be sitting right next to you in class! I know many teams that started working together on student projects and went on to form their own companies.

Much like the *Dungeons and Dragons* tavern, **online forums** bring like-minded people together to swap tricks, share experiences, form teams, and promote their games. The official development forums link to updates and tools. If you need a quick answer, some feedback on your game, or just to meet some new people, the forums are the best place to start.

---

[9]If you want to know where to go to school for video game design, the Princeton Review releases a list of the top 50 schools: http://www.princetonreview.com/top-undergraduate-schools-for-video-game-design.aspx.

Here are links to just a few of the forums available online:

- ○ **Android development forums:** `http://www.anddev.org`
- ○ **Apple development forums:** `http://devforums.apple.com/`
- ○ **Game Dev:** `http://www.gamedev.net/index`
- ○ **iDevGames:** `http://idevgames.com/forums`
- ○ **Indie Gamer:** `http://forums.indiegamer.com/`
- ○ **iPhone Dev SDK:** `http://www.iphonedevsdk.com/`
- ○ **Touch Arcade:** `http://forums.toucharcade.com`
- ○ **XDA developers:** `http://forum.xda-developers.com`

Already working in the video game industry? Many mobile gaming teams have formed while working on other titles. Sometimes the team is working on a game they aren't that interested in and want to make something more inspiring or interesting. Sometimes a team isn't given a chance to make a game out of an idea of their own. Sometimes a team wants to make a game "after hours." Sometimes a team is laid off but still wants to work together. Just be careful if you are going to create a game that you aren't getting paid to make. Avoid using your employer's equipment and check your legal rights: Many companies have "non-compete" clauses in their hiring contracts. New development teams will also need a contractual understanding of how their game is funded, who owns the game, and how profits are to be distributed. If you make the next *Angry Birds* you don't want the lawyers deciding these things for you!

Now that you've assembled your team, it might be a good point to assess your next steps and get organized.

Organization: Start by creating a ***schedule.*** List all the tasks required to create your game. Talk to your teammates to determine time estimates for how long it will take them to complete their tasks. Use an organizational tool like Microsoft Excel to create a task list. Don't forget to assign an end date based on those time estimates. Then it's up to your team to stick to those dates. However, it's not going to happen. Not because you are a bad producer, but because *games are made by people.* And people are only human.

Take the human factor into account when creating your schedule. There will be slippage on your schedule: People get sick, need to take days off, aren't as productive as they could be, have family issues, and so on. Be aware of these issues and prepare for them in advance.

If I were to sum up the experience of being a producer, it would be "hope for the best . . . and prepare for the worst." Follow this producer-ly advice as it may save your bacon if and when things go wrong:

○ Build a team . . . but be prepared to not have enough people.

○ Make a schedule . . . but allow for slippage of your dates.

○ Make a budget . . . but be prepared to go over it.

○ Design your game . . . but be prepared to cut content.

○ Build your game . . . but be prepared for things to break.

○ Test your game . . . but be prepared to act on the feedback.

As they say about riding a motorcycle, "It's not a matter of if you are going to crash; it's a matter of when you are going to crash." Being prepared will make the crash hurt a lot less, cause a lot less damage, and will be one you can walk away from.

Another thing a producer can help with is organizing game assets. Even if you don't use file-sharing software, it's good to devise a **naming convention** for your design, art, and sound assets.

I recommend the following naming convention: Project, description of the file, date, and file creator initials for identification purposes. Make sure you use hyphens (-) and not under-scores (_) to help with file sorting purposes.

For example, the first draft of my game design document for my new game *Rad Game* would be titled:

RadGame-GDDFirstDraft-20XX0614-SR.doc
Simple, right? Being organized is vital to making your project run smoothly. It's just as vital as good communication.

Communication: Take the time to regularly meet and discuss the progress on your game with all your teammates. Constantly assess completion times and adjust accordingly. Let teammates know as soon as possible when changes in direction have been made. Make sure documents are delivered to all team members to keep everyone on the same page.

The most important thing to do as a producer is to make games. The more games you make, the more you will learn. Experience is the best teacher. Learn from your mistakes (and there *will* be mistakes, so get used it!) and repeat your successes. It's just that simple.

Production Pointers

Oh my glob, there are so many things to learn about the production of a touchscreen video game that I could write an entire book about it! But since I'm almost finished writing this book, those details are going to have to wait. Instead, here a few pointers to help make your game better and production smoother:

- **Theory of Unfun.** During production, teammates will ask you if your game is "fun." The problem with the term "fun" is that it is too subjective. It's like "funny" or "sexy." Everyone has a different idea of what fun is. Sometimes a game idea or design feature might sound like it would be fun, but when you get it into the game, it isn't. While you can't always tell whether something will be fun, you can tell when something is *unfun*. This is where the Theory of Unfun helps. The Theory of Unfun states: "Start with a fun idea. Then start making your game. If something is not fun, remove or change it. When you are done removing all the unfun, all you should have left is the fun." How do you determine whether something is unfun? If everyone hates it, then it's unfun!

- **Gray box.** Before you make your game beautiful, make your game playable. Create your game in gray box form—simple, untextured levels and gameplay elements—that lets you play your game in its most basic form. You can resolve problems pertaining to physics, controls, camera, and spatial relationship while in gray box form. If you can get players hooked on your game even without it looking pretty, then you know you are on to something good!

- **Iterate, iterate, iterate.** Play your game. Find problems (or **bugs**). Remove bugs. Improve game. Repeat until your game is perfect!

- **Take it easy.** During the production of your game, you will be the best player of your game in the universe! But don't let that make you make the game too hard. Remember that the rest of your audience will be noobs. Don't be cruel to the noobs. Don't make your game too hard. Try to look at your game through the eyes of the newcomer.

- **Find the fun, then repeat.** If something is fun in your game, then make the player do it more than once. I find that three is always a good number to start with.

- **Let your mom play.** Rovio co-founder Niklas Hed tells a story about how after nearly abandoning *Angry Birds*, he watched his non-gaming mother burn their Christmas turkey. The reason? She was distracted by playing the game! The lesson? Don't cook and play games at the same time. The other lesson? Let everyone play your game. You should try to get feedback from gamers of all ages and levels. Ask them for ideas too! You never know where a good idea is going to come from.

Okay, that's enough production advice[10]! Let's talk about something that no one likes to talk about.

The Topic No One Likes Talking About

Face facts: It costs **money** to make games. Since the goal of making games[11] is to make money, we need to make money so we can keep making games. So how do you make money? Charging for your game is one way to start. Blog.Betable.com, an excellent blog on game monetization, elegantly sums up the conundrum:

> *The problem and opportunity raised by monetization in modern social and mobile games, especially freemium games, is that making money must be integrated into the game itself. For game designers, this means that their decisions will impact not only the user experience, but also how much money the game makes. Instead of getting paid $50 upfront for a game, your game's monetization hooks translate directly into revenue. Often times, this means game designers have to make trade-offs between gameplay and monetization. So how do you monetize your game effectively without tarnishing your game's creative vision?[12]*

---

[10]Got to save something for the next book!

[11]You can tell me that the goal of making games is art or social commentary or story telling or some other lofty creative goal, but in the end, it is a business.

[12]http://blog.betable.com/the-principles-of-game-monetization/#more-322

The best ways to design in monetization is to figure out how you are going to get players to pay for your content. In his talk[13] at Betable's event, Roger Dickey, the designer of *Mafia Wars* (Zynga, 2008) identified the many ways people pay:

- **Chance:** Dickey found that even when players had no idea what they were getting, they were still willing to buy the chance to find out.

- **Competition:** Beating an opponent, whether by having a better weapon, a tactical advantage, or just more stuff, is a strong motivator to have players pay. Dickey found getting the competitive edge appeals especially to hardcore male players.

- **Exclusive features:** Want to play the latest feature or a new gameplay mode? It only costs a bit more. *Justin Smith's Realistic Summer Sports Simulator* offered five events for free and ten more events for a fee.

- **Fun:** Items that make the game more fun and relieve player's pain such as the crystals that consolidate items and robots that kill bears in *Triple Town* are often worth paying for.

- **Identity expression:** Anything that makes your character, farm, or vehicle more interesting and personal can motivate players to pay. Companies like Valve, Roblox and Zynga have made fortunes off of hats alone.

- **Stat Progress:** Need to get to the next level in a jiffy? *Jetpack Joyride* lets players pay a small fee to skip missions.

- **Story:** Dickey was surprised to learn that players would pay to advance the storyline. He surmised that the feeling of progress the player gained outweighed the cost of the payment.

- **Vanity:** The more limited the item—whether by amount or time—the more desirable it is to the player. And they are willing to pay for that exclusivity and collectability.

Dickey suggests that you create your "master plan" for monetization. This outlines the way you are going to make money and what aspects of the game design will be impacted by whether the player has the option to buy or not. Many games allow the player to grind his way through the game, slowly earning the in-game currency at a slow rate. Players can buy things, but not as quickly as if they spend real money in the game. There are several game design mechanics that can be impacted by monetization including:

---

[13]An excellent talk which covers many topics about monetization. Watch it at http://vimeo.com/32161327.

○ **Collection completion:** Many games, especially those by Zynga, require players to complete collections to progress. In some cases, the players can have other players donate these items to them, acting as a *de facto* recruitment tool. The alternative is to have the players skip all the time and embarrassment of constantly harassing their friends for things and just pay for the items to complete the collection. Be wary of this mechanism as it has created user backlash from players who find that the constant demands for money can get tiresome.

○ **Consumables:** Particularly popular in Asian-made games, items can be bought with limited uses or a "rental time." Consumables are a pretty popular way to earn money (they remind me of the "just one more quarter" play of the vintage arcades) as are time periods where the player can earn a benefit or play a mode that they normally don't have access to. Some games have limited quests that, if not completed within a time frame, end prematurely, require another purchase to restart.

○ **Energy:** Do players have to buy energy to continue playing? It's better to let players get a little energy when starting out and decide whether they want to buy more energy to extend their play sessions. When offering energy to the player, give them escalating deals on larger volumes. The more you buy, the more you save!

○ **Territory expansion:** The player can have the option to expand her playfield. This is particularly noticeable on social games in which players are building farms or towns like *Smurf Village*.

○ **Wagering:** Letting the player change the outcome of the gameplay is very desirable to the player, especially if the outcome result is clear. King Cashing has purchasable items that let the player skew the percentage of when a hero, enemy, or weapon item comes up on its one-arm bandit style gameplay.

Now that you've determined how and what you are going to monetize, it's time to determine a price for these virtual goods. There are a wide range of prices to choose from. The prices range from as little as 99 cents to $9.99—and everything in between. Do your research and see what other comparable games are selling for. The answer to determining how much a customer will pay for your game is "as little as possible."

You can always lower your price point, but you can never raise it. So start with a price you feel comfortable debuting your game at with the intention of lowering it later on. Or you could go the other way and sell your game using the "freemium" model: offering it for free, with the intention of gaining revenue from other methods later on. I asked a few developers about the freemium model. This was their advice:

Chris Ulm (*Spellcraft School of Magic*, Appy Games):

> *Fair disclosure: Appy has transitioned from a "premium" model to a "freemium" model with all of our new releases. We feel that the only way to achieve volume and acceptance around the world is through games that have no friction to the end user. In order to make this work, you have to design games that have enough interaction and fun that players will find it worthwhile to buy virtual goods and support the game. We believe that players will pay for our work if we give them the opportunity to experience it and give them original games that they "want" to upgrade with virtual goods rather than games where they "have to" buy the good in order to keep playing.*

Not everyone is "down with the freemium" model. Casey Holtz offers another perspective:

> *The danger is in player fatigue, in being "nickeled and dimed" for their game content. I have played a bunch of "freemium" games, and most of the time their core gameplay is such a grind and a bore that I have no intention of spending money on what other games give me with the price of admission. They can set a precedent and a fear in the players' minds that they will have to continue spending if they want to continue enjoying the game. Oftentimes, it is better to know your complete investment right when you buy the game.*
>
> *"Freemium" games are currently so clearly designed to be a constant vacuum on your wallet that they [developers] currently forget to make them fun or provide a minimum amount of fun and value to make me care. They need to work on earning the players' time and trust before trying to shill their virtual goods on you. They are currently balanced so harshly that micro transactions are the only way to progress without going insane. A lot of "freemium" top-down, twin-stick shooters will give the player one weapon, with new weapons unlockable via in-game currency earned through killing enemies or for cash. The player is expected to grind in one arena, killing enemies to earn currency, to buy weapons, to kill more of the same enemies in the same arena . . . .*
>
> *The diversity, gameplay mechanics, and quality of content do not warrant the player time or financial investment. I could see this model tricking younger gamers who might be more impulsive to buy content, especially if the visuals are polished. I think these gamers will either grow to expect deeper, more engaging games or stop playing games.*

Clearly the debate isn't going to be answered here. Don't come away thinking that monetizing your game is a bad thing; you just need to be responsible while doing it. Right now, there are two ways to monetize your game: **in-app purchases** (covered in Chapter 9) and **advertising revenue.**

Advertising revenue is when you are paid by advertisers to feature their ads or products in your game. While an in-game ad generates revenue for your team, many players view ads as distractions that cheapen their gaming experience. Make sure you evaluate several ad networks and integrate your **software development kit** (or **SDK**) of choice as early as possible in the design process. SDK integration will almost always consume more development time than you budgeted, especially when you upgrade your app to a new version of the SDK. If you have ads in your game, try some of these techniques to keep them from getting too annoying:

○ **Make them skippable.** If the players don't want to click on the ad, don't force them. Let them get to the game.

○ **Make them interactable.** If you can make your game fun, then why not your ad? Give your ads some funny sounds, animations, or reactions when touched.

○ **Theme them.** The worst ads stick out like sore thumbs. Design your ads to look like they belong in your game's world.

○ **Put them in the game.** Some players don't mind having their in-game health power-ups represented as a bag of Honey BBQ Cheetos, while others might view it as a crass advertisement[14]. If you show the ad too often (or don't have enough sponsors to have a variety of products), seeing only one ad over and over will get repetitive.

○ **Deliver what they click.** If your player clicks on your ad, then make sure that it leads to the correct website! Check all your links before you ship!

The key to having in-game ads is to not be too demanding or greedy. Let the players decide when they are going to spend their money, and give them a good reason to spend it. It's just that simple.

Ship It!

Hooray! You're finally finished making your game! Congratulations! Now all you have to do is get it into the hands of your players. How are you gonna do that? **Market your game** and **submit your game**.

---

[14]. . . and a sneaky way to get the fine folks at Frito-Lay to send you a case of these delicious snacks.

Marketing Your Game

Marketing is letting people know about your game. There are hundreds of ways to do this seemingly simple task, and your marketing strategy can literally make or break your game. No pressure. I asked Charley Price (*Bag It!*, 2011) to share his team's marketing plan:

> *Use every social outlet you have. Every friend, family member, or random person who owes you a favor. For something to go viral, you need to get as many threads active as possible all in one "burst" and hope that something catches the mainstream and takes off.*

> *One of the most valuable things you can do as a developer is define your core target audience, so that you can hit a particular subset of the total population early and often to build awareness within that space. Our first game is themed around the supermarket, so we have endeavored to contact a wide variety of opinion leaders within that space—from major grocers to coupon providers to industry periodicals. By building awareness with those who can readily evangelize our product to our target consumer, we're hopefully earning honest, earnest recommendations of our product, which are by far the most valuable asset at your disposal.*

I asked Indie developer Andy Reeves (*Die Zombie Die*, 2010) the same question:

> *This is the hardest part of the indie game creation: to actually make money with your title. Here is the standard procedure:*

> 1. *Timing of the upload is very important. Make sure the game will launch more or less on Friday/Saturday. Your title will be in the "NEW GAMES" category for about 3 to 4 days until the newer games push your game out. This is the most important period for you. The visibility is huge. Your game icon should be catchy, the game name should be awesome, and so gamers will get interested. If your games don't go up in the rankings in these 3 to 4 days into the first 200, that's it for your game. Better thinking on the next title.*

> 2. *Create a new thread with your new game's info in the forum section on the major mobile game review sites (toucharcade.com being the most popular). Talk about your game a lot there, so you bump your posting to the first position (visibility).*

> 3. *Create a YouTube trailer and gameplay video of your game (very important). Post it in all the forums.*

> 4. *Ask gamers that use your promo codes to post a good review on the iTunes App Store.*

5. *Post promo codes in the forums where you featured your games; ask gamers that use you promo codes to post a good review on iTunes.*

6. *Wait a few weeks and see how your game does, then create a free version and launch it. The free version will do wonders.*

7. *Your free version HAS TO BE in the first 200 (rankings); otherwise, your game will not be visible ANYWHERE in the store. It can be searched only by name.*

Here is a valuable trick: There are 19 subcategories in the game store. At the upload you have to choose two. Choose wisely. The two strongest are Action and Arcade. It's very hard to keep your paid or free game in the first 200 in these categories. A good alternative is: Adventure and Puzzle category. These are heavy-duty categories where games do well, but still not as crazy as Action and Arcade. When I launched Die Zombie Die, *in the Action and Adventure, it went up in rankings to about 80, then in a few weeks slowly descended to over 200 in Action. But in Adventure, it stayed in the first 200 for months.*

Thanks for the good advice, guys! To sum it all up:

○ Get your friends involved. Have them spread the word about your game.

○ Select the right categories for your games. Apple lets you pick two categories (like Games, Entertainment, Travel, etc.) upon initial release—which you can change every time you submit an update.

○ Have a web presence, be it a blog, website, or social media page.

○ Pick the right partners. Interested parties will help you promote your game.

○ Send a test build to review sites ahead of the release of your game. Don't forget that press kit with a description of your game, links to where they can download it, and some great looking screenshots.

○ Release demo codes to get fans playing. They will spread the good word about your game.

○ Pick a release date and stick with it. Tell your fans when they can buy your game. Do your very best not to miss that date and risk disappointing or angering your audience.

○ Once you release a game, you are just starting! Marketing persists long after launch. Updates, whether they have new features or not, require their own marketing efforts.

You're not just marketing your game, you are marketing yourself: Don't pretend you are a big-shot company, unless that's the way you want your company to be perceived. In the words of Han Solo, "Don't get cocky, kid." But, you do need to be your biggest fan when communicating with the world. Don't insult or belittle your work. Don't give someone the opportunity to say, "Yeah, you are right. Your game does suck."

Remember that the first person you show your game to is your first audience member. So make sure whatever you show is up to the level of quality you need it to be when you are ready to show your game to the world.

You Can Make a Game, But Can You Do the Paperwork? (Submitting Your Game)

Your game is done, the word is out, the reviews are popping up online, and now it's time to submit your game for the world to play. Whether you are submitting to the Android Market or the App Store, you need to follow the correct guidelines. Mistakes in this process can cost timely delays and even cause you to miss your release date. Before you submit your game, make sure you have everything ready to go. Have you answered everything on this checklist?

- ○ What is your game's name?
- ○ Do you have a short description of your gameplay?
- ○ What compatibility: It is platform-specific (phone, tablet) or universal?
- ○ Have you got your copyright info prepared?
- ○ Do you have your game's SKU (stock keeping unit) ready?
- ○ What two categories fit your game's genre?
- ○ What keywords will you use to describe your game?
- ○ What is your contact URL?
- ○ What is your contact e-mail? You probably want to create an account specifically for your company or even your game.
- ○ What is your End User License Agreement (EULA)?
- ○ When will your game be available? You should always "hold for developers," which means you pick the day of your release. This allows you to create marketing that targets an exact day. The last thing you want is do is have an "automatic release" which sometimes releases your game at the worst possible date like after the traditional two-week freeze after the Christmas holiday.

○ How much does your game cost?

○ Do you need to **localize** your game for other countries? This means translating text or even changing some art assets to make your game more relevant (or less offensive) to other cultures.

○ Have you created all the artwork you need for the store? These include:

- Up to six screenshots of gameplay

- An app icon

- A store icon

Diversion #4: How to Design an Icon

An **icon** is one of the most important assets you will create for your game. Let's look at some well-known icons for inspiration:

Cut the Rope: The great thing about this icon is the whole game is right here! Om-Nom, the rope, the candy, even the scissors. It's like a mini-tutorial in icon form!

Angry Birds: According to the team at Rovio, they fell in love with the character first and came up with the game later, which makes perfect sense to why they featured it on their icon. But even more importantly, their color scheme of a red bird on a light blue background pops.

Jetpack Joyride: Some icons not only feature the character but also the feel of the game. I really like this image of a very excited Barry Steakfries blasting forward on his stolen jetpack. It looks like so much fun that I want to do it too!

Spider: The Secret of Bryce Manor: Rather than using the realistic art style found in Spider, the icon designer went for a cleaner, more representational image.

Creating a visual symbol for your game allows you to sum up the game in icon form—and if it's good enough for Batman, it's good enough for me[15]! Here are my ultra-secret tips to designing an iconic icon:

- ○ **Clarity:** Make the images in your icons easy to see. Remember when we talked about character silhouettes in Chapter 7? You want to do the same thing here. The stronger the silhouette your image has, the easier to see on that tiny mobile device screen.

- ○ **Iconic:** If you could sum up your game in one image, what would it be? Once you've figured that out, *that image* should be your icon. An icon is often the first thing a player sees in the online store. Make it memorable, cool, funny—whatever you think will best sum up your game. Since your icon will become your game's identity, make sure it looks great!

- ○ **Color:** Learn some color theory, son (or, er, daughter!)! Yellow, red, and bright green grab the eye more than dark blues, purples, and blacks. Bright colors are easier to see on small screens. Contrasting colors make images pop. Look at the most compelling icons and see what they do to grab your eye.

- ○ **Avoid text and numbers:** If you use raster art, then text runs the risk of aliasing or blending together to make it unreadable—especially when reduced down. Consider skipping words altogether if you want an international audience to enjoy your game.

You can use any graphic tool (Photoshop, Illustrator, and so forth) to create your icon; just make sure it's the correct size! iPhones and iPads have a standard size for their icons (an iPhone App icon is 57 × 57 pixels [px], iPhone 4 is 114 × 114 px, and an iPad App icon is 72 × 72 px), while the icon used in the App Store is 512 × 512 px. The Android store uses a scalable scale depending on the density of the item viewed: 36 × 36 px for low density, 48 × 48 px for medium density, 72 × 72 px for high density, and 96 × 96 px for extra high density. If you need more guidance and inspiration, you can find plenty of examples and tutorials online.[16]

---

[15]Maybe this should be the "Batman Rule"?

[16]The best app icon guide I've found is here: `http://mrgan.tumblr.com/post/708404794/ios-app-icon-sizes`.

Now Where Were We?

Andy Reeves has this to say about the Apple App Store submission process:

> The App Store submission is awesome. A perfectly thought-through system. It has a workflow that HAS TO BE followed. I have a nice 5- to 6-page note in my notebook on the steps, and I always follow them. My apps and games have never been rejected. Test your games before you submit; don't be sloppy. The game should be unbreakable. Read the suggestions on the Apple site and don't break the rules. For example, don't put: "coming soon" buttons in your game. Also: All buttons should work. Don't use copyrighted logos or names. Also, if the user can type in anything, then a profanity-preventer system HAS TO BE built in; otherwise, your app will be rejected.

> Other notes on the App Store approval process: Uploading is a breeze, but prepare all your graphics in advance (icon, five splash screens, description, keywords [max. 100 characters, no spaces, only commas between the key words]), support e-mail name, support website, company website. All info has to be correct and working (i.e., e-mail).

> There are few key tricks that should be followed in the game compiling process, that require trial and error, but when you get it, it will work all the time. Just follow the workflow precisely. The App Store uploader will check your binary for specific codes, so if something is missing the uploader will reject it and you can try it again. The approval takes about 4 to 7 days (more before holidays). The App Store and approval process is halted between Christmas and New Year's. This is the biggest down time that needs to be calculated.

> Don't try to put a specific date for the launch date. You might miss it because of the approval process, and it will mess up your ranking among the new apps. Just upload it when you are ready and keep it at the default date (launching on the approval date). All in all, the App Store works perfectly. Trust it.

Well, there you go!

Post-Release Strategies

Finally your game is out, your marketing has been effective, and your monetization is bringing in income. You're pretty much done with your game, right? Wrong! Unlike the "fire and forget" days of arcade and cartridge system gaming, your audience expects you to follow up your initial release with more content!

Fixing bugs can be done with ***patches:*** updates to your code and art that solve problems, improve gameplay, or even just make the game look prettier. Many developers offer **content updates** that add new quests and missions, store items, or theme their games to the holidays.

Design your game plan for these updates even before you release your game. Stick to your schedule. If you are confident that you can make your deadlines, then let your audience know when they can expect new content. Their excitement and online discussions about your game will hopefully create some great (and free) word-of-mouth marketing.

Be aware that app updates on iOS require your game pass through approval all over again. Games that passed approval in your 1.0 version could be flagged as objectionable in version 1.1 and fail submission. Different judges have different opinions about content. If you are fixing a critical bug, you can request an expedited review from Apple, but otherwise assume that an update will take the same time (about 2 weeks) to be approved as your initial release.

Updates are not only great opportunities to fix everything that is wrong with your game, but to improve content including your game's name, icon, metadata, keywords, and categories. During one update, Halfbrick added fat and skinny scientist characters to *Jetpack Joyride* just to add a little visual variety to the game. Each update also give you 50 fresh promo codes from Apple to distribute to reviewers and other people you want to see your game. Use these updates as marketing opportunities to promote your game to fans as well as customers who might have not wanted your game in the first place because of a problem you have fixed! You definitely want to make sure you communicate any content changes to your audience. For example, knowing that an annoying bug is being fixed should create some goodwill with your audience—it shows that you care enough to make sure the game is as fun as it can be.

The key to additional content is to think ahead to what the player might want, quickly resolve game problems, and address customer concerns as they happen. Put yourself in your audience's shoes: The customer is always right!

What to Do for an Encore?

The first step is to flip back to the beginning of this book and start again! If your game is a success, you might want to create a **sequel.** Take a critical look at your game and determine what you could do better the second time around. Maybe there is a gameplay idea or story point you weren't able to get in the first time. Now is the time to get it into the game. Some developers feel that the first game is where you figure out how to do everything in your game, and the sequel is where you make the game you wanted to make the first time. AAA game producer George Collins has a rule about sequels that I call the ***"70/30 rule."***

The 70/30 rule states that every good sequel keeps 70% of the game content the same as the first game while adding or changing 30% of the content to offer something new. My additions to this rule are: (1) Keep anything that worked the same. This can be controls, camera, or combat systems. Don't make the player relearn core systems. (2) Throw out anything that doesn't work (remove the unfun, remember?) and find a way to improve it. If it can't be improved, maybe it doesn't belong in the game. (3) Advance the adventure! What's the next step of the journey that your player and characters are on? Players have fallen in love with your game for a reason. Keep them in love; don't go switching characters or key elements without having a good reason that is clear to your audience.

Even if your game isn't a success, **NEVER GIVE UP.** Did you know that "overnight success" *Angry Birds* was the 52nd game that Rovio developed? If they can stick with it and create a massive success, then so can you! So hop to it! Start making that game! I can't wait to see what game you create!

GAME DESIGN SPOTLIGHT 6

Angry Birds

Format: iOS (available in lite, HD, and "Seasons" versions)

Developer: Rovio

Designer: Jaakko Iisalo

The survival of the Angry Birds *is at stake. Dish out revenge on the green pigs who stole the birds' eggs. Use the unique destructive powers of the* Angry Birds *to lay waste to the pigs' fortified castles.* Angry Birds *features hours of gameplay, challenging physics-based castle demolition, and lots of replay value. Each of the 288 levels require logic, skill, and brute force to crush the enemy.*

If you haven't heard of *Angry Birds* by now, then you probably live in a cave. So, Batman, it's like this: Players slingshot colored (and angry) birds into rickety structures to collapse them onto green pigs. Yeah, it's a physics puzzler. As of this writing, *Angry Birds* has become the most downloaded game ever[1]. To the casual observer, the game might seem like an overnight sensation, but *Angry Birds'* success is due to a series of very smart design choices.

---

[1]http://www.reuters.com/article/2011/11/02/us-rovio-idUSTRE7A137Q20111102

Angry Birds' primary action is flinging. The player pulls back on a slingshot and lifts her finger to launch the bird across the screen. A process made simple by limiting the player's options. Players don't have to worry about reloading their sling-shots or the order in which birds are launched. Players can only fire at a 60-degree arc. (You can "fire backward" and waste a shot: one of the few player-unfriendly actions in the game.) This makes accurate aiming a matter of inches, or rather degrees, than feet. This isn't a bad thing. Players play better under limitations. Why have them make unnecessary decisions? Let the player concentrate on playing. Little touches help the player succeed. For example, a dotted line guide marks a launched bird's path to help the player "aim" the next shot.

Launching a bird by a different degree yields a totally different result. This is the benefit of physics, the inherent randomness that gives the player predictable yet unpredictable results. The building designs capitalize marvelously on this notion. A wooden beam that will shatter if a bird hits it dead on will become a support for the rest of the structure if only knocked down by a glancing hit. This means that although there are definitive ways to win (and win efficiently with only one or two birds), there is plenty of room for variation.

The birds evolve, keeping things interesting. Some birds split into threes, others speed up when touched a second time. Others explode like bombs, poop out explosive eggs, inflate four times their size, or boomerang around to smash on the backend. And then there's the sardine loving Mighty Eagle, a gigantic bird that obliterates everything in its way . . . for a one-time payment.

But it isn't the flinging or the variation of the birds that makes the game so fun; it's the destruction. Destroying things is satisfying. We don't get to do it very often in the real world. It's the best part of the game: *Angry Birds* lets players indulge in one of their most basic desires, presented as good, clean fun. Once you see *Angry Birds* in action, you understand *Angry Birds*.

Detractors are quick to point out that the *Angry Birds* game mechanic isn't original. Armor Game's *Crush the Castle* debuted as a flash game online in early 2009 and migrated over to the App Store in September of that year. *Crush the Castle* has players using a trebuchet to knock down structures and crush knights and

their king. Sound familiar? But the difference between *Crush the Castle* and *Angry Birds* is inclusiveness. *Crush the Castle*'s trebuchet requires skill in launching; the arc of the projectile makes it challenging to get a precise shot. The rocks often leave the screen, adding to the tension of where they will hit. The *Angry Birds* slingshot requires skill to use, but the arc is not essential to making successful shots. The camera zooms out to let the player always see what's going on. *CTC* has *Monty Python and the Holy Grail*-esque characters that squirt blood when smashed. *Angry Birds* has cartoony pigs that poof into smoke when crushed. *CTC* is not a bad game, it's just a niche game: one definitely catering toward the trebuchet crowd[2]. What it was missing was ***inclusiveness.***

---

[2]While there are over 11,000 trebuchet launching videos on YouTube, ask the man-on-the-street what a trebuchet is and you'll probably get blank stares.

The entire *Angry Bird* experience is well crafted. The start screen is lively and draws you in. Backgrounds scroll by as birds fling about. Madcap music plays. The game certainly seems fun even before you start playing. A large PLAY button beckons the player to jump right into the game, while five simple but clear icons sit at the bottom of the screen. A gear represents options; an award podium leads to leaderboards; a grail links to achievements; a sinister eye links to the Mighty Eagle, a pay-to-own "solve-all" cheat system; and finally, an arrow links to social networking like Facebook and Crystal. It might be because developer Rovio is European[3], but the simple and (mostly) text-free interface screens are very approachable. This extends to the cutscenes, which are text-less and voice-less screens showing scenes of the "story."[4] It reminds me a lot of the stories in the LEGO games. The game relies on physical comedy and nonverbal communication to get the story across, and it works. Charlie Chaplin and Mickey Mouse won over international audiences the same way almost 100 years ago.

After pressing play, the crafty level select screen appears. Seven selection screens each contain 21 puzzles, for a grand total of 147: The player's mouth waters just to see all of that delicious gameplay. Unfortunately, the majority of the puzzles are locked, meaning you're going to have a lot of bird flinging to do. Fortunately, completing puzzles takes only a few seconds to a minute and the player whizzes through puzzles at a pretty good clip. It is here that the thankfully-for-the-rest-of-the-iOS-industry-not-patented-by-Rovio three-star system first made its appearance. It's an elegant system. My only complaint with the star rating setup is that it isn't implemented as clearly as it could be. As far as I can tell, it's one star for crushing all pigs, no matter how many tries you take. The second star is for using less than the allowed birds. The third star is awarded for beating a predetermined high score that isn't revealed to the player. However, the bars for earning these aren't that high and it's enough to motivate the player to "catch them all." Stars become the new Pokémon . . . and there's less unique art for the team to create as well.

---

[3]Finnish, to be exact.

[4]Apologizes for quotations, but it ain't Shakespeare: Pigs steal eggs, birds get angry, birds get eggs back. Whoops, Spoiler Alert!

Speaking of characters made from simple shapes and primary colors, the *Angry Birds* character designs use primary shapes (circles and triangles) and colors (red, blue, and yellow), which make them easy to distinguish even in mid-flight. According to designer Jaakko Iisalo, the *Angry Birds* characters were created before the gameplay was developed. Were the simple but easy to see designs a happy accident or savvy design? It was probably a little of both. Simplicity makes each bird and enemy easy to distinguish even with a zoomed-out camera—nice consideration for the player who prefers to see the whole screen.

I have to acknowledge the cleverness of the pig enemies' design too. Their bright green color contrasts with the birds nicely[5] and makes them easy to see amidst the clutter of wooden beams and stone slabs. The filthy smirk they have when you fail to smash them all is a great motivator for the player. It just makes you want to crush those little so-and-sos all the more. Multi-stage pigs (that wear a helmet) and the King pig are scaled differently from "grunt[6]" pigs, making them appealing targets.

---

[5]Remember, good guys wear primary colors, bad guys wear secondary colors.

[6]Sadly, pun intended.

Puzzle complication comes from the game's designers rearranging the limited number of elements in increasingly more challenging configurations, from sturdy constructions to complex cause-and-effect structures. There are a few clever setups, like a wheeled vehicle and an airplane. The building materials also escalate in durability, from wood to glass to stone. TNT boxes show up to provide a little flash and help crack some of those tougher items. A little perplexing is the appearance and disappearance of a few physics objects over the course of the game. What happened to that smiley-faced rolling ball? Was it too unpopular and phased out? Oh well, sometimes these things happen.

Sound design gets as much attention as the rest of the game. From the twittering of the birds, to the crash of the breakable items, to the chipper victory sting, *Angry Birds* is minimalist sound design at its best[7]. Only the important events have sound cues and all else be hanged. Not everything needs to make noise: only the right things. The main theme song is sufficiently wacky, and I'm sure we'll be hearing more of it until we are sick of it when *Angry Birds: The Cartoon Series* premieres. So why is *Angry Birds* so good? I chalk it up to the following:

- ○ Simple controls that showcase the touchscreen
- ○ Well-designed characters for both personality and functionality
- ○ Physics add just enough variation to make the same puzzle feel different
- ○ Destruction never gets old

Angry Birds HD is available on iTunes.

---

[7]Danish modern, Ikea, minimalist sound design . . . It must be something in the Nordic water.

App-pendix 1
The Class of 2008

MESSAGE BOARDS BUZZED with excitement as gamers eagerly awaited the opening of the Apple iTunes App Store. Since spring 2008, Apple had teased its debut into the gaming market, showcasing a wide variety of games for the iPhone 3G. Among those games: *Backgammon*, *Super Monkey Ball*, *Enigmo*, *Cro-Mag Racer*, *Spore Origins*, and *Kroll*[1].

When the App Store finally opened on July 10, more than 160 games were available for purchase. A wide variety of developers were represented on launch day—including big players such as EA, Sega, and Namco, and independent developers like Pattern Making Co. and Bootant. Several debut games wisely played to the strengths of the iPhone, including the accelerometer, tilt functions, and touchscreen. Other games shot straight for the heart of the casual gaming audience. For example, 18 sudoku games were available for purchase the first day alone.

After scouring through hundreds of blogs, user videos, message boards, and websites, I've been able to re-create the list of games available on the App Store that day for the first time. On it, you'll see which publishers were eager to dive into this new format (Hudson Soft, SEGA, Namco, and EA) and which up-and-coming publishers (Chillingo, Gameloft, and Jirbo) were attempting to make their big grab into the new market. It's surprising to see how many games from the dawn of gaming were back for one more go. Most compelling is the number of independent developers on this list: they were the pioneers of this new market and some of them reaped small fortunes (and some big ones) simply from being there on "day one."

It's important to note which genres were popular at the dawn of iPhone gaming and how far the market has come in a few short years. Surprisingly (compared to other gaming systems) many of those early games are still available for purchase (and have even migrated over to other gaming systems). Games available for purchase have been marked with an asterisk (*).

Arcade Games
- **Air Hockey*** (Personae Studios)—Inspired by the classic arcade game
- **Air Hockey Fingertip Sports** (Sea Lion Games)—Flick the puck to score
- **Alien Invasion*** (PHD Gaming)—Awful-looking "touch to destroy" game

---

[1]While featured prominently during Apple's App Store promotions, both *Spore Origins*, a simplified version of Will Wright's evolutionary simulation and *Kroll*, a fantasy action-adventure game from Digital Legends Entertainment, were scheduled for a September release.

○ **Bomberman Touch!—The Legend of Mystic Bomb*** (Hudson Soft)—Explode bombs to defeat enemies and explore mazes

○ **Bounce*** (Jirbo)—*Whack-a-Mole* clone

○ **Break*** (Jirbo)—Cartoony *Breakout* clone

○ **BreakClassic** (Bootant)—*Breakout*-style game

○ **BreakTouch 3D** (Bootant)—Sister product to *CubeRise 3D*, complete with rotating playfield

○ **Bullfrog*** (Outer Level)—Hop a frog around to eat bugs

○ **Chimps Ahoy!*** (Griptonite)—Bounce a coconut to break bricks and collect prizes

○ **Comet Cowboy*** (Maverick Software)—Draw on the touchscreen to lasso asteroids

○ **Cybersaurus 3D*** (Darxun)—FPS featuring a robotic dinosaur

○ **Dactyl** (John Allen)—Touch bombs to defuse them

○ **Discovery Channel Cannon Challenge*** (Discovery Communications)—Artillery combat game promoting the Discovery Channel's show, *Future Weapons*

○ **Dreigit (aka Space Rocks)** (crajcdesign)—Nice-looking *Asteroids* clone

○ **Ikanoid** (aka Space Buster*) (Storybird)—*Arkanoid* clone

○ **iTilt Pinball*** (Random5)—Substandard pinball game

○ **Ms. Pac-Man*** (Namco)—Port of the 1981 arcade classic

○ **Pac-Man*** (Namco)—Port of the 1980 arcade classic

○ **Solar Quest*** (Neon Surge)—Side-scrolling game where player avoid hazards and collects coins

○ **Space Monkey*** (Glu Mobile)—Spin monkey to collect and deflect space trash

○ **Space Out*** (Binary Square)—*Space Invaders* clone

○ **Space Trader*** (Kechbs Software)—Sci-fi asset management RPG

○ **StarSmasher*** (espressosoft)—3D sci-fi rail shooter a la *Star Fox*

○ **Super Pong** (Coby King)—*Pong* clone

○ **Tank Ace 1944*** (Chillingo)—3D tank combat game

○ **Tap Tap Revenge** (Tapulous)—Fast-paced music rhythm game

○ **UEIpong** (UEI)—Bare-bones *Pong* game with network sharing

○ **Ultranium 4*** (Julien Meyer)—Space-themed *Breakout* clone

○ **Vector Pong** (Gyrocade)—*Pong* clone with *Tron*-style graphics

○ **ZEN Pinball Rollercoaster*** (ZEN Studios)—Pinball where player tilts game to view board from different angles

Breaker Games

○ **Aurora Feint** (Danielle Cassley and Jason Citron)—Fantasy-themed puzzle/RPG hybrid and harbinger of the Open Feint mobile social gaming network

○ **Bejeweled** (Popcap)—iPhone version of hit game

○ **Bejeweled 2*** (Popcap)—iPhone version of hit sequel

○ **Bubble Bash*** (Gameloft)—Pacific Islander–themed *Bust-a-Move* clone

○ **ColorRise 3D*** (Bootant)—*Tetris* clone with rotating playfield

○ **CubeRise 3D*** (Bootant)—*Bejeweled* clone with a rotating playfield

○ **Critter Crunch*** (Capybara Games)—Swallow and spit out critters to break lines with cute graphics

○ **Diamond Twister*** (Gameloft)—*Bejeweled* clone with accelerometer features and storyline

○ **JawBreaker** (Mundue.net)—Simple candy-themed *Bejeweled* clone

○ **Picnic Poker** (Sea Lion Games)—Poker-themed *Bejeweled* game where player matches poker hands rather than colors

○ **Rockfall** (Pyrofer's Projects)—*Boulder Dash* clone

○ **SEGA Columns Deluxe*** (Sega)—Classic falling gem breaker game; also includes *Puyo Pop*

○ **Spinblox*** (Binary Square)—*Bejeweled* clone with cartoon graphics

○ **Tap-a-Brick 3D** (Balazs Vagvolgyi)—*Breakout* clone

○ **TetoTeto!!** (Macer Software)—Lame *Tetris* knock-off

○ **Tetris*** (EA)—Classic handheld puzzle game nicely presented

○ **Touchcris** (Nigel Williams)—Poor *Tetris* clone with 3D viewing option

○ **Tris** (Noah Witherspoon)—Decent *Tetris* clone

○ **Trism*** (Demiforce)—Slide rows of triangles to make a color match

Classic Games

- ○ **3D Card Games** (Freeverse)—Classic card games
- ○ **5 Card Touch*** (Griffin Technology)—Poor video poker game
- ○ **AcidSolitaire Collection HD*** (Red Mercury)—Solitaire with photographic backgrounds
- ○ **Aki Mobile Mahjong Solitaire** (Ambrosia Software)—Classic Chinese-themed Mahjong game
- ○ **Backgammon*** (PosiMotion)—Basic backgammon game
- ○ **Blackjack 21*** (MobileAge)—Blackjack with impressive selection of environments and themes
- ○ **Blackjack Run*** (Seahorse Software)—Blackjack game
- ○ **Blip Solitaire*** (Maverick Software)—Another solitaire game
- ○ **Carrom*** (Personae Studios)—English version of pool
- ○ **Cookie Bonus Solitaire** (Free)—Cookie-themed *Klondike* game
- ○ **Demon Solitaire***/**Demon Solitaire free** (Cliff Maier)—Bare-bones solitaire
- ○ **Disney's All-Star Cards** (Disney Mobile Studios)—Classic card games (*Go Fish, Hearts*, and so forth) with Disney characters
- ○ **Five Dice*** (Pelted Software)—*Yahztee*-style game
- ○ **Freecell*** (MobilityWare)—Standard *Freecell* game
- ○ **iMahjong*** (Jirbo)—Mediocre version of classic game
- ○ **Las Vegas Solitaire*** (Cliff Maier)—Standard solitaire
- ○ **Lucky 7 Slots*** (Griffin Technology)—Poor Vegas-style slot game
- ○ **Mahjong Solitaire*** (Sunsoft)—Bright graphics for this standard game
- ○ **Mondo Solitaire*** (Ambrosia Software)—Excellent game with more than 100 variations
- ○ **Moonlight Mahjong*** (Michael R. Howard)—3D presentation for expert players
- ○ **Motion X Poker** (Fullpower Technologies)—Shake dice poker game with impressive lighting effects; early fan favorite to show off the iPhone
- ○ **Platinum Solitaire*** (Gameloft)—Nice presentation but a basic solitaire game
- ○ **Pyramid*** (MobilityWare)—Basic pyramid solitaire game
- ○ **Pyramid Solitaire*** **(Free)** (Seahorse Software)—Egyptian-themed game

- **Shanghai Mahjong*** (MobileAge)—Excellent mah-jong game with lots of graphics and play options
- **Sol Free Solitaire** (Smallware)—Solitaire game with many variations (*Klondike*, *Demon*, *Yukon*, and so forth)
- **Solebon Solitaire** (Smallware)—20 game variations
- **Solitaire*** (MobilityWare)—Standard game
- **Solitaire CAO** (Mike Orr)—Mediocre solitaire game
- **Solitaire City*** (Digital Smoke)—Includes 13 games and leaderboard functions
- **Solitaire Forever*** (Mike Sedore)—3D playfield and 150 games
- **Solitaire Top 3*** (PosiMotion)—Basic solitaire game
- **Super Jong*** (Jirbo)—Another mah-jong game, this one's by Jirbo
- **Texas Hold'em*** (Apple)—Play poker against digitized characters
- **Vegas Pool Sharks Lite*** (Chillingo)—Average billiards game
- **Wee Spider Solitaire*** (Smallware)—Spider-themed solitaire
- **Yulan Majhong Solitaire*** (Maverick Software)—Standard mah-jong game

Puzzle Games

- **2 Across*** (Eliza Block)—Crossword game
- **ACTSudoku/ACTSudoku Easy** (Houdah Software)—Straightforward sudoku game
- **Aqua Forest*** (Hudson Soft)—Liquid dynamic physics puzzles
- **Big Bang Chess** (Freeverse)—Computer chess game
- **Big Bang Sudoku*** (Freeverse)—Space-themed sudoku
- **BlockPuzzle** (Telconi GmbH)—Sliding block puzzle
- **Brain Challenge*** (Gameloft)—Brain twisters and puzzles in the vein of *Brain Age*
- **Chess and Backgammon Classics** (Gameloft)—Chess and backgammon together at last! And in 3D!
- **Crosswords*/Crosswords lite** (Stand Alone)—Classic crossword game
- **Cubes*/Cubes Light** (Manta Research)—*Rubik's Cube*-style puzzler

○ **CubicMan Deluxe*** (TeemSoft)—Roll the cube with an eye to the end of the maze. Bizarre.

○ **Enigmo*** (Pangea Software)—*Incredible Machine*–style game where players fill jugs with water or fire. Players can download user-created levels.

○ **Enjoy Sudoku (aka Enjoy Sudoku Daily and :) Sudoku*)** (Jason T. Linhart)—A long-running sudoku game with new challenges updated daily.

○ **FLOverload*** (DS Media Labs)—*Pipes* clone

○ **Game Pack Vol. 1*** (On-Core)—Features *Suduko, Wordfind,* and *Picture Flip.* All mediocre.

○ **Hangman RSS*** (Finger Arts)—Classic word guessing game

○ **Imangi** (Imangi Studio)—*Scrabble* meets *Rubik's Cube*

○ **Jirbo Match*** (Jirbo)—Match item game

○ **Kamicom Suduko*** (Sans Pereil)—Changing backgrounds can't make this version any better

○ **KillerSudoku** (Houdah Software)—Ugly-looking version of classic

○ **KuGon/KuGon lite** (IV Realms)—Solve number puzzles to reveal mosaics

○ **Lumen*** (Bridger Maxwell)—Bounce lasers by using mirrors

○ **Match It*** (MobilityWare)—Match item game

○ **Morocco*** (Thomas H. Aylesworth)—*Reversi* clone

○ **Mr. Sudoku*** (Ambrosia Software)—Charming bee-themed game

○ **Nikoli SUDOKU Vol. 01*** (Hudson Soft)—Sudoku by the "creator" of the game

○ **Numba*** (Cobra Mobile)—Based on the game *Bookworm* but with numbers instead of words

○ **Platinum Sudoku** (Gameloft)—Impressive version that also features *Kakaro*

○ **Quordy*** (Lonely Star Software)—*Boggle* clone

○ **Radius*** (Pattern Making Co.)—Rotate ball controller to locate targets

○ **Rubik's Cube*** (Magmic)—Based on the popular 1970s puzzle game

○ **Rubik's Cube 3D** (Balazs Vagvolgyi)—*Rubik's Cube* clone

○ **Satori Sudoku*** (Kevin Kozan)—You guessed it, another plain sudoku game

- ○ **SUDOKU*** (EA)—Nicely presented, but average sudoku title
- ○ **Sudoku (Free)*** (Mighty Mighty Good Games)—No-frills version
- ○ **Sudoku** (Hudson Soft)—Game features English and Japanese fonts
- ○ **Sudoku** (Shekhav Yadav)—Substandard version of classic game
- ○ **Sudoku Classic*** (Phase2 Media)—Stripped-down version of *Sudoku Unlimited*
- ○ **SudokuManiak** (Alexandre Minard)—A plain variant of sudoku. Available as *PuzzleManiak**.
- ○ **Sudoku.MD*** (Rightsprite)—Japanese-themed sudoku
- ○ **Sudoku Pro** (Out of the Bit)—Mediocre sudoku game
- ○ **Sudoku Unlimited*** (Phase 2 Media)—Robust sudoku game including clever "hand-written" graphics
- ○ **Surf Shack Sudoku** (Surf Shack Software)—Blandly presented sudoku game
- ○ **TSudoku +** (James)—Poor sudoku game
- ○ **Tile Sudoku*** (Magnetism Studios)—Basic wood tile sudoku game
- ○ **Trivial Sudoku** (Trivial Technology)—Bland presentation of standard game

Racing Games

- ○ **Crash Bandicoot Nitro Kart 3D*** (Activision)—Based on the popular console game series
- ○ **Cro-Mag Rally*** (Pangea Software)—Caveman-themed tilt racing game
- ○ **Wingnuts MotoRacing (aka Motoracer & Motochaser*)** (Freeverse)—Use the accelerometer to steer your cycle and collect coins

Rolling Games

- ○ **aMaze*** (Redwheels)—Labyrinth-style game
- ○ **De Blob*** (THQ)—Roll, tilt, and bounce De Blob as he paints the city
- ○ **Dizzy Bee*** (Igloo Games)—Tilt bee to collect items and avoid hazards
- ○ **Labyrinth*/Labyrinth Lite** (Codify AB)—Based on wooden tilt toy

○ **Marble Mash*/Marble Mash Lite** (Jirbo)—Labyrinth-style game

○ **South Park Imaginationland*** (RealNetworks)—Tilt and roll the South Park character Butters to collect items

○ **Spinner Prologue*** (Fuel Industries)—Tilt game with arcade-style graphics

○ **Super Monkey Ball*** (Sega)—The first big game on the iPhone. Port of the GameCube game

The Others

○ **Battle of Waterloo** (Touch Tomes)—Sloppily made historical, choose-your-own adventure

○ **BattleAtSea*** (Pelted Software)—*Battleship* clone

○ **ChartFightSP** (Mutant Piano Software)—Clever cartography-themed battleship game. Available as Chart Fight SP*.

○ **Cube Runner*** (Andy Qua)—3D dash game. Don't hit those blocks!

○ **Galcon*** (Hassey Enterprises)—Space-themed strategy game similar to *Risk*

○ **iGotchi*** (Smack Fu)—Tamagotchi game

○ **Paper Football (aka Jirbo Paper Football*)** (Jirbo)—Flick the football, just like in high school detention class

○ **Vay*** (SoMoGa)—Port of the classic Japanese RPG

App-pendix 2
Touchscreen Template

IN ORDER TO design a touchscreen game, you need to consider how it is going to look on-screen. You also need to think about how all the elements (avatar, enemies, environments, puzzle elements, UI, HUD, and so forth) will fit on-screen as much as how your game is going to play. Creating a mock-up is a great way to quickly start visualizing a game. Here's how you use this handy-dandy template:

1. Place the following page face down onto a copy machine.

2. Make a photocopy of the page[1].

3. Close book, set it aside for future reference.

4. Using a pen, pencil, marker, crayon, brush, or any other writing implement, draw your best representation of what your game will look like. It doesn't have to be pretty, but it must convey all the elements you feel are necessary. (If your game has multiple modes, you should make a representation for each one.)

5. Show your drawing to someone else (co-worker, spouse, relative, stranger) and see if he understands what is going on in your drawing. Ask him how he would play the game you drew. Use your fingers to simulate gameplay. Use your mouth to make sound effects if you have to. If the individual understands your game idea, then go to Step 6. If not, go to Step 7.

6. Congratulations! You have successfully communicated your idea. Now go make what you drew into a game (hopefully with better art).

7. Crumple the page up, recycle it, and start over again with Step 1.

---

[1]You can also rip the following page out of the book, but then you'd have to buy another book. Hmmm. Maybe Step 1 should be "rip the following page out of the book."

screen template

landscape view

portrait view

App-pendix 3
Gameplay Storyboarding Template

SAY YOU HAVE a great idea for a gameplay mechanic but you aren't the one coding the game. You could wave your arms around or use sock puppets to communicate your idea, but I find nothing works better than a good ol' pencil and paper. But because things in games move, you are going to have to ***storyboard*** your ideas to help get them across.

Making a storyboard is just like drawing a comic strip. You want to show a sequence of actions that happen in the game. For example, if you want to show how a character jumps over a deadly pit of spikes, you would draw the first panel of the character approaching the pit of spikes, the second panel of the character jumping over the pit of spikes, and the third panel of the player landing safely on the other side and going on his merry way.

Storyboards are simple to use. Just photocopy the template found on the next page. Then grab a pencil or a pen and use the template to help you design any of the following:

1. **Movement:** How do elements in the game move (from the player's avatar to puzzle pieces)? How will players navigate their character past a mechanic and hazard? How does a vehicle steer? How does the player select and place a puzzle piece? Or flick an object?

2. **Combat:** How do enemies attack or how does a specific combat move work?

3. **Cause-and-effect gameplay:** If the player does something in panel 1, then what happens to him in panel 2?

4. **Camera:** How does a game camera move to showcase an element in the game?

5. **UI design:** What happens when the player loses health? Or gets a high score? Or beats a level? Or reveals a major plot point?

6. **Cutscenes:** Storyboard cutscenes or instructional sequences.

7. **Interface design:** How does the player enter a level or access an option screen?

Just think about what you want to show in your game and draw it! You don't even have to be an artist. Just do your best!

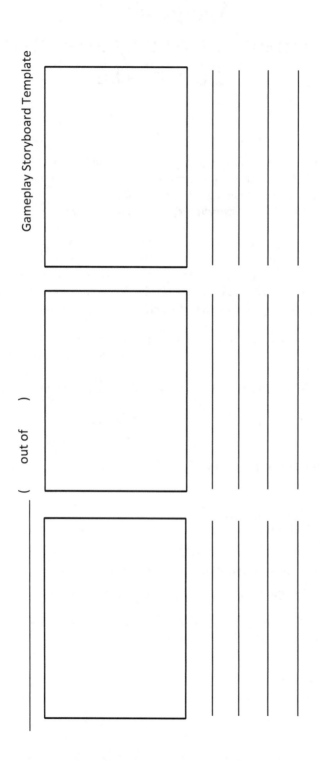

Gameplay Storyboard Template

(_____ out of _____)

App-pendix 4
The Game Designer's Checklist

COMING UP WITH a great idea for a touchscreen game is one thing, but getting all your ideas organized is a totally different thing. A good game design document covers the following topics:

- ○ Game's name
- ○ Player's primary action
- ○ Control scheme (virtual vs. gesture controls)
- ○ Core gameplay examples
- ○ Game story (if applicable)
- ○ Character descriptions and model sheets (if applicable)
- ○ List of mechanics, hazards, and enemies
- ○ Leveling/progression system details
- ○ Economy system/game store details (if applicable)
- ○ Art style guide
- ○ Navigation wireframes
- ○ Sound and music requirements
- ○ Cutscene and cinematic scripts and storyboards
- ○ Plans for any future content updates

Just remember to give enough details to get the idea across and use images whenever necessary. Be kind to your readers and write a GDD that your teammates will *want* to read, not just *have* to read.

Afterword

AS KIM KARDASHIAN once said, "Writing books is hard," and for once, she was right. I have learned that writing a book is not a solitary experience. A lucky writer has many, many family members and friends to lean on. Fortunately, I am a lucky writer. These are friends and family to whom I could not have made this book:

Brenda Lee Rogers: The hardest working editor I am related to and best friend a writer could ever have. I love you.

Evelyn Rogers: Who knows the location of the secret message in this book. Maybe one day you'll let me be player one. xoxo

Jack Rogers: An excellent game player and budding game designer in his own right. Keep going , buddy! xoxo

To my excellent and inspiring interviewees: **Andy Ashcraft, Andy Reeves, Blade Olsen, Casey Holtz, Charley Price, Chris Ulm, Colton Phillips, Erin Reynolds, Matthew Hall, Sam Farmer, Sam Rosenthal.** You all rock! The rest of you should buy all their games.

Paul O Connor: Old Grimtooth himself who stepped up to the plate and helped a friend in need. Many thanks and even now, Death approaches you.

Hardy LeBel: The best sounding board and steadfast rock a pal could ever have. Go make another Tyrant game already!

Akira Thompson: For the good art advice. Also for putting on Indie-Cade, the best and most inspiring game conference in the known universe. You're better than Donald Glover in my book.

Jaclyn Rogers: Thanks for being my biggest fan. And for that whole giving birth to me thing.

Brett Rogers: For poetry polishing, constant intellectual stimulation, and keeping me up to date with what "the kids" have been doing.

Colleen and **Paul Delany-Rivera:** For not only being great friends but for buying more copies of *Level Up!* than anyone else I know.

Chris Webb: The guy who keeps commissioning me to write these books regardless of my lackadaisical writing and drawing schedule.

My fantastic team of editors, artists, and marketers at John Wiley & Sons, Ltd.: **Julian Dye, Gareth Haman, David Mayhew, Ellie Scott, Kate Parrett** (who gracefully dealt with all of my "blue rocking"), and the ever-patient **Sara Shlaer.**

Noah Stein: Thanks for calling me on all my bs, but you are still wrong about story.

To my **friends** who visit me online at www.mrbossdesign.com, get my tweets at mrbossdesign, and visit my *Level Up! The Guide to Great Video Game Design* and the *Swipe This! The Guide to Great Touchscreen Game Design* Facebook fan pages. I love your messages and e-mails. Keep 'em coming!

The hardware teams at **Nintendo, Sony, Microsoft,** and **Apple:** Thank you for creating such wonderful devices.

Steve Jobs: The visionary who will always be with us.

The two best touchscreen sites on the interwebs: **Touch Arcade.com** and **SlideToPlay. com**: Thanks for keeping me up to date and hipping me to the greatness of Kitty games.

AppShopper.com: The best damn app search engine online. Without it, this book would have taken a lot longer to finish.

And last but definitely not least, **you,** who bought and read this book all the way to the last word.

Index